THE STORY OF
SOHO

About the Author

Mike Hutton is a London social historian. His other books include *Life in 1940s London*, also from Amberley. He lives on the borders of Leicestershire and Northamptonshire.

THE STORY OF
SOHO
The Windmill Years
1932–1964

MIKE HUTTON

AMBERLEY

This edition first published 2013

Amberley Publishing
The Hill, Stroud
Gloucestershire, GL5 4EP

www.amberley-books.com

British Library Cataloguing in Publication Data.
A catalogue record for this book is available from the British Library.

ISBN 978 1 4456 1449 6

Typesetting and Origination by Amberley Publishing.
Printed in Great Britain.

CONTENTS

Introduction

Toe in the Water

'How old are you?' The middle-aged matron in the ticket kiosk leant forward to get a better look at me. 'Eighteen,' I replied, unconvincingly. My well-rehearsed bass baritone started as a croak before climbing to a schoolboy alto. Behind me, my fourth form friends skulked in the shadows, aware that they looked even younger than me. For a moment she hesitated, then, with a look of distaste mingled with one of weary amusement, she issued the tickets. To my horror, as we made our way across the foyer my school cap slipped from its hiding place beneath my raincoat. So it was that red-faced with embarrassment I made a dash for the welcoming darkness of the Windmill Theatre.

Only half an hour earlier we had been singing like angels (or so our mothers thought) at our school carol concert, which was held each year in the austere surroundings of St Martin's in the Fields. Having persuaded our parents that we were going for tea at Lyon's Corner House and then on to a film at the Empire, Leicester Square, we headed instead for forbidden territory – Soho. On that cold, damp late afternoon in 1953 we pushed our way through crowds of Christmas shoppers towards an area we only knew through schoolboy gossip. This was by reputation the most exciting and tempting part of London. This was to be an adventure, part of our growing up. Just a year ago we had been children with only childish interests. The arrival of adolescent spots had coincided with our awareness of girls and sex. Everything had changed.

I have no idea what we really expected as we left the bright lights of Leicester Square, but our sense of anticipation was high. We plunged into the darkened streets of Soho and discovered a different world. There was the smell of ripening cheese and salami as we passed a delicatessen. Whiffs of rich coffee borne off on a breeze to be replaced by heady, cloying perfume coming from a darkened doorway. People lingered. Men with trilbies pulled down over their faces as if attempting to avoid prying eyes. Groups hung around in clusters. They talked and puffed at cigarettes, watchful as if expecting something out of the ordinary to happen. It didn't. As we moved on, women's voices floated towards us from the shadows. Murmured invitations to passers-by. There were young, heavily made-up women standing under street lamps. They were smoking. Everyone was smoking and some of these girls twirled a bunch of keys from fingers sporting garish nail polish. One, an attractive redhead, linked arms with an elderly man and attempted to shepherd him down an alley towards her flat. He broke away but after a hurried conversation he followed her. He stayed several paces behind her, like a Prince Consort behind his Queen. Amongst a sea of trilbies he sported a bowler. He glanced around him constantly, hoping not to be recognised, but only our small group showed any interest.

Further back in the shadows, away from the street lights, were other women. Older, much older, absolutely ancient. God, they were even older than our mothers. I was shocked. The continuing sense of difference was underlined by snippets of conversation we overheard. French, Italian, Spanish and other languages we could only guess at.

Sitting in the half-empty Windmill, I reflected on the uniqueness and excitement of London's 'naughty square mile'. Not that either naughtiness or excitement extended to the performance at the Windmill that day. There were a couple of comedians, one of whom I think was a young Bill Maynard. The patter fell on deaf ears – the punters were only interested in the girls. For three schoolboys there was an overwhelming sense of anticlimax. Sure, the Windmill girls were lovely and nude, but standing absolutely still they seemed no sexier than the white marble statues at the British Museum.

Travelling home on the underground that evening I realised I had been seduced. Not by one of the lurking prostitutes, but by Soho like many before me. I already sensed it was a place of stark contradictions. Somewhere to have fun and yet remain wary. Sometimes warm and welcoming, yet also mean and threatening. It walks a fine line between the exhilarating and the sordid.

The years that the Windmill stayed open marked huge changes for Soho, whilst never quite mirroring those taking place in society generally. It remained something of an enigma, continuing to shock and entertain in equal measure. They were years that witnessed huge changes in morals and social equality. The music of Al Bowlly, skiffle and the emergence of rock 'n' roll. From the sedate tea rooms of the 1930s to coffee bars where youngsters sipped their espressos, perched on mock coffins at Le Macabre in Wardour Street. There was the changing face of cinema and the theatre which plays such a huge part in Soho's life. The war years brought hardship, bombings and American GIs; many decided these were the best years of their lives. Somehow, Soho managed to sideline much of the austerity of the 1950s, which was a golden era for the area. Then, always in the background, there were the gangs and organised crime. The Sabinis, who ruled in the 1930s, through to the Messina brothers, to Jack Spot and Billy Hill, with the Kray twins waiting in the wings.

The period offers a journey of endless strands. Of artists and writers. Of deadbeats, whores and drunks. The talented, feckless and clueless, the hopefuls and the hopeless. The crooks, pimps and twisters. People drawn from all over the world and poured into one crowded, dingy, fabulous part of London, hemmed in on all sides by its more fashionable West End neighbours, none of whom has such an amazing story to tell.

PART 1

THE THIRTIES

1

Let's Start at the Beginning

Grim-faced office workers hurried along a crowded Shaftesbury Avenue. A traffic jam around Piccadilly Circus clogged the surrounding roads. Buses, cars and the occasional horse-drawn cart edged forward. It was a day that called for sunshine but that was asking too much of an early February morning. The year is 1932, and symbolic, dark clouds hung over central London. Britain was still in the grip of the Great Depression. It was as if the pedestrians jostling their way along the crowded pavements could sense the even greater problems that lay ahead, culminating in the outbreak of war seven years later.

Almost all the men wore hats. Trilbies, bowlers, the occasional Homburg and a sea of cloth caps. Dress indicated quite clearly your background. The women and office girls were more difficult to pinpoint. Certainly the frivolity of 1920s fashion was no longer in evidence. The Bright Young Things had gone to ground. So too had the cropped hairstyles and the desire to acquire a boyish figure. Cloche hats had been discarded in favour of brimmed hats, some worn at a rakish angle allowing only one eye to be visible to a passer-by. Skirt lengths had dropped, reflecting more serious times, measuring just ten inches off the ground.

For respectable office girls, Shaftesbury Avenue was perhaps the only street in Soho where they felt totally at ease. Their mothers would have issued dire warnings about the area. They were advised that it was unwise to stop, even to window shop or to pause to look at the billboards outside the many theatres that lined the road. There were rumours (unsubstantiated) of young girls being plucked from London streets and shipped off to some beastly foreign country to endure a fate worse than death.

Shaftesbury Avenue had been built in the late nineteenth century, cutting a swathe through the slums of Soho and St Giles. Alleys and yards with no sanitation and where the sun never penetrated were bulldozed away to make a modern thoroughfare linking Piccadilly Circus to Charing Cross Road. The construction of theatres surrounding it and along its length created London's answer to Broadway. The Empire and the Alhambra rose in 1883 with the Prince of Wales being built a year later. The Garrick, Daly's and the Duke of York followed. In 1886 the Criterion Theatre was developed by the actor-manager Charles Wyndham at the Piccadilly end of the road. Further building on Shaftesbury Avenue saw the arrival of the Shaftesbury and the Lyric. Just down the street at Cambridge Circus, Richard D'Oyly Carte's massive Palace Theatre was built in 1891. Still new theatres continued to rise along Shaftesbury Avenue with The Apollo, Globe, The Prince's and The Ambassadors following in quick succession. These establishments brought a degree of respectability to an area that was still viewed with distinct suspicion by Middle England. Not that the acting fraternity were thought of very highly either. Until recently actresses were reckoned to be little better than the prostitutes who lined the surrounding streets. As for the men? Well, most of them were surely queer!

Many thought of Soho as a strange, foreign enclave. This was at a time when all foreigners were viewed with suspicion. To others it was the last surviving London village. An island of entertainment and temptation. It was also a stronghold of endangered craft trades which were already under threat from a growing tide of corporate enterprises. Whilst Soho was so different in character from its neighbours, it was not immune from the overwhelming difficulties of the time.

The country was being run by a national government led by a Labour Prime Minister, Ramsay MacDonald. In truth, it was the Tories that held the real power. As usual, Britain was staggering from one crisis to another. The country had never recovered from the crippling debts incurred during the Great War. Matters came to a head with the stock market crash of 1929. Developed countries sought to weaken their currencies in order to help exports. Britain abandoned its long-held commitment to free trade. The Board of Trade imposed huge duties on goods from outside the British Empire.

It is unlikely that these concerns were uppermost in the minds of those pedestrians weaving their way along Shaftesbury Avenue that morning. Unfortunately, few would escape the implications. The Tories demanded wage cuts and a reduction in public spending (sounds familiar!). This would lead to further unemployment, which already stood at over 13 per cent in Southern England and higher still in Wales and the North. So the mood in the country overall was sombre. Those office and shop workers who glanced up Great Windmill Street that morning might have had their spirits lifted slightly (or, alternatively, muttered their disapproval). Later, a new, daring form of entertainment was to be launched at the Windmill Theatre featuring NUDITY! Soho, so long associated with risqué entertainment, was again pushing against the boundaries of outward British respectability. How was it that Soho had acquired its colourful reputation?

Soho derives its name from an old hunting call dating back to the sixteenth century. It is recorded that London's Lord Mayor hunted in the fields to the west of town, killing hares and the occasional fox. These hunting fields were overwhelmingly the property of the Crown. With London expanding so rapidly, these rural lands were increasingly under threat. By the end of the century, a few scattered dwellings had appeared. Then the Earl of Leicester had two large mansions built on the land. Gradually, Soho began to evolve with as many as sixty further modest houses being built in the area prior to the Great Fire of London. It was this catastrophic event in 1666, with thousands of Londoners being made homeless, that led to a rash of speculative building.

A windmill recorded in 1585 was demolished and Great Windmill Street was developed. Centuries later, its iconic theatre was to become the focal point for Soho at its very heart. New Crown tenants, including Sir Edward Wardour, allowed further development with the building of Rupert Street and (Old) Compton Street. Demand for homes continued to be strong and Berwick Street and Poland Street followed soon after. The stately homes of former years were swallowed and surrounded by a tide of speculative building.

A foreign connection was established early on. The French Huguenots and the Greeks were the first to arrive in the 1680s, fleeing oppression at home. The French influence was particularly strong, bringing a distinctly Continental atmosphere to the area. Like many refugees newly arrived in a foreign country, they stayed close together, speaking their own language and transferring their way of life and cuisine to their new home. They also brought their expertise in trades, some of which were poorly represented in London at the time. Already, by the first quarter of the eighteenth century, only half of Soho's population was English. What had started as a country retreat for aristocrats had been overrun by jerry-built houses and foreigners. It was time for the 'toffs' to decamp to Mayfair. They had no wish to be contaminated by the proximity of trade surrounding them. Instrument makers, weavers and lace makers plied their trade from narrow streets and alleys. Shops sold foul-smelling sausages and cheeses. It was time to go to where the air was fresh and your servants understood an ordered society.

Now an artistic influence became established in the area. The formidable Sir Joshua Reynolds came to lodge in Great Newport Street. He was followed by Canaletto, John Zoffany and J. M. W. Turner, all of whom were residents of Soho, as was William Blake, who grew up in Broad Street. The connection with the arts, generally including writers and musicians, continued and is maintained today.

Most areas in London go through periods of change and desirability. Districts which were once sought after become slums and then later reinvent themselves, gaining respectability again. By the end of the nineteenth century, Soho had declined further. During the 1840s, sizeable Jewish and Irish communities had descended on an overcrowded Soho. Initially, the eastern European Jews settled around Newport Market. They quickly established a synagogue in Dean Street and a school for Jewish girls in Greek Street. As the men found work, mostly in the rag trade as outworkers for the smart West End tailors, they tended to migrate and set up home around Berwick Street Market.

The huge influx of Irish escaping the potato famine led to a further deterioration in local living conditions. Whilst most were confined to the hellish rookeries of St Giles, many found Soho more to their liking. Why? By the 1860s, conditions were being compared with the worst areas of the East End. Immigrants were still drawn here because of continuing persecution in Eastern Europe. By now, living conditions around Newport Market were quite appalling. Soho was filthy. Open sewers and slaughter houses competed with animal dung to offend the senses. There was a fatal outbreak of cholera which claimed hundreds of lives before the source was traced to a contaminated water pump in Broad Street.

Crime and prostitution have always been associated with Soho. For the most part, whores through the ages have found Soho a tolerant place to ply their trade. It was in Victorian times that a high, moral tone etched with hypocrisy saw the number of prostitutes in the West End soar. Where there were whores, invariably there were men who sought to live off their earnings. The earliest prostitutes were usually English, many of them country girls who had come to London in search of employment and were duped into selling themselves. Often befriended by seemingly trustworthy men or women who lurked around stagecoach destinations, they soon found themselves trapped. Increasingly, it became foreign girls who were exploited, often met at the docks and sent to work within days. Many were Jewish girls, arriving alone from Eastern Europe and unable to speak English, who fell prey to men, some of whom claimed to be relatives. Increasingly, they were joined and exceeded in numbers by French and Belgian girls who became known as 'Fifis'. They could earn up to 10s or a pound from a well-heeled client, although at the low end of the trade a 'fourpenny touch' in Lisle Street was more likely.

By the beginning of the twentieth century, Soho's reputation was obviously at a low ebb. A Royal Commission reporting in 1906 commenting on Greek Street stated that 'crowds gather there nightly who are little else than a pest'. It concluded that 'some of the vilest reptiles in London live there and frequent it'. In the 200 years since the first Greeks had arrived to escape the religious persecution of the Ottoman Empire, their street was now reckoned to be one of the very worst in London.

In 1905 an Alien Act was passed by Parliament to restrict the wave of foreigners coming into the country. Aimed predominantly at restricting the numbers of Eastern European Jews, there were also worries about the Italians. Whilst many had settled around Clerkenwell and were involved in traditional trades, such as mosaics or knife grinding, others had branched into the catering industry. Italian restaurants were well established in Soho by the mid-nineteenth century, but it was their well-organised crime gangs that worried the British public. Damned by an 1888 Parliamentary select committee as 'immoral, illiterate and vicious', a hard core seemed hell-bent on confirming their unflattering reputation. The Sabini gang preyed on Soho businesses for protection money. Pubs, cafés and clubs were all targeted. Few dared to refuse. Those who did were attacked and ended up in hospital. We will meet the

Sabinis again as they were still a power to be reckoned with in the 1930s.

The 1920s had been a decade of excess, typified by the Bright Young Things' generation. They helped create a market for drug trafficking which was largely supplied by the Chinese community. A leading figure, 'Brilliant' Chang, had restaurants in Regent Street and Gerrard Street from where he is thought to have dispensed his 'oriental delicacies'.

So foreigners continued to be thought suspect at best by many British people. Yet this extraordinary mixture of nationalities lived, for the most part, in harmony in London's most cosmopolitan square mile. A significant Swiss population lived alongside families from Scandinavia and Germany, and there were even a few Americans. White Russians, who had fled the revolution, set up home in drastically reduced circumstances. Like the majority of immigrants, they worked hard to better themselves and in time many moved to more affluent areas. Yet most records report a tolerant society, albeit one where only gradually did the nationalities mix socially and intermarry.

Into this unlikely mix of hard-working artisans, shopkeepers, whores and criminals is pitched a wild card. A wealthy, grey-haired eccentric English woman, who decided to buy a theatre. Most of her contemporaries would have thought her to be quite mad. Perhaps she was, but Laura Henderson brought a touch of glamour to Soho that was to last over thirty years.

2

And Here's to You, Mrs Henderson

Eighty pounds a week! Not bad for a relatively young man in 1932. The equivalent of an annual salary of almost £200,000 at today's values. Born into a London middle-class family of Dutch/Jewish extraction, Vivian Van Damm had already made a name for himself in the burgeoning British film industry. He had progressed from humble beginnings in the provinces to be a leading manager, familiar with the wheeling and dealing of studios on Wardour Street. A born showman, he even employed dozens of men to provide sound effects for the epic silent film *The Four Horsemen of the Apocalypse*. They were placed behind a screen to produce the noise of galloping horses and gunfire. It was the sort of stunt that brought him to the attention of Sidney Bernstein, who was in the process of building up his chain of Granada cinemas. They had a series of meetings and found they had similar thoughts about the future of the film industry. With only a few minor details to be clarified and the contract awaiting his signature, Van Damm decided it was time to celebrate with his wife Natalie. He was pondering on which restaurant to book when his thoughts were interrupted by the shrill ring of the telephone. This was a call that was to change the whole direction of his life.

Bernard Issac was a friend and an influential businessman. Issac was very pressing, insisting he had someone he was anxious to introduce to Van Damm. Intrigued, Van Damm took a cab to Issac's flat in Sackville Street, where he was introduced to 'a bundle of dynamite'. Introducing Mrs Laura Henderson. Given that she was a diminutive, grey-haired figure of under five feet in height, these two represented that strange attraction of opposites. With little time for small talk, the sixty-nine-year-old socialite bubbled over with excitement. She explained that Issac was a director of a rundown cinema she had bought in Great Windmill Street. With the confidence of a woman who was obviously used to getting her own way, she informed Van Damm that he was the very man she wanted to run it. He found himself engulfed by her infectious enthusiasm. He was whisked off by car to her lawyer's office. On the way he tried to explain that he had only just received a wonderful job offer. She seemed utterly impervious to his concern. Her lawyer, the tall and elegant Leslie Perks, also expressed severe reservations. She gave no indication that she was even listening as she ushered them all back into her chauffeur-driven limousine. It was off to the Windmill Theatre in Great Windmill Street. On the way Perks enquired if Mrs Henderson had given any thought to a salary for the General Manager of her theatre. She said £8 per week might be appropriate.

Who in their right mind would accept £8 a week when £80 was on offer? But then, who in their right mind at the age of nearly seventy would think of buying a theatre with absolutely no experience of any form of previous business activity? On that level at least they were well matched. It is not recorded if poor Natalie was ever treated to that expensive supper, but Vivian Van Damm was giving this strange proposal real thought. On the surface it seemed crazy even to consider such an outlandish idea. And yet…? Laura Henderson had already shown a massive commitment to the project by completely gutting the former Palais de Luxe and constructing a state-of-the-art modern theatre.

Still unsure, but intrigued by the possibilities of being able to run his own operation, Van Damm agreed to meet this mysterious lady for lunch at Claridges the next day. Obviously well known at the hotel, she was fussed over by the staff. Severe doubts had formed in his mind overnight. Who was this Laura Henderson? Probably just a spoilt, rich widow pursuing a half-baked idea. As the meal progressed, however, he found himself warming to her. They shared an enthusiasm and belief in their own ability to succeed. A bond, a form of chemistry, was forged, helped by some excellent claret. Their relationship was to be volatile, lurching from true affection to outright irritation. When Van Damm informed Bernstein of his bizarre decision to follow his instinct rather than reason, the film mogul wished him good luck. 'You may need it,' he added. He was right.

Eccentric is an overused word, but Laura Henderson represents a genuine eighteen-carat version. Born at the beginning of the second half of the Victorian era, she was brought up in the days of strict parental discipline. Manners and appearance were constantly monitored. She was expected to be 'a lady' at all times. By her teens any chance of being left alone in the company of a man was unthinkable. Still, by the age of twenty-two she was married. Not, as her parents would have hoped, to a member of the aristocracy but to a jute merchant. True, he was a rich jute merchant, but trade was still something of a dirty word in the higher realms of London society. Her sheltered upbringing was underlined by her first visit to the theatre, where she was supposedly scandalised by seeing bare-legged dancers, albeit sporting black net stockings. Was this, perhaps, the start of her love of the theatre? Early in her marriage it became obvious that here was a young woman who was not prepared to sit at home making small talk and doing embroidery. She accompanied her husband on arduous, far-flung trips to Australia, India and China. She developed a love and taste for all things Chinese and her drawing room in Rutland Place was furnished with exquisite fabrics and antiques from her travels. Crimson banisters inlaid with gold leaf dominated the entrance hall, and the main living rooms featured several miniature shrines. She was prone to welcoming guests wearing one of her collection of colourful kimonos. In addition to her long-suffering chauffeur, she employed a cook, a lady's maid, a uniformed footman and an imposing butler.

She was a complex mixture, capable of great kindness and hurtful dismissiveness. She was at today's values a multi-millionairess, although she appeared to give very little thought to, and not to have any real understanding of, money. She had unimpeachable blue-chip connections which were to prove invaluable for the Windmill over the years. Against all this she was a great supporter of the oppressed and underdogs generally, an energetic social worker who devoted much of her time to good causes. She was a keen supporter of the Women's Guild of Empire and a club for women in the dockland settlement at Hulton House. Tellingly, her interest in entertainment was emphasised by her being on the committee of the Musicians' Benevolent Fund.

So it was that this diminutive socialite formed a partnership with the young, cigar-smoking, self-made showman. The first play Laura Henderson had launched at the Windmill had been *Inquest*.

Although well received, it failed to find favour with the public and closed after a short run. She reverted to film, but avant-garde offerings also failed to draw in the crowds. Van Damm, on his arrival, continued to show films, but these had greater popular appeal, such as *The Blue Angel*. This was just a holding phase whilst he sought a viable future for the theatre. Given the theatre's seating capacity of only just over 300, he realised it was going to be impossible to compete with the glamour of the huge West End picture palaces. A few weeks after joining the Windmill, Vivian was approached by a French producer, Lucien Samett. He had the idea of transforming the Windmill by offering a 'non-stop show of flesh and blood vaudeville'. Van Damm, although naturally cautious, was also intuitive. He was intrigued by the possibilities of non-stop entertainment. Quick-fire variety, with customers coming and going as they pleased, would be revolutionary for a British theatre, although it was already well established in France. He visited Mrs Henderson at Rutland Gate. She was fascinated by the proposal but for once in her life she considered the financial implications. She asked what her loss would be if the venture failed. Van Damm had already done his homework. He estimated £10,000 (over £450,000 at today's values). Thoughts of money were cast aside – people interested her more. Was he thinking of engaging British or foreign artistes? 'Only British,' came the reply. That settled matters.

The theatre and particularly variety were going through extremely difficult times. The Depression continued to eat away at employment. There were thousands of entertainers on the dole. The talkies had devastated much of London's live theatre. The public had been swept away with the escapism offered by the silver screen. For many working people the cinema offered them a chance to enjoy themselves in palatial surroundings at a price they could afford.

The philanthropic side of Laura Henderson was now in full flow. Non-stop revue would provide jobs for talented 'resting' entertainers. She threw a huge sherry party for all her well-connected friends to publicise the Windmill's new strategy. In December 1931, the Windmill Theatre Company formally applied for permission to open a variety house. Auditions began and a twelve-piece orchestra recruited. Ever the showman, Van Damm arranged for the *London Evening Star* to organise a contest for an original title for the show. A Mr Arnold Kite's suggestion saw the birth of *Revudeville*, although he never claimed the £5 prize. The opening night was fixed for 3 February 1932.

The new business partners went to work on the press. Van Damm trumpeted his confidence in his variety company, insisting there was absolutely no competition. Laura Henderson proclaimed they would be offering 'big acts, but not necessarily big names'. The Windmill would be featuring a rolling revue, giving West End opportunities to largely unknown talent who hopefully would become the stars of the future. A slightly bemused press was informed that she had been a talent spotter for years. This was unlikely to be true but by now she was on a roll. She continued to maintain that the shows would include 'plenty of fun and gaiety, but with no sex silliness'. As she looked at the pressmen over rimmed spectacles, few doubted her.

Although Samett was only offering average wages, he was overwhelmed with the hundreds of hopefuls seeking an audition. The standard was generally quite appalling. People were desperate. Some walked tens of miles for the chance. Others were weak from hunger. Laura Henderson, who attended many of the auditions, was visibly saddened. The most pathetic of the down-and-outs were surreptitiously slipped a banknote, highlighting her complex character. She could also be incredibly mean over little things, whilst wildly generous on other occasions.

Eventually, Lucien Samett was able to engage forty-two artistes for his first edition of *Revudeville* and more than another 100 for the next three shows, for which rehearsals were to commence immediately. There was to be a complete change of programme every fortnight. All of this would have been fine, but it soon became clear that the bookings for the first show would have disgraced an average amateur dramatic society. Who was going to pay to see a juggler of apples, whose trick was to eat one whilst keeping the rest airborne? The comedians were dire and to cap it all the chorus girls were described at the time as strangely flat-chested.

No matter, the show must go on. It was announced that shows would run continuously from 2.30 p.m. until 11 p.m. There would be four performances, each lasting two hours. It was established that the maximum time for an act would be seven minutes. The band members were to be alternated during the shows, with only nine of the twelve ever playing at one time.

With two weeks to go to opening night, it was realised that the show lacked star quality. There was only a loosely connected bunch of rather second-rate turns. A top of the bill was urgently needed. Talented but cheap – not normally a combination easy to find. The star arrived, shabbily dressed, in the form of a salesman trying to sell space for a variety magazine. Van Damm wasn't buying but something about the man's rather pompous pitch appealed. Vivian's instinct went into overdrive. Rather rudely he suggested that if the chap could be as funny on stage as his sales patter he would give him a job. After an initial protest and ruffled feathers, John Thompson agreed. Van Damm sent him across the road to get a coffee and something to eat. The poor man was starving. Suitably revived, Thompson took to the stage whilst Van Damm looked on from the stalls. There was something of Stan Laurel about him. An air of innocent incompetence. With hair parted down the middle with quiffs like devil horns, he started with a lugubrious voice, 'Mind if I make you laugh?' Vivian didn't mind at all and Thompson made the showman laugh until tears ran down his cheeks.

He gave a talk on the current economic situation. Combining a mixture of extreme nervousness with an air of superiority – and using all the correct, if jumbled, economic jargon – he had many of the cast who gathered to see him laughing out loud. Assuring Van Damm he had many other monologues already written and ready to be used, he was signed on the spot. His previous experience in the forces' concert parties became obvious. His name was changed at his request to John Tilley in honour of the only person who had ever predicted that he would become famous. And he did. Although he signed a contract with the Windmill for two years, he was released when other work was on offer. He was featured regularly on the radio and appeared at the London Palladium as a scoutmaster lecturing his troop on how to tie knots, with predictable results. Unfortunately, his fame was short-lived for, after marrying a Windmill girl, he died tragically whilst still a young man in 1941.

A new problem arose just a week before opening. Two chorus girls were threatening to go on strike because they claimed their costumes were too revealing. Here again, it was probably a publicity ruse dreamed up by Van Damm. In any event the news had the effect of highlighting the interest in the Windmill. The opening performances were totally sold out. The audiences were a mixture of high society, coerced into attending by Laura Henderson, and a public anxious to judge if the show was as risqué as various newspaper articles had suggested.

Laura Henderson, who was dressed in a coat of intricate Chinese brocade, threw a lavish reception in the theatre's lounge after the show, whilst they all waited for the critics' verdict. She was joined by Princess Helena Victoria, Princess Marie Louise and an entourage, most of whom featured in Debrett's. Hopefully, the champagne fortified them as the reviews were almost entirely negative.

The first to arrive was damning. 'A mixture of revue, variety and unemployment relief,' the *London Evening News* read. 'The most tragic theatre in London. Wind needed for the Windmill.'

The *Daily Sketch* was even more cutting: 'Surely there must be more real talent that has fallen on evil days than the first bill of the Windmill seems to disclose. I hate to say this but at least half of the turns we saw last night are obviously unemployable on any stage, however humble, that has to pay its way!'

Van Damm acted decisively by sacking half the company. The second *Revudeville* was much improved. Younger, brighter and altogether more professional. Even the press was more encouraging. The *Daily Mail* offered a crumb of comfort: 'When Mrs Henderson started her continuous variety shows people applauded her motives but were sceptical. She has proved herself right.' So after a shocking start things were looking up. By the end of the second edition weekly attendances were nudging 5,000. A public nerve had been touched and the theatre was full most days from mid-afternoon.

Van Damm kept the papers interested, never missing an opportunity to photograph his scantily dressed girls in a series of bizarre publicity stunts. He fed the papers stories of human interest – office clerks and glamorous shop girls seeking stardom in the West End. He didn't miss a trick. A chorus girl fell into the orchestra pit, but the plucky trouper clambered back on stage and carried on despite chipping her front teeth. Van Damm lost no time informing the press that he had insured the Windmill girls' teeth for £10,000. She was pictured smiling, teeth repaired, under the headline '£100 a tooth'.

No good idea survives long without being copied. Situated just round the corner from the Windmill, a rival continuous variety show was staged at the London Pavilion, under a banner headline, '2s 6d and come down when you like and leave when you like!' Sensing variety was back in vogue, Lucien Samett left the Windmill and joined the Phoenix Theatre Club in Charing Cross

Road. The show was to be continuous and a cast of over 120 were engaged with prices ranging from 7d to 3s 6d. Something had to be done. Financial problems were already becoming acute at the Windmill. The girls' costumes had been reduced to a bare minimum. Van Damm was convinced that the time was right to follow the French. 'Nudes are the way forward,' he declared. 'You will never get away with it,' he was constantly told. But he did, or rather, Mrs Henderson did.

Sheila, Van Damm's daughter, maintained it was Vivian who persuaded the Lord Chamberlain, Lord Cromer, to allow nudity on a modern British stage for the first time. It has to be remembered that, not long before, a country steeped in Victorian moral values viewed nudity with outright horror and outrage. Even the crazy 1920s generation had failed to break down that particular barrier. It seems unlikely with all her social connections that Mrs Henderson was not behind the decision to loosen the law. Cromer had been Assistant Equerry to King George V, the ultimate arch traditionalist. So he was perhaps an unlikely target for overseeing what many saw as a shocking lowering of moral standards. However, ten years into the job he was obviously his own man. Was it Laura Henderson's lobbying or Van Damm's powers of persuasion? Who knows, but he agreed that nudes could appear on stage providing they remained static and the presentations were wholly artistic. Another stipulation insisted on subdued lighting. Van Damm was to stick rigidly to this brief and still attendances soared. The Windmill had found the key to its success, which was to last three decades. The Public Morality Council was outraged. Cromer was deluged with letters and deputations. There were calls for a ban on all nudity in public places. 'What, and close every art gallery in the country?' was the response. The genie was out of the bottle. Life was never going to be quite the same from now on.

Vivian Van Damm, sitting in his cluttered office, could afford himself a smile as he lit his Corona. The Windmill had established its unique selling point. At least, for the time being.

3

The Windmill's Neighbours

In the 1930s, myths and preconceived perceptions tended to cloud Soho's reputation. It wasn't a place populated solely by foreigners and dangerous gangs of violent criminals. True, there was a hardcore criminal element and Soho's streets had a vaguely Continental atmosphere, but many native-born Londoners still continued to live within its borders.

Just down the road from the Windmill Theatre, Harriet Rees, the landlady at the Red Lion, was pulling pints for the princely price of 7*d*. Samuel Berry sold gobstoppers and liquorish sticks from his sweet shop – row upon row of glass jars filled with barley sugar, lemon sherbets and aniseed balls, his counter stacked with Continental chocolate. From early in the morning the wonderful smell of freshly baked bread rose from the ovens of Drewry's Bakery. James Healey was listed as a pavement light maker, whilst at No. 39 Regent & Co. strived to keep pace with the demand for their popular permanent-waving machines. Musical instrument makers had been active in Soho for centuries, but Raymond Casey, a violin dealer, confirmed that the music trade was not just confined to the Continentals. Nearby, Fuller & Mead were wholesale stationers, well placed to supply the numerous neighbouring offices. The British influence in Great Windmill Street continued with William Clowes & Sons, who were printers. Butler Screen Company, manufacturers of cinema screens, represented an outpost of the film industry centred on Wardour Street. Hugh Lane ran his upholstery business from No. 28, whilst nearby dentist Harold Wilton was extracting teeth with the aid of gas. Several of the street's cafés were also run by Londoners. At Charles Dones's Eating House, customers could get a good 'fry-up' whilst British cuisine was further upheld by Lizzie Henman's traditional fish and chip shop. Of course, there were also foreign-owned restaurants, although the food they served wasn't the fine dining found deeper in Soho's heartland. Lorenzo Franchi ran his café from 32 Great Windmill Street, whilst next door were dining rooms run by Guiseppe Speroni. Benoit, a leading kitchen outfitter, operated out of No. 29. The little community of Great Windmill Street was completed by St James and St Peter School, a dancing academy and a dingy billiard hall where petty criminals gathered. The street may not have been typical of Soho but it gives a flavour of the mix of small businesses existing at the time.

In Soho, every available space was occupied. A bewildering range of goods was sold from attics, backrooms and basements. Rents were cheap, with rooms to let on short leases for a few shillings a week. Many were tucked away in ancient courts and down darkened alleyways. People worked above stables where the warm smell of hay and horse flesh helped mask the stench of damp and decay. Many buildings were still without electricity or running water. Buildings had been neglected by landlords and the interior of most properties differed little from those of Victorian London. Dangerous, evil-smelling paraffin stoves often provided the only heating available. Once a week most residents would treat themselves to a visit to the public baths in Marshall Street. Towels were provided but you were expected to take your own soap and flannel. It was a great meeting place for a chat, whilst you waited your turn. Ten minutes lying back in the luxury of the warm water was all you were allowed before the attendant starting pounding on the door. Ten minutes of solitude in a crowded Soho where you were seldom alone.

Although life for many was very tough, with a minority going hungry, at least food was relatively cheap and plentiful in Soho. There were two vibrant street markets in Berwick Street and another situated in Peter Street. Berwick Street stallholders sold mainly fruit and vegetables. As well as seasonal produce they offered exotic fruits and unfamiliar vegetables from around the world. Much of what was on offer was unavailable across most of London, unless you could afford a visit to Harrods' Food Hall. The markets were also where stolen goods were sold on. Some barrow boys would openly boast, ''Ere you are, ladies, look at this, straight off the back of a lorry.' The chances were that the goods were 'straight' but few could resist a supposed bargain.

It was claimed that by the 1930s over 70 per cent of the population surrounding Berwick Street were Jewish. It had become a centre for the 'rag trade', outworkers beavering away in sweatshops supplying the swanky West End tailors. There were embroiderers, button holers, gown makers, trimming dealers. Every service required for the industry was available on the one street. Huge sacrifices were made by newly arrived immigrants to better themselves. Space was at a premium and owners would often sleep under a counter so that work could continue all around them. These Jewish traders had a work ethic that in many cases allowed their children and grandchildren to prosper in the years ahead.

Even around these seething market streets a few local businesses survived. London butchers and fishmongers continued to trade in Berwick Street, as did billiard table maker Blandford & Co. The Premier Drum Company, soon to become a backbone of the music industry, also had an office on Berwick Street. The market was open from Monday to Saturday and was constantly thronged with people seeking a bargain. There was perpetual shouting as the stallholders fought to make themselves heard. Street bookies stood on corners taking bets, shifty-eyed, always on the lookout for the law. The windows of the kosher restaurants were steamed up and the smell of salt beef wafted skywards as the doors were opened. On the crowded pavement, standing back from the stalls, shop owners tried to usher punters into their emporia. It was live theatre with an ever-changing cast.

With its rich mix of nationalities, Soho had long earned a reputation for the quality of its restaurants. British food languished, unloved and ridiculed abroad. Even food served in the grandest English homes tended to be plain and predictable. For those not employing a cook, meals usually revolved around the Sunday roast, which was often kept warm in the ovens of the local bakers and collected on the way back from the pub. The joint would then be served cold on a Monday and rehashed as mince later in the week. Most people cooked their meat to death and vegetables were reduced to a watery mush. Food for most was just eaten to fill a hole and stave off hunger. Bulky stodge rather than tasty flavours was what was required. The Joe Lyons Corner Houses were leaders in guiding the Great British public towards an appreciation of good food, attractively presented in rather grand surroundings. Rising like palaces in Coventry Street and Tottenham Court Road, they gave a glimpse of the future. On each floor there was a different-themed restaurant, many with their own orchestra. They offered a touch of glamour, with waiters dressed like foreign princes swaying between the crowded tables with trays piled high. On the ground floor, there was a huge array of cakes and delicatessen, ranging from rollmops to chocolate éclairs, all at affordable prices. More basic Joe Lyons Teashops were also scattered all over London, whilst if you were feeling flush you could go to a rather grand tea dance at the Trocadero on Shaftesbury Avenue.

For the well-to-do residents and visitors to London with a more adventurous palette, Soho had an obvious attraction. Leaving their luxurious hotels or West End apartments, they were offered a bewildering array of cuisines. In Greek Street alone, there was Au Bien Venu or the famous Au Petit Savoyard, as well as first-rate Italian food available at Rinaldi's. Further down the road at No. 8 was Canton, one of the relatively few Chinese restaurants in Soho. Back in 1927, Escargot Bienvenu had opened on the site of an ancient cock fighting pit, and it remains a mystery as to how Georges Gaudin managed to persuade Londoners to eat snails at the renamed 'L'Escargot'. But he did, perhaps helped by the serving of Chambéry, his favourite apéritif. Dolin Vermouth de Chambéry is made from wine in which are immersed leaves and berries collected from the Alpine meadows above Chambéry and it obviously had the desired effect ... after three or four, that is!

Around the corner in Old Compton Street was another renowned favourite. Wheelers had originally opened just for the sale of oysters but by the 1930s it had developed into one of London's best-known fish restaurants, offering Dover sole cooked in dozens of variations. Its founder, Bernard Walsh, who lived in Whitstable, obviously saw a niche for his local oysters, but he could have hardly imagined that from its humble beginnings Wheelers would become a favourite haunt for the rich and famous for generations to come. Other iconic restaurants from the period and still serving today include Kettners and Quo Vadis. Kettners in Romilly Street had existed since 1867. It had been a favourite haunt of Oscar Wilde and Edward VIII, both of whom used one of the private upstairs dining rooms for their assignations. Quo Vadis was opened in Dean Street by Peppino Leoni in 1926. The business started modestly with just seven tables, but Leoni's welcoming manner and attention to every detail helped its rapid expansion. Within a few years the restaurant was serving over 400 covers a day. Leoni's philosophy was to welcome all comers, no matter how modestly they wished to dine. Someone requiring just one simple dish was made to feel as welcome as a party sitting down to a five-course meal. He helped popularise eating out for the aspiring classes. Visitors would come 'up to town' on the tube and take in the heady Soho atmosphere. The ladies turned a blind eye to the prostitutes who lined the streets and propositioned their husbands as they paid off the cab. The strange light from the gaslit street lamps, the wine, the rich food and the people lurking in the shadows all added to the experience – in small doses, that is. Fine for birthdays and anniversaries but, honestly, they felt more at ease when they were safely back on the underground and heading home to the suburbs.

A typical set dinner in Soho at the time would cost about 3s 6d. Perusing a variety of à la carte menus gives an idea of the scope available. The average price for a bowl of soup was about 6d, whilst hors d'oeuvres could set you back 1s. Moving to your main course, you might be tempted by Tournedos Rossini on offer at 2s or veal Holstein at 2s 6d. Salmon and chicken were both expensive before factory farming and also cost about 2s 6d, which was generally the price charged for a fillet steak, with vegetables costing extra. Still hungry? Right, it's time for the sweet trolley. Fresh fruit salad was available from 1s 3d, whilst an apple fritter served at a leading Chinese restaurant was charged at 8d. Moving on to the cheeseboard, followed by coffee, would add a further 8d to your bill. Even allowing for inflation these prices appear to offer good value, but maybe it was time to go easy on a bottle of good claret priced at 18s 6d (about £45 at today's value).

For those who wanted to go on to a nightclub, there was a huge selection for them in Soho. They ranged from the grand, offering food and lavish floor shows, to mean dives, spielers and clipjoints. The 1920s had seen a proliferation of clubs, many falling foul of the law prohibiting the sale of alcohol after ten o'clock. The licence was extended to 12.30 a.m. where food was served. One frail lady club owner was constantly in trouble. Kate Meyrick ran a number of clubs including the Manhattan in Denman Street and the Silver Slipper in Regent Street. Her most famous outlet was the 43 Club in Gerrard Street. Here, a bizarre mixture of aristocrats, artists, writers, film stars and gangsters rubbed shoulders to drink champagne at inflated prices. The attraction is hard to imagine. Dirty sackcloth covered the ceiling and the guests sat on rickety chairs at chipped tables. It didn't matter. It was the place to go and be seen, and to be greeted in person by the shabby-looking Kate, with a cheery 'hello, dearie'. The entrance fee would vary seemingly on a whim, depending on her mood. She spent several spells in Holloway for ignoring the licensing laws, which probably contributed to her early death in 1933.

The Gargoyle Club on Meard's Street also opened in the twenties, founded and owned by the Hon. David Tennant, supposedly as a place where he could dance with his fiancée Hermione Baddeley whenever they felt so inclined. Membership was restricted to the cream of London society and celebrities from stage, screen and the arts. Those who were considered interesting but poor had their membership subsidised by the wealthier members. Distinctive decor by Lutyens and a huge mosaic by Matisse helped emphasise the perception of exclusiveness. The club opened late and continued into the early hours, often attracting stars like Noël Coward, who would relax there after appearing on stage. Although he never appeared in cabaret at the club, Hutch was a regular visitor, as was Augustus John. It became a place to stargaze, to rub shoulders with Marlene Dietrich or Cole Porter. The cult of the celebrity was already gearing up.

Coventry Street, which links Piccadilly to Leicester Square, was the location for possibly the most iconic and ill-fated nightclub. The Café de Paris opened in 1924 and became the favourite haunt of the Prince of Wales. Set in a basement, it was the exact replica of the doomed liner RMS *Lusitania*, which had been torpedoed in the First World War. The entrance and central lobby led to the bridge. From here twin staircases, each of twenty-one steps, swept down to the dance floor, ensuring that all arrivals made a dramatic entrance. It was an instinctive reaction for your eye to be drawn to each newcomer and it added to the charged atmosphere. Formal dress was essential, with gentlemen in tailed suits escorting their ladies to a table allocated by the head waiter. The table directly adjoining the dance floor was permanently reserved for the Prince of Wales and his party. The band was required to play non-stop whilst the Prince was on the dance floor. Appearing in cabaret at the Café de Paris was considered to be on a par with heading the bill at the London Palladium. As such, it attracted the top international stars, including Maurice Chevalier, Al Bowlly and Marlene Dietrich. Foreign royalty flocked to the venue, as did the Aga Khan and a host of Indian Maharajas. Up on the balcony, less influential guests were permitted to wear dinner jackets or suits but were not allowed onto the dance floor. The café employed five hostesses, who were chosen for their poise and style. Although they ate at their own table on the balcony, they were required to provide company and conversation for any lonely men. Liaisons after hours were strictly outlawed and sex quite out of the question. The future Lady Docker and Merle Oberon both acted as hostesses for a time.

Another lavish, but less exclusive, venue was the London Casino on Old Compton Street. Formerly the Prince Edward Theatre, it had endured a number of flops since opening in 1930. It was purchased in 1935 for £25,000 and transformed into a cabaret restaurant. The stage was converted into a semicircular dance floor and a modern kitchen constructed in the basement. The auditorium was altered so that the former dress circle could be reached by the stalls stairs. The effect was dramatic, with banks of tables tiered slightly so as to give an unimpeded view of the cabaret and dance floor. The decorations and furnishings were spectacular and supplied by Maples. Guests were required to wear evening dress, adding to the sense of occasion. The concept of dining whilst watching a spectacular show, at prices to appeal to the growing middle class, was something of a forerunner to the Talk of the Town established later at the London Hippodrome.

The most extraordinary show staged at the Casino was presented by the impresario Clifford Fischer. *Folie Parisienne* proved difficult for the reviewers to pigeon-hole. Staged by Jean le Seyeux, with choreography by Natalie Komarova of the Folies Bergère Theatre in Paris, it was described as a sumptuous, lavish, Arabian-nightish, Spanish-esque sort of review. A bizarre mix of ballet, fashion show and strange speciality acts, it featured mannequins leading dogs around the stage against a backdrop of dramatic spouting fountains, whilst showgirls were decked out in the style of leading fashion designer Jean Paton. There were aerialists, illusionists, songs from Polly Frank and a superb troupe of chorus girls. Everything about the production was designed to create the maximum spectacle. With the show containing over thirty acts and running for over two hours, it's amazing that the audience had time to eat their supper.

As the audience filed out of the London Casino, Soho nightlife was still in full swing. Nest, a tiny club in Kingly Street, was popular with leading musicians, who held frequent, noisy, impromptu jam sessions. It was another favourite of the Prince of Wales. It was a place where he was able to let his hair down, get drunk and play the drums. Staff were consigned to clear the road of onlookers when he was the worse for wear and had to be driven back to St James's. Frisco's in Frith Street was a popular piano bar and drinking club, whilst Jig's, at the corner of St Anne's Court and Wardour Street, was an illegal gambling joint whose doors were firmly shut at eleven o'clock each night.

Gay clubs, now such a part of the Soho scene, were not unknown in the 1930s. Billie's Club in Little Denmark Street was being kept under police surveillance in November 1936. They reported witnessing degrading scenes. They described the people in the club as being of the 'Nancy Boy' type, men dancing with each other, some wearing rouge. Shockingly, these 'queers' referred to each other by girls' names. Even the cabaret featured a man in evening dress singing in an effeminate falsetto. The judge was not impressed, jailing the club's owner Billie Joyce for fifteen months.

Normally, it was daybreak by the time Soho revellers made their way home. At about the same time, bleary-eyed stallholders from Berwick Street were making their way to Covent Garden to collect their day's produce. Alarm clocks were waking shopkeepers, café owners and Windmill dancers. It was time to greet another day in the heart of Soho.

4

The Dark Side

It is strange how often dictators, despots and violent criminals have a soft side to their character. Darby Sabini, whose gang controlled much of the West End, was no exception. His father had died when he was only two, and the influence of his Irish mother remained with him and manifested itself in some unusual traits for a feared criminal. He hated swearing and blasphemy. He also insisted that all women were treated politely and with respect. This is significant because the one area of crime that he never became closely involved in was prostitution. That left a huge area of illegal activity for him to indulge in, including extreme violence, and yet even here there was a contradiction. He was squeamish when it came to slashing with a razor. He just couldn't look. No problem seeing an enemy being coshed or whacked with a chair leg, but then we all have the odd weakness in our CVs.

Darby Sabini was born in Saffron Hill, Clerkenwell, known as Little Italy, in 1889. Although he was one of the youngest of six brothers, it was Darby who emerged as the leader. They had all been educated at the local Roman Catholic school and found employment on leaving at thirteen. One brother, Joseph, even served in the Great War before being wounded and invalided out. The eldest boy, Fred, worked as a bookmaker and had little to do with the rest of the family. The brother most closely connected to Darby was Harry Boy, a good-looking young man known as Handsome Harry.

After the war, racing was booming and the Sabinis moved in and established a lucrative protection racket on the southern tracks. They charged the bookies not only for their pitch but every other essential required for them to trade, right down to the chalk to mark up the odds. This was achieved right from the outset by extreme violence. Darby had recruited a gang of hardmen to back up his family. Many were Jews from the East End. The gang's reputation spread – they were ruthless. Anyone challenging or even questioning them found themself in hospital. Here was the first example of violent organised crime in London since the end of the war. Any bookie hoping to appease or deflect them had fights develop outside his pitch so that the punters were unable to place their bets. Any further prevarication led to their whole pitch being destroyed and the bookie nursing a sore head. Nobody was going to help them – certainly not the police, who were already on the Sabini payroll.

By the 1930s, Soho and the West End were on their menu. Their methods were simple and effective. A fight would be started in a pub or club. Tables were broken, glasses smashed. Next morning, enter a sympathetic member of the Sabini organisation. The owner was informed that small regular payments would guarantee that no such trouble would ever be encountered again. Business could continue serenely and everyone would be happy. Few refused. Rumours spread that Darby Sabini had Mafia connections. True or not, the Flying Squad allowed the gang to continue unimpeded with their 'protection' or, put more crudely, their demanding money with menaces. Savage reprisals were visited on the few who challenged the gang. It was reckoned that they could call up to twenty thugs at a moment's notice. Their foot soldiers always carried weapons. They had rusty razors in the peak of their cloth caps. To be slashed with a razor was bad enough, but a rusty blade helped spread infections. These were not men to be provoked. They carried coshes and lead piping concealed down their trousers.

A hush would spread through the Admiral Duncan in Old Compton Street when the boys entered. Darby would look round the room and if in a good mood would order drinks all round. It was not his physical presence that spread fear. He was under average height and certainly not a snappy dresser. He always wore a wide, flat cap which made him appear even smaller, but there was something, a tension, a look, that put those who met him on their guard. He always wore a dark-brown suit. His crisp white shirt had no collar, but he sported a black silk cravat. He also favoured a high-buttoned waistcoat. It was rumoured that he often slept fully clothed, always on guard, a gun tucked under his pillow.

The Sabinis' activity spread across the whole of Soho like a stain. Bottle parties, so popular at the time, were targeted. Hardly a club, pub, café or shop escaped their scrutiny. Money was demanded and given. Sometimes they even employed a subtle approach, with police raiding premises and finding minor breaches in regulations which could lead to a court appearance. Enter a Sabini boy to soothe the troubled proprietor with the promise that no further action would be taken providing small regular payments were made and maintained. There was now another profitable area for Darby and his gang to exploit. Slot machines were installed and leased. They were all the rage and a nice little earner. Still the Sabinis sought new revenue streams and found them right amongst the criminal fraternity. It was time for them to pay their dues too. The Sabinis preyed on those they knew had recently 'pulled off a job'. They expected a cut or else! Known crooks who were stupid enough to travel up to Soho for a night out were targeted. Drinks ordered at clubs controlled by the Sabinis were charged at outrageous prices. Anyone hinting at complaint would find themselves lying in a gutter covered in blood.

The Sabinis had been challenged once by a combined gang from Hoxton and Holloway. They were routed in what became known as the Battle of Ham Yard, and the Italian boys then reigned supreme for years. Ham Yard was a dirty little backwater off Great Windmill Street and home to grubby clubs which constantly changed their names. It was quoted as being frequented by 'men and women of the worst character'.

By the mid-twenties, Harry Boy had extended the family's activities to include greyhound tracks, which were attracting massive crowds. Business was good but trouble was brewing. A group from the Elephant and Castle had gone on the rampage in Great Windmill Street. Although this was swiftly dealt with, there were problems from within the gang. Alf White and his extended family, who had loosened their connection to the Sabinis, now sought to challenge them. The trouble rumbled on until a henchman of White's, Michael MacAusland, was killed in an attack in King's Cross. Things were getting out of hand. Both Darby and White had always maintained a low profile where the courts were concerned. It was time for compromise. It was agreed that the Sabinis would confine their activities to the West End, and White to King's Cross. Darby was already showing signs of seeking a quieter life, drifting off for weekends in Brighton, where he had bought an apartment overlooking the sea. In his absence Harry Boy kept control.

At this point another character enters the cast. A man who is to feature strongly in Soho's criminal history. Jacob Comancho was an East End Jew who claimed that he had offered protection to the Jewish community from the Blackshirts of Oswald Mosley's British Fascists. He became known as Jack Spot because he maintained that he was always on the spot when there was trouble. The less charitable attributed it to a nasty mole on his ugly mug. In 1938 Spot was given a ten-month sentence for assault. It was whilst he was in prison that he found himself in a fight that made his reputation for being a hardman. Anti-Semitic feelings ran right through British society at the time. Antonio 'Babe' Mancini made his loathing obvious by spitting in Jack Spot's food. Mancini, a leading 'enforcer' for Darby Sabini, was generally feared. Enraged, Spot tore into Mancini and, as an onlooker put it, 'did him up'. News spread quickly throughout the underworld. The Jew was the one to watch. They were right.

Corruption in the Metropolitan Police was endemic. In November 1931 in a surprise move, Hugh Trenchard, former Marshall of the Royal Air Force, was appointed Commissioner of the Met. Although reluctant to accept the post, he was eventually persuaded by King George V. What he found on starting deeply disturbed him. Discipline was lax, discontentment with pay and conditions rife. He felt that many of his senior officers were evasive on the question of corruption within the force. This seemed to be exacerbated by widespread membership of Freemasonry, which divided loyalties. Trenchard was quoted as saying, 'You can't measure corruption as exactly as you can measure crime.' He really didn't know who he could trust and, besides, there were many other problems which were easier for him to address. By the time he left his post in 1935 police corruption in Soho remained and was to get worse.

Before the arrival of the Messina Brothers from Malta, prostitutes tended to work mostly freelance or were controlled by their ponce. Many were French or Belgian girls who married British men to enable them to work the streets. They were known

as 'Fifis' and as if they weren't obvious enough they opted to wear
a chain around one ankle just so there was no doubt. The year
1935 saw the start of a series of murders involving prostitutes.
Business remained difficult due to the economic climate and the
girls were being forced to take lower prices and go with the type
of punter they would previously have turned down. The killing
started in November when Josephine Martin was found in her flat
in Archer Street strangled with one of her own stockings. Although
known as 'French Fifi', she had been born in Russia. Married off
to an Englishman to gain citizenship, she was also helping to
distribute drugs for her ponce, Max Kessel, known as 'Red Max'
because of his ginger hair. Her brother was questioned by police
but as he relied on her for his sole income he was unlikely to be
implicated and was released. Less than two months later, Max
Kessel was murdered. His body was discovered in a ditch near
St Albans, but forensic tests showed he had been shot in Little
Newport Street in a flat rented by Frenchman Marcel Vernon. A
larger than life character, Vernon had been sent to Devil's Island
in 1924 for assault and was one of the very few to escape. There
appears to have been an intense love triangle involving a beautiful
prostitute, Suzanne Bertrand. She and Vernon escaped to France
but were arrested upon arrival. They were sent for trial at the
Paris Assizes and the *United Press* reported it under the banner
headline 'Murder in Soho'.

French law didn't permit extradition but allowed French citizens
to be tried in France for crimes committed abroad. Vernon's
defence was exposed by British pathologist Sir Bernard Spilsbury,
as six bullet wounds and a severe beating around the head hardly
smacked of self-defence. As the two men had links to prostitution
dating back many years across the Continent and in Canada, it
seems likely that the murder related to an attempt to set up and
control prostitution in Soho. Vernon was sent back to Devil's
Island but, intriguingly, the killings continued. Jeanette Cotton
was found strangled with her own silk scarf in Lexington Street
and within weeks Constance Hines was also strangled in her flat
in Old Compton Street. Then Elsie Torchan, who worked a stretch
in Wardour Street, was also found strangled. The police reaction
was strange. They were obviously worried that a connection
would be made to the Kessel killing and that organised crime
was rife. They preferred, for some reason, to let the public believe
that 'Jack the Strangler' was on the loose. We will never know the

truth as no arrests were ever made. The killings stopped but the suspicion remained that the police were not that keen to find out who was responsible.

If the public was really concerned about organised crime, a new team had just arrived in Soho to justify those fears. Brothers feature prominently in British crime and the Messina Boys were just about to introduce a new meanness and professionalism to the oldest profession. With the leading French operators out of the scene, the Messinas showed exquisite timing. The brothers Alfredo, Carmelo, Salvatore, Attilo and Eugenio had an impeccable pedigree. Their father had worked at a brothel in Valetta before moving to Alexandria, where he built up a successful chain. The boys had learnt the business well but Guiseppe was deported from Egypt in 1932 and within a couple of years the others followed. Because their father had Maltese citizenship they were able to take British nationality. They started in a small way with Eugenio's wife Colette working the streets. Steadily, they brought over girls from the Continent. They now assumed English names – Arthur Evans and Charles Maitland had a comfortable ring to them. They started buying up Soho property, rundown and filthy but cheap. Paul Raymond was to start building up his Soho property portfolio some twenty years later, a decision that helped make him one of the richest men in Britain. Slowly, the Messinas recruited English girls using the old trick of flattery, gifts and even hints of marriage before requiring them to go and earn their keep. The brothers were laying the foundations for their future empire.

In the 1930s homosexuals faced the twin threats of prison and blackmail. It was a golden age for blackmailers, often referred to as 'murder of the soul'. Harry Raymond was a former West End actor who had appeared in Edgar Wallace's racing thriller *The Calendar* at Wyndham's Theatre in Charing Cross Road. It was not long before he was using his skills to more lucrative effect. He set out to target members of the establishment who had a liking for young men. Often married, they proved easy quarry when set up by Raymond. Whilst several danced to his tune, frightened by the stigma of exposure, there always seemed to be a strong character who would not be cowed and who went to the police. This was a lesson he was always slow to learn, but not before he brought misery to many lives. In January 1933 Raymond was sentenced to five years for extortion. Rather than being deterred, he used his time inside to refine his operation. Released on licence in October 1936, he rented a café in Lisle Street which he used as a base to train and groom a small army of attractive young men to be used as bait. They were smartly dressed and strategically despatched to fashionable hotels and restaurants. They were rehearsed in the art of entrapment as thoroughly as if they too were to appear on the West End stage. Slowly and steady wins the race. A drink at the bar, maybe followed by a second 'chance' meeting during a visit to the theatre or at a late supper. Then, finally, the visit to the bedroom – the door left ajar. Enter another member of the team posing as a brother or father of the poor young man who is reduced to tears. Raymond went to huge trouble in making the interruption look genuine.

The quarry had been carefully chosen: former senior army officers, retired judges, leaders of industry. All seemed willing to pay, sometimes huge sums, to avoid the shame of public exposure. One poor man had over £10,000 extorted from him. Raymond was ruthless in pursuit of his victims. Business was booming. He extended his activities by controlling a small collection of prostitutes from his seedy café. He was living the high life. It couldn't last. It didn't. Finally, a man known simply as 'Mr A' realised there would be no end to the demands and went to the police. A trap was set at Victoria Station, where Raymond was heard to say, '£5,000 – you know I can ruin you unless you pay!' His reign was over. This time the sentence was ten years.

Soho has always attracted 'characters' but possibly none stranger than Willy Clarkson. He was a wig maker and costumier to leading West End theatres. He was also a victim of blackmail and an insurance fraudster. King George V had appointed him as Royal Perruquier and Costumier. He was part of the twenties establishment, running his business from premises in Wardour Street. Opposite was a notorious public lavatory in Dansey Place known as 'Clarkson's Cottage'.

Clarkson's appearance was, in a sense, also one of disguise. Short and overweight, he had curly red hair and his moustache was described as being like the horns of a cow. His clipped beard was dyed. His face was powdered and rouged, creating an impression so grotesque that many, including John Gielgud, felt extremely uncomfortable in his company. During the height of his success in the 1920s, he was able to purchase the Duchess Theatre in Catherine Street. By the 1930s, the emergence of the film industry had led to a decline in his fortunes. Although still always seen at opening nights, he became increasingly miserly. Then, in October 1934, he died in suspicious circumstances. A post-mortem carried out by Sir Bernard Spilsbury was unable to pinpoint foul play, but doubts remained. The chances are that this master of disguise was being blackmailed. Rumours circulated about his homosexuality and visits to the public toilet in Dansey Place. What was certain was a will dated 1929 leaving the bulk of his estate to a convicted blackmailer, William Hobbs. This was challenged in the High Court by Max Brezinski and his daughter, who claimed they were close to Clarkson and that he treated them as family. They had a will dated 1931 which had been witnessed. In 1935 the probate court found in favour of Brezinski, and Hobbs was subsequently convicted of forgery and sentenced to five years.

Still the plot thickened. Insurance companies started looking into a series of claims submitted over the years by Clarkson for fire damage. A search revealed that he had made nine claims over some forty years. In 1937, London Assurance and Lloyds Underwriters filed suits against the estate. It appeared that they were able to prove that a 1931 claim had been fraudulent and another made two years later refused. Further investigations led to the trial of Leopold Harris. An insurance assessor, he had organised a fire-raising gang and had been involved with Clarkson in making false claims. The insurance companies were now able to reclaim their money from the Clarkson estate. So a man who had been admired for his amazing skill as a costumier, but laughed at behind his back for his mincing ways and coarse Cockney accent, remained an enigma as he went to his grave – a man who had dressed the leading lights of British ballet and theatre, who supplied disguises to Crippen and, quite possibly, Jack the Ripper. Disguises allow for concealment and deception. Surely this is a fitting epitaph for Willy Clarkson.

5

The World is a Stage

It was probably the smallest lift in London. A single occupant felt constrained and claustrophobic as it shuddered its way to the top floor. Upon joining the formidable Dame Mary Tempest in its confined space, a callow, young actor found it impossible not to make contact with her mountainous bosom. After such intimate contact she demanded that he should do the honourable thing and marry her. Horrified, the young man scuttled away. The only other access to this lair above the Globe Theatre in Shaftesbury Avenue involved climbing a steep, concrete staircase. Either way, those arriving on the top floor were often discomforted or out of breath. Their unease was not improved by their being led down a darkened corridor and shown into a tiny, cramped office. Sitting at an elevated desk, to put his visitor at further disadvantage, was a man who was to dominate London's theatre for some forty years.

Binkie Beaumont's arrival on the public scene strangely coincided with the opening of the Windmill and continued during the theatre's lifetime. Although not a man to seek publicity, it was in June 1932 that he first came to the public's notice. The *Daily Mail* headline read: 'Foyer Lounge Suit. "Fanfare" Manager's Dress Suit Stolen'. It went on to report that theatrical tradition had been shattered when Hugh Beaumont, the manager of the 'Fanfare' company being staged at the Prince Edward Theatre, was dressed in a lounge suit, rather than the customary evening dress. Binkie's flat, just off Park Lane, had been broken into. The thief took not only his cufflinks and tie pins, but also all his waistcoats, dress shirts and his evening suit. Binkie, although the employee of Howard

& Wyndham, the theatrical agents, was already working with
Harold Tennant. By 1936, they felt confident enough to found
their own company and H. M. Tennant increasingly came to
be the overwhelming major force in London's theatre world.
Whilst C. B. Cochran continued to be known for his lavish
musicals, Beaumont originally opted for serious drama and
light comedy.

Unlike Vivian Van Damm (whose headquarters were just
round the corner from the Globe), Beaumont sought to cloak
his early life in mystery. His modest upbringing in South Wales
didn't suit the persona he projected. He was, and remained,
a terrible snob. Like Van Damm, he was a perfectionist in his
own field, with an eye for detail but, more importantly, with an
instinct for what would work. This intuition covered seemingly
the commissioning of unlikely scripts and the inspirational
casting of actors. Something of a social butterfly, he was also
skilful at making and maintaining influential contacts.

None of these attributes appeared forthcoming during the
early months of the newly formed H. M. Tennant. The sure
touch demonstrated whilst working for Howard & Wyndham
appeared to desert him. Although he had judged it imperative for
his first show to be a roaring success, he was to be disappointed.
He turned down plays by George Bernard Shaw, Eugene O'Neill
and Ivor Novello before deciding on the smash Broadway hit *The
Old Maid*. He brought Lilian Gish across from the States to star.
His choice of the aggressive lesbian Leontine Sagan to produce
the show led to huge friction. It didn't even survive the provincial
run before being put to death in Manchester. His humiliation
was such that Binkie's usual impeccable social manners deserted
him. In a sign of his immaturity, he didn't even thank the cast or
Lilian Gish for their efforts. The knives were out. He didn't only
look ludicrously young – he was also acting like a spoilt child.
Without the protection of a large organisation behind him it was
reckoned he would struggle. Things were not about to improve.
His second production, *The Ante Room*, fared little better. It
at least made the West End but was damned by the critics and
closed after ten miserable performances. Still he struggled; where
was the Midas touch that had catapulted him to prominence at
such a young age? His next effort, *Farewell Performance*, seemed
aptly named, running for just eleven shows. The star impresario
was becoming an embarrassment, losing his backers' money, his

confidence in his own ability and his reputation. This was crisis time for a young man previously admired but not universally liked. His upbringing in South Wales had been cloaked in a mist of his own making. He didn't like his modest background and had no intention of returning to it. He had acquired the trappings of success, together with a clipped, cut-glass accent. Binkie was a snob and a social climber. This was a time when he could have disappeared from public view. Instead, he used his ability to meet and greet those who were influential in the theatrical world. He was convinced that opportunities would not be long in coming. It was time to regroup.

Whilst Binkie Beaumont was searching for a success to reverse his fortunes, business just around the corner at the Windmill was brisk. Making worthwhile profits was still a struggle, but whilst Laura Henderson was prepared to bankroll the company, much of the stress was taken away from Vivian Van Damm. He had worry enough with the logistics of changing shows every three to six weeks. The layout of the building didn't help, with dressing rooms split between the basement and upper floors, even though they each had loud speakers to give early warning of entrance calls. Above the auditorium, stage and lounge were shower rooms, the wardrobe department and rehearsal rooms. Offices were tucked away wherever a space could be found and on the top floor were the kitchen and canteen. During show times there was a constant rush as artistes squeezed by each other to make their entrance.

By 1935 the Windmill had become something of a West End fixture and a popular tourist destination. Even the critic for *The Times* was warming to *Revudeville*: 'The sixty-fifth version of the Windmill Theatre's continuous revue preserves the easy going friendly atmosphere that has always been its distinguishing characteristic.' It went on to praise the tableau entitled 'Bees Wedding' as being beautifully posed. The critic praised the 'hard working young ladies called "the Windmill Girls", as they flitted and pranced, displaying perfection in the outline of their limbs'. The punters would probably have described them rather more graphically.

Laura Henderson continued to be an almost daily visitor to the shows. She had her own private two-seater box fitted with brocade curtains which she drew if anything in the show displeased her. She would regularly take an irrational dislike to some of the girls. Her dislike was never directed towards a male member of the cast, all of whom she appeared to love. This quirk was attributed to the loss of her beloved only son in the Great War. She could be really vindictive if she took umbrage at some poor, unsuspecting chorus girl. She would turn away or even make a dramatic exit when the offender came on stage. Van Damm, to his credit, never let any of Mrs Henderson's prejudices affect his judgement and he just ignored her constant harping. Laura Henderson could be very intimidating. If the girls heard her coming along the corridor, they tended to turn the lights out in their dressing rooms in the hope she would go away. There was little common ground between a seventy-year-old millionairess and chorus girls surviving on a few pounds a week. Normally dressed in black, Laura had the appearance of a maiden aunt. Sometimes she would arrive in the evening after a dinner engagement, in an expensive gown which was crowned by her wearing a glittering diamond tiara.

Her relationship with Van Damm continued to be largely friendly and supportive, and yet she always maintained enough distance between them to establish their employer/employee relationship. She rarely dropped her formal guard except by referring to him as Bop. Her letters to him, although often affectionate, were always signed 'Laura H' or just 'LH'.

Although her upbringing came out in her formality, her eccentricity was seldom far from the surface. Bizarrely, she amused herself by gaining entry to her own theatre dressed in a series of outlandish disguises. She even went to the trouble of going to the famous costumier and master of disguise Willy Clarkson. He once accompanied her to the theatre when she was dressed as a man, complete with tailed coat and grey felt hat. So good was the disguise that Vivian Van Damm failed to recognise her. She also took a childish delight in duping the staff when she dressed as a Chinese woman, and then with a blackened face as an African. It remained unclear why she derived so much pleasure from these seemingly crazy impersonations. Still not satisfied, she subsequently turned up at auditions, first dressed as a polar bear and then as a giant rabbit.

Away from these distractions, Van Damm hit upon an important new source of revenue with the introduction of the *Windmill Souvenir Programme*. The first edition cost only 1s and set an entirely new trend by containing photographs of nudes. Although he probably didn't realise it, Van Damm was opening up a lucrative market for girlie magazines. At the time, photographs of nudes were not openly available and largely confined to 'under the counter' purchases imported from the Continent. The first edition sold out in a matter of days and was a forerunner of the increasingly sexualised magazines that followed over the years.

In 1935 Vivian Van Damm became aware that Doris Berry, one of his dancers, was the sister of ballerina Alicia Markova. Following visits to see Markova dance, Van Damm, in consultation with Mrs Henderson, decided that they would form their own ballet company. It was confirmed that the company would tour the provinces and, although this proved to be an expensive failure, ballet played an increasingly important role in the staging of Windmill shows.

By 1936, there was a renewed chorus of complaints about the amount of nudity to be seen on the West End stage. This was prompted by the Palladium including nudes in their latest production. Van Damm remained untroubled by the furore, mainly because he had a rather more pressing problem. To his horror, two girls informed him they were going on strike. They had worked out that at a weekly rate of £2 10s they were only earning 1s 8d for each of their performances. A friendly statistician had estimated that in the course of a year they covered 35 miles from their dressing room to the stage. That didn't seem too excessive, but how about having 5,000 changes of costume? Worse still, they were required to complete 75,000 high kicks. No wonder they went through seventy-five pairs of shoes in a year. Confronted with this evidence, even the rather autocratic Van Damm had to give way. The cast's wages were increased by 5s a week every two weeks until they reached £4 per week. In fact, the girls weren't doing that badly when fringe benefits were included. There was a subsidised canteen and they also enjoyed the services of a company doctor, dentist and an accountant who was also on hand to help with any tax or financial problems. A sun lamp was even provided for those who wanted to top up their tan, which would also have been possible courtesy of a canvas plunge pool situated on the roof during the summer. Not much work was done on the top floor of surrounding offices on those sunny Soho afternoons.

The Windmill was not the only niche theatre in Soho. The Arts Theatre Club performed from a basement in Great Newport Street. It specialised in quirky, experimental plays and those considered not commercial enough for the major West End venues. Occasionally, a new play did make the transition, such as *Richard of Bordeaux*, which was directed by John Gielgud in 1932. Several West End theatres were struggling against the onslaught from the cinema. Daly's Theatre in Cranbourn Street suffered a series of short runs. A revival of the popular *Charley's Aunt* failed to save it from closure. Following a final performance of *The First Legion* the management gave up the fight and the old theatre was demolished to make way for the ultra-modern Warner cinema. The Crosse & Blackwell factory in Charing Cross Road was another landmark which had been replaced by the Astoria cinema. Manufacturing on a large scale was becoming a rarity in the West End. By the end of the 1930s it was mostly only pockets of small workshops (many within Soho) which were actually making products.

The popularity of the cinema was irresistible. Seats were cheaper than at most theatres and the scope of the silver screen was infinite. It was possible to be transported all over the world in the company of international stars. For the most part the attraction of the theatre paled by comparison; revues and musicals remained popular but serious theatre was having a tough time.

Binkie Beaumont was only too aware of this as he still awaited his first popular success. The year of 1937 was important for him both on professional and personal fronts. His production of George Bernard Shaw's *Candita* opened at the Globe to excellent reviews. He had widened his circle of influential friends to extend beyond the theatre to politics. His good looks and wit had attracted Clementine Churchill and he found himself being invited to her luncheon parties. Never happier than being surrounded by the rich and powerful, he made a lasting friendship with Foreign Secretary Anthony Eden. To sit alongside Noel Coward, Sir Thomas Beecham,

Lord Beaverbrook and the Duke and Duchess of Kent marked his arrival as a fixture in London's top social scene.

His good fortune was accelerated by his meeting with John Perry, a languid, good-looking actor from a rich, aristocratic, Irish background. Only one snag: Perry was living with John Gielgud. Obviously, there was a mutual attraction and in no time at all Perry decamped to Binkie's Piccadilly flat. The two had similar interests. They seldom missed an important race meeting and they enjoyed the thrill of the gaming tables. They were to spend a lifetime together, punctuated by one or two jealous hiccups. Later in their relationship, Perry was made a director of H. M. Tennant.

Binkie normally steered away from being involved with charity performances, which he thought were generally miscast and under-rehearsed. When royalty was guaranteed to attend, his prejudices were instantly cast aside. At the beginning of 1938 he presented *The Importance of Being Earnest* at the Globe. The first performance was given in aid of the Soho Hospital for Women and attended by Queen Mary. Binkie could not have been happier. At just thirty-one, he was already an established figure in the West End. He had a new and loving partner. The outlook was bright except for that ghastly Mr Hitler. Binkie always tried to ignore unpleasantness. In July 1938 he declared, 'This silly war is just not going to happen.' At the Windmill there was a much more pragmatic approach. Tin helmets hung amongst the sequins and feathers. Brown cardboard boxes containing gas masks littered the dressing rooms. Sandbags were being placed outside public buildings. All along Shaftesbury Avenue people wearing service uniforms began to outnumber civilians. Attendances at theatres, which had been poor for some months, slumped alarmingly during August. By early September barrage balloons floated above the Windmill. Binkie Beaumont had been fooling himself. This war was going to be frightening and devastating for Britain and London. For Soho too, but, as ever, its experiences were to be subtly different, its reaction more complex. Foreign neighbours would be betrayed whilst others from around the world welcomed. There would be death by bombing, but by murder too. There would be tragedy but also laughter and love. There would be rationing, shortages, the black market and spivs. Soho was to become a magnet for servicemen on leave. The restaurants would attempt to serve edible meals for the allowed maximum of five bob. The whores would be working overtime, and at Soho's centre stood the Windmill Theatre, whose wartime slogan was to become immortalised.

Top left: 1. A rather scruffy-looking Frith Street in the 1930s, despite the bunting.

Bottom left: 2. The Lyric Theatre, one of many that lined Shaftesbury Avenue in London's answer to Broadway.

Below: 3. The irrepressible Laura Henderson, owner of the Windmill Theatre.

Above: 4. An early photograph of the Windmill auditorium.

Right: 5. A young Vivian Van Damm captured during his early years at the Windmill.

Windmill Theatre

GREAT WINDMILL STREET. PICCADILLY CIRCUS. W.1

THE SITE OF THE WINDMILL THEATRE AND SCOTT'S RESTAURANT

Programme

6. A programme for *Inquest*, the first play to be staged by Laura Henderson, which closed after a short run.

7. A charming publicity shot of Windmill girls taken in August 1932.

8. The company celebrating the first anniversary of the Windmill, taken on 4 February 1933.

REVUDEVILLE

CONTINUOUS VARIETY

WINDMILL THEATRE

Directors:
L. HENDERSON   L. V. PEARKES

Licensed by the Lord Chamberlain to
Mrs. Laura Henderson

**GT. WINDMILL STREET
PICCADILLY CIRCUS, W.1**

TELEPHONES
BOX OFFICE: GER. 7413-4
MANAGER'S OFFICE: GER 4841

August 1st 1933.

AM.
Eric Barker Esq.

Dear Sir:-

This is to confirm that your contract has been extended for a further week commencing August 7th 1933.

Yours faithfully,
WINDMILL THEATRE CO.LTD.,

V. Va Dann

General Manager.

9. A letter confirming the appointment of comedian Eric Barker.

The London Casino Restaurant

10. The London Casino on Old Compton Street was a spectacular setting for a night out in Soho.

11. Programme for the London Casino, whose premises are now the Prince of Wales Theatre.

12. Programme for *Black Velvet*, the popular 1938 revue.

Above: 13. Dancing at a crowded Café de Paris in 1932.

Right: 14. Peppino Leoni, owner of the famous Quo Vadis restaurant in Dean Street.

15. The Café de Paris in 1935. The most fashionable nightclub venue in town was tragically destroyed by a German bomb in 1944.

Above: 16. The only known photograph of the infamous Sabini gang.

Right: 17. From his office on the top of the Globe Theatre in Shaftesbury Avenue, Binkie schemed and plotted his way to unrivalled influence.

18. An early 1930s shot of a young Binkie Beaumont, who was to become the major force in the London theatre.

THEATRES OF WARTIME LONDON REVIEWED BY ARTIST AND CAMERA: No. 14. REVUDEVILLE NON-STOP REVUE AT THE WINDMILL.

19. A collage of early Windmill performers.

20. Laura Henderson poses with the company to celebrate the eighth anniversary of the opening of the theatre. Seated second from the left in the front row is Doris Barry, sister of the ballerina Alicia Markova.

21. 'Snake Hips Johnson', the band leader who was killed together with many others when the Café de Paris was bombed on 18 March 1941.

22. Windmill girls sunbathing on the roof of the theatre.

Above left: 23. Snatching some sleep despite the bombs.

Above right: 24. Some Windmill girls described the period of the Blitz as like being back at school.

Revudeville No. 139
"THE COCKTAIL PARTY"
Margaret and Nugent Marshall

25. Pin-up girl Margaret McGrath pictured with fellow performer Nugent Marshall. It was Margaret who helped rescue the horses from blazing stables in Ham Yard.

26. Margaret McGrath, pictured with fellow artiste Valerie Tandy.

27–29. The notorious Messina brothers, who virtually controlled the vice trade in Soho for two decades.

Above left: 30. Windmill girl Jill Anstey with American film star George Raft.

Above right: 31. The Rainbow Corner, a Soho sanctuary and home from home for thousands of American troops during the war.

Top: 32. Evelyn Oatley, one of the victims of the 'Soho Ripper'. She claimed to be an ex-Windmill girl, but this is disputed.

Middle: 33. Victory celebrations in Piccadilly Circus. Note that the statue of Eros was boarded up.

Bottom: 34. A Jean Straker photograph of GIs getting to meet the locals in a Soho club.

Above: 35. Chez Auguste in Old Compton Street, captured by Jean Straker.

Right: 36. Arthur English, the archetypal spiv, on stage at the Windmill.

PART 2

THE FORTIES

6

It's War

The reedy voice of Neville Chamberlain concluded, 'Now may God bless you and may He defend the right. For it's evil things that we shall be fighting against, brute force, bad faith, injustice, oppression and persecution. And against them I am certain that the right will prevail.'

The wireless was switched off and for a moment there was silence. Then, as if on cue, the first wartime air-raid siren wailed its way down Shaftesbury Avenue. Edith Evans, losing any semblance of a stiff upper lip, shrieked, 'I'm an actress – I can't do anything but act.' War with Germany was bad enough but the compulsory closing of London's theatres was too much to bear. Alec Guinness guided her out into the late summer sunlight in an attempt to calm her down. Meanwhile, Binkie Beaumont, in an extravagant gesture, took the whole cast of *The Cherry Orchard* for lunch at Scott's.

Round the corner at the Windmill, there were no such histrionics. Vivian Van Damm realised that wartime would eventually offer his theatre the chance to cash in on the huge numbers of servicemen likely to visit the West End. He arranged to pay his staff until the theatre was allowed to reopen. As the company attended rehearsals each day during that twelve-day period, he was famously able to claim, 'We never closed.'

The country, meanwhile, was understandably apprehensive. Londoners almost expected bombs to rain down on them immediately. It appeared to many that just as the country was overcoming many of its ills, due to complacency and appeasement Britain was again drifting into a catastrophic war. So much had improved. People were generally healthier. Life

expectancy had increased and, significantly, child mortality had
halved since the end of the Great War. Earnings had increased
substantially and the number of industrial deaths had fallen
dramatically since the General Strike. Violent crime represented
less than 1 per cent of the total.

Despite the dire warnings of air attacks, nothing happened.
This was a phoney war, although life was certainly different.
Thousands of children were being evacuated to the country.
There was a plague of rats. Throughout London thousands
of pet dogs and cats were put down, either through concern
for their well-being or, more likely, to save on feeding costs.
Despite sandbags, gas masks and barrage balloons, it was
still possible to convince yourself that little had changed. At
the end of September it was decided that price controls rather
than rationing would be instigated for bread, eggs and fish.
However, by January 1940 everyone had to register with a
grocer or butcher as general food rationing was progressively
introduced.

As news of the war worsened with the fall of Belgium and
Holland, Britain's tendency to xenophobia increased. In Soho,
where for centuries people of different nationalities had lived
in harmony, suddenly many started showing resentment
towards their Jewish and Italian neighbours. Bizarrely, many
Jewish refugees who had sought sanctuary in this country were
rounded up and sent to internment camps. With Mussolini
entering the war in June 1940, the anger and resentment was
now directed at the Italian community. Placards appeared in the
windows of Italian-owned shops claiming the proprietors were
Swiss, but with little effect. A group of Soho women marched
down Old Compton Street threatening Italian businesses.
They were dissuaded from smashing windows by Rosie Blau,
a brave Jewish woman who confronted them and reminded
anyone who was prepared to listen that most of the Italian
families had lived in Soho all their lives. Rather shamefaced,
the march broke up. This didn't influence gangs from outside
the area who rampaged through Soho smashing up Italian
shops and restaurants. Churchill didn't help. He issued orders
'to collar the lot'. People were snatched from their homes.
Well-known Italian figures, like delicatessen owner Ennio
Camisa and leading restaurateur Peppino Leoni (owner of
Quo Vadis), were rounded up by police. They were taken to

Lingfield racecourse and later to a disused cotton mill in Bury whilst their future was being decided. The unlucky ones were chosen for deportation to Canada. They were despatched on former Blue Star cruise liner *Arandora Star*. The ship carried over 1,500, mainly Italian deportees and 400 British service personnel. It has never been explained why the ship did not carry the Red Cross emblem. It was torpedoed by a German U-boat off the coast of Ireland with the loss of almost 700 men, 200 of whom were British.

In all, about 39,000 people were interned during the war. Their absence was particularly noticeable in Soho, where they had formed such an important sector of the community.

The day of 7 September 1940 witnessed the first night of a bombing campaign that became known as 'The Blitz'. For months to come, Soho roads were seldom free from shrapnel, broken glass and piles of debris. On the night of 18 September, the area endured a particularly heavy raid that saw the demolition of the John Lewis store in Oxford Street and widespread local damage. In the same month, Soho suffered its first major loss to the Luftwaffe when St Anne's parish church was destroyed on the evening of the 24th. Only the tower remained; the rest of the seventeenth-century building was burnt out. Two months later, a huge bomb smashed through the roof of St Patrick's Roman Catholic church in Soho Square. Amazingly, the bomb was buried in the nave and didn't explode. During the same raid, the Queen's Theatre in Shaftesbury Avenue was also badly damaged. The auditorium was wrecked and the front façade destroyed. Thus ended the successful run of Daphne du Maurier's *Rebecca*, in which Margaret Rutherford (formerly known as a comedy actress) appeared as a frightening Mrs Danvers to rave reviews.

By now many Soho dwellers were using either Leicester Square or Piccadilly Circus underground stations for sleeping. For those who didn't fancy stretching out on platforms, the Lex Garage in Brewer Street offered a good alternative. The building had been partly converted into a well-planned shelter. It had a canteen, doctor's surgery and, most importantly, relatively comfortable bunks. Some, though, brought their own chairs and blankets or slept on the floor. It developed into its own community centre, with card schools and sing songs being organised. As the Blitz continued, fewer people used the shelters. A feeling of invincibility became commonplace, with many not bothering to take cover even during air raids.

18 March 1941 was one of the blackest days for Soho as it saw the bombing of the Café de Paris in Coventry Street. The Rialto cinema had been built in 1912 and the basement converted into a nightclub in 1924. It was, without doubt, the place to be seen and ironically advertised as 'the safest place to dance in town'. Its resident band was the West Indian orchestra led by 'Snake Hips Johnson'. He had been appearing earlier in the evening at the Embassy Club. He rushed back to the Café de Paris to the noise of ack-ack fire and falling bombs. Standing well over six feet in height, he appeared his normal debonair self as he led his band in the opening number of 'Oh Johnny' right on time at 9.30 p.m. As the band continued playing, a bomb fell straight down an airshaft and exploded on the dance floor. There was pandemonium. Survivors in torn and tattered evening wear staggered out onto the street. 'Snake Hips', like several other victims, died totally unmarked. The nearby Honeydew Restaurant was used as a mortuary, whilst survivors were taken off to Charing Cross Hospital. In all, thirty bodies were recorded and more than fifty revellers were seriously injured. Eventually, the death toll was to rise to a distressing eighty. How ironic that a club designed to replicate the decor of the doomed *Lusitania* should be witness to so much death and destruction.

At almost the same time as the Café de Paris was wrecked, another bomb brought misery to Soho. The Madrid Restaurant in Dean Street received a direct hit, killing a further seventeen people. Within a month even worse was to come. A tumbledown block of tenements was hit and destroyed on 17 April 1941 in Newport Place, which was amongst the most deprived districts in Soho. Sleeping residents were trapped in the tangled debris. Despite the frantic efforts of rescue teams, a further forty-eight people were killed. Ugly gaps were appearing in the streets like missing teeth. Children used these bomb sites as playgrounds, climbing through the rubble that had once been people's homes and where their neighbours had recently died. To many of them, war was just as exciting as their visit to the Saturday morning 'pictures' at the local cinema.

After twelve days of compulsory closure, the Windmill reopened for the 126th edition of *Revudeville*. The first show attracted an audience of less than a hundred. Soon, however, long queues snaked their way down Great Windmill Street. Already servicemen were well to the fore, pushing their way towards the stage by leapfrogging the seats in what was to become known as the 'Windmill Grand National', in order to get a close-up view. Each morning, the resident handyman had to tighten the bolts holding the seats down. *Revudeville* and the Windmill came to symbolise London's refusal to lie down under the Nazi threat. Increasingly, people were looking for a few moments' distraction from the continuous, gloomy news regarding the progress of the war. The Windmill provided a bright and cheerful interlude and also a chance to see bare flesh. It seems strange to us today, but back in those dark days many young men had never seen a bare female body. It was not uncommon for married couples to keep themselves almost totally covered even when making love. Young men arrived in London full of hope and testosterone. Luckily for them, rationing and the need for the cast to share costumes led to the shows being far more revealing. What covered a slender chorus girl left little to the imagination when her better-endowed colleague took over for the next show. The Windmill fast became the first stop of choice for servicemen on leave or stationed close to London.

For the girls at the Windmill, it was also a time of huge excitement and whirlwind romances. Life was for living *now*. It was perfectly possible that anyone could be killed, either in action or by a falling bomb. The stage doorkeeper was an important man. All the girls tried to keep in his good books. Stage-door johnnies were kept waiting whilst the particular girl of interest was contacted by phone and the admirer described in detail by the doorkeeper. Looks, rank and personality were all reviewed from the dressing room. It was noted that, generally, Army personnel were rather shy and tongue-tied. The Naval boys fared a little better, but the outright favourites were 'the boys in blue' – the young RAF pilots and crew, who had little time for regulation uniforms and who wore their service hats at a rakish angle. These young daredevils didn't take no for an answer. They had a cab waiting and a table booked. What was a young girl supposed to do? Romance and passion often followed, but so did tragedy. Although very occasionally these initial, rushed dates led to marriage, more often death or hideous injury intervened. Life was being lived at a hectic pace. Morality was being turned on its head in a dash for instant excitement.

It would seem that even Vivian Van Damm was caught up in the changing climate. Being surrounded by so many beautiful girls was obviously a temptation as reports of him resorting to the 'casting couch' emerged. Even so, VD, as he was known by the company, remained an admired and respected boss. Tough, but caring, he had arranged for all the staff to be given specific wartime duties, including first aid and fire watching. Some became ARPs (air-raid precaution wardens), whose duties included patrolling the streets during blackout. With the commencement of the Blitz, many of the company moved into the theatre. Van Damm insisted that on their days off all staff wore tin hats and carried gas masks. He also set his own curfew hours, requiring everyone to be back at the theatre by eleven o'clock. Some likened the atmosphere to that of boarding school. Lights out was set for 11.15 p.m. in order for everyone to get a good night's sleep. The boys slept in the downstairs dressing room, whereas the girls had mattresses in the bar, whilst others cosied up in Mrs Henderson's private box. Van Damm, a notorious snorer, was consigned to one of the smallest dressing rooms. To many, the camaraderie and excitement were fondly remembered in later life.

With the decision for most of the company to live in the theatre, they were, in effect, working in the front line. They showed great courage and spirit each night as they went onstage against a background of ack-ack fire and falling bombs. On 19 October 1940, there was a particularly heavy raid. One of the girls asked Valerie Tandy to pop out and get her a sandwich. She rushed across the road to the café opposite. The fact the café had run out of egg and tomato saved Valerie's life. As she returned to see if cheese would do, there was a fearful explosion. She was blown headlong into the theatre. The café she had just left was completely wrecked. There were no survivors, but she lived to tell the tale.

The same incident resulted in the only death experienced by the Windmill staff. Although Joan Jay, an eighteen-year-old dancer, had promised her father not to go out during raids, there had been a lull and she decided to risk it. Together with male dancer Nugent Marshall and Peter Rock, a seventeen-year-old electrician, they went out of the stage door to the pub opposite. Joan said, 'Suddenly, I experienced a sensation I can't explain!' No wonder. In the ensuing panic she would have been just vaguely aware of the smell of gas and cordite. People were yelling and screaming. Everything was very confused. Marshall was hailed as a hero for pulling her out of the rubble. Later in life she insisted they climbed out together. Marshall suffered shrapnel wounds to his neck, but Joan had far worse injuries. One wound in her thigh was so deep that she had to ram her fist in it in an attempt to staunch the bleeding. Girls from the Windmill, several of whom had first-aid certificates, piled blankets on her and desperately tried to find an ambulance. The whole area was in turmoil but eventually they managed to wave one down in Shaftesbury Avenue. Joan was operated on in Charing Cross Hospital and it was decreed she would never dance again. How wrong they were. After a series of skin grafts, she was back on stage at the Windmill some three months later. A sad postscript to that night was that Peter Rock, the young electrician, was killed.

Margaret McGrath was generally acknowledged as the Windmill's number one pin-up in 1940. On that awful October night, she volunteered to look for the missing electrician. It was a gruesome business. There were over a dozen mutilated bodies covered by blankets lying in the street, and none of the Windmill men could face the task. So it was left to the glamorous Margaret to identify the poor boy.

Within days, Margaret was back in action. She was in one of the remaining cafés in Great Windmill Street with her friend Annie Singer. Hundreds of firebombs were being released by the Nazi planes above. As the girls ran towards the theatre they heard the whinnying of horses. The stables at the back of Ham Yard were ablaze. The horses were frantic but the girls, undaunted, plunged in and released them. Eventually, holding onto their halters, they led three horses each out onto the street. Trying to calm them down was not easy with the sound of gunfire and fire alarms going off. In due course, with the help of passers-by, they managed to pacify the poor horses. What do you do with six horses in the middle of an air raid in the heart of the West End? First they tried a garage but were turned away by the fire brigade. So they set off down Shaftesbury Avenue. When they encountered a perplexed policeman, he suggested taking the animals to the nearest police station. So they set off round a still crowded Piccadilly Circus. Trying to lead three horses each isn't easy at the best of times. They received many offers of help, not all of them related to equine safety. What a sight, two very pretty girls leading six bucking horses. For a moment, it was possible to forget the falling bombs. But not for long. They drew even more attention to themselves by singing 'I've Got Sixpence' as they went along. They felt a strange sense of exhilaration until another bomb fell nearby and the horses broke loose. It was half an hour before they managed to catch them all, firstly from Regent Street and later from Burlington Street. Eventually, the horses were passed for safekeeping to an astonished duty sergeant at Vine Street police station.

Despite the bombs, rationing, power cuts and endless queues, Soho adapted – but, as always, in different ways. Whilst there were tales of sacrifice and bravery, criminals realised that war was to be a period of endless opportunities.

7

Parasites and Killers

The war provided a perfect backdrop for criminal activity. Shortages brought on by rationing created a ready market for a deprived population willing to pay over the odds for almost anything that was not generally available. The spivs, wide-boys and career criminals were helped further by the more active policemen being co-opted into the armed forces. Darkness was also their friend, with the observance of the blackout.

The National Service Act of September 1939 imposed conscription on all men aged from eighteen to forty-one, unless they were in a reserved occupation. Amazingly, Jack Spot signed up, doubtless fuelled by his loathing of anti-Semitism. He fancied himself as an officer and a gentleman. He was neither, but still angry at being denied a commission. He survived in uniform until 1943 when he was discharged from the Marines on medical grounds. Not all of Soho's finest demonstrated such patriotism. Billy Hill, one of twenty-one children from a famous criminal line, decided smash-and-grab raids would offer him quite enough excitement. Far more lucrative prospects too. The Messina brothers simply ignored orders to present themselves to recruiting centres. They adopted a low profile whilst fine-tuning their hold over the vice trade and making a fortune over the duration of the war. Gino even had a custom-built hiding place behind a bookcase in his Lowndes Square apartment.

The one crime family who bitterly regretted the outbreak of war were the formerly all-powerful Sabini brothers. Although Darby had partially retired to his penthouse above the Grand Hotel in Brighton, the authorities were out to break the gang in the existing climate of xenophobia. No one was going to stand up for an Italian, albeit an anglicised one with a Cockney accent. Darby was described by Inspector Ted Greeno as 'a gangster and racketeer of the worst type. One who is most likely that enemy agents would choose as a reason to create and lead violent internal action against this country.' Total rubbish, of course, but facts were not going to be allowed to cloud the issue. Harry Boy was described as 'a dangerous man of the most violent temperament who has a heavy following and strong command of a gang of bullies of Italian origin'. Their imprisonment led to the break-up of the gang and to a power vacuum in Soho. This was filled, in part, by the White gang from King's Cross.

Darby was released from internment in 1943 following his prison sentence. He and Harry returned to being small-time bookmakers. When Darby died in 1951 he left very little money – a sad husk of a man, yet one who had been feared for years throughout the West End. A sense of sadness had overwhelmed him when his son was killed on active service with the RAF, whilst Darby was in prison. The irony would not have escaped him: the father considered to be a security risk, and yet his son able and willing to make the ultimate sacrifice for king and country.

Whilst the spivs and small-time crooks warmed to new opportunities, for a time Soho was menaced by a new threat: a gang of youngsters known as 'The Dead End Kids'. Under the age of conscription and with little parental control with their fathers away in the forces, they were considered a nuisance, rather than a danger. Police in Soho continued to patrol the streets in pairs in an attempt to stamp out disturbances that continued towards businesses with Italian or Germanic names.

With the introduction of rationing across a whole range of food, clothing and fuel, a thriving black market was soon in operation. There was a perceptible swing in public attitudes. Whilst most declared loudly that spivs and racketeers should be locked up, many, given the chance, were not above buying goods in short supply 'under the counter'. The authorities, in an attempt to set an example, arrested a number of celebrities. Ivor Novello was jailed for offences relating to petrol consumption. Noël Coward was also arrested for failing to hand in his US dollar holdings to the Treasury. Whilst several leading companies, including Joe Lyons, Sainsbury's and even swanky hotels (including the Savoy and Grosvenor House), fell foul of the authorities, the perception was still that there was one rule for the rich and another for the rest.

Each night it was reckoned the West End was hosting 200–300 bottle parties. The Anti Vice Squad had been formed in 1937 and it was to them that the regulation of clubs was consigned. As fast as illegal establishments were closed down, new ones appeared under a different name. Touts stood outside theatres and cinemas handing out cards advertising rip-off clubs and bottle parties. Gullible members of the armed forces looking for a good time in Soho were fleeced of their money. They were charged for admission and then inflated prices for watered-down beer. Attractive hostesses encouraged the young men to buy drinks for them too. The organisers of bottle parties were making massive profits. Some parties claimed to be legal by asking guests to sign order forms, with drinks being brought in from all-night wine shops. The Anti Vice Squad raided a club in Old Compton Street and its owner was fined a hefty £50. In May 1940, Mother Hubbard, a sleazy club in Ham Yard, was also raided and the owner on this occasion jailed for three weeks for serving drinks after hours. Clever club owners, however, kept a low profile, allowing front men to take the rap when the law came calling.

Soon, clubs and bottle parties were offering added attractions. Heroin was seized at a club in Fouberts Place. Illegal gambling was frequently on offer. War had brought a new recklessness to many and Faro, a simple game but with massive opportunities for cheating, helped line the club owners' pockets. The outwardly respectable Piccadilly Club in Denman Street was happily fleecing its members when raided by the police. Threats of draconian sentences did little to dampen down activity. Everyone knew the prisons continued to be full of internees. The rewards of running illegal clubs were huge, the risks worth taking. Added to the cocktail of booze, gambling and the odd offer of drugs was striptease – a rather racier version than offered by the regulated Windmill.

Within months of the outbreak of war, it became obvious that Soho was a magnet for deserters. In March 1940, the police made the first of a series of raids in the area on a club in Leicester Square. They discovered six deserters amongst a gathering of known crooks who were found to be in possession of piles of petrol coupons and stolen road fund licences. Whilst bars and clubs continued to be raided, Soho was a major magnet for many of the 20,000 deserters reckoned to be on the run by the end of the war. It was an area where few questions were asked by a constantly changing population.

By the spring of 1941, single women were also required to register for war service. For once, the Messina brothers insisted that all the girls under their control should fill in the forms honestly. The occupation of 'prostitute' did the trick. The authorities had no wish to expose virtuous British women to the influence of vice girls. They were left free to ply their trade. The Messinas, seldom missing a trick, now required their girls to try and inveigle the punters to hand over any petrol coupons they had. The Messina boys, courtesy of their customers, patrolled the streets each night in their flashy cars, keeping an eye on their hard-working girls. They had already introduced the ten-minute rule. This was the maximum time allowed for any punter and even a minor deviation was likely to prompt a violent response. Time and motion study had reached the sex industry.

1941 didn't turn out to be a vintage year for Antonio 'Babe' Mancini. In April, there had been a number of fights between Jews (the Yiddishers) and the few remaining Italian criminals who, together with the White gang, were seeking control of Soho. The Italians ran three clubs at 37 Wardour Street. The Palm Beach bottle parties were organised from the basement, whilst the Casio Club traded on the ground floor. Upstairs was the grand-sounding West End Bridge & Billiard Club. In a previous confrontation, Eddie Fleisher, known as Eddie Fletcher, had been beaten up and banned from the premises. Just over a week later, Fletcher sought out Mancini (who was the quasi-manager/doorman) and trouble broke out again in the Billiard Club. It appears 'Babe' Mancini wanted to avoid any more confrontation so he went to change out of his evening dress, presumably hoping things would calm down. Later, assuming the coast was clear, he went upstairs to see what damage had been done. As he climbed the stairs he claimed to hear someone say, 'There's Babe, let's knife him!' Mancini was convinced it was Fletcher. Turning, he realised he was being followed by Harry 'Scarface' Distleman. Fighting broke out and in the ensuing melee Distleman staggered back clutching his chest. He was heard to cry out, 'I'm terribly hurt. Babe done it.'

At his trial, Mancini's defence was not helped when it was explained that he had chased Fletcher, inflicting a terrible wound, almost severing his arm. Claiming he had arrived unarmed and had picked up a dagger he had found lying on the floor, Mancini pleaded guilty to manslaughter. He was encouraged that a similar case earlier in the year had resulted in a manslaughter verdict. He was given further hope by a favourable summing up by the judge. The jury had other ideas and found 'Babe' guilty of murder. It is quite possible that his Italian background weighed against him in the prevailing hostile climate. His appeal was rejected by the Lord Chamberlain and the House of Lords. 'Babe' Mancini was hanged at Pentonville prison on 17 October 1941. He was the first victim of Albert Pierrepoint since being appointed Chief Executioner by the Home Office. As the hood was placed over his head, Mancini bid the attending officials an upbeat 'cheerio'. 'Babe' was the first Soho gang member to be executed for twenty-five years, and it served as a poignant reminder to career criminals to be extremely careful not to inflict fatal wounds.

The Blitz that started on 7 September 1940 was still raging whilst 'Babe' Mancini was fighting Soho's own version of warfare. It seems amazing that amidst the ack-ack fire and falling bombs, criminals could find time to fight amongst themselves. In truth, the Blitz was a blessing, a distraction, improving their ability to prosper against a background of death and destruction. They spared little thought for the thousands of London's dead and injured. They dedicated their lives to personal gain. Small gangs patrolled the streets following, rather than avoiding, the crash of falling bombs. Shops and warehouses were looted as well as private homes. There were even dark tales of watches and jewellery being taken from corpses. Looting was subject to the death penalty in Germany, but it was generally treated just as theft in Britain. So the odds were stacked in the looters' favour for, even if caught, the penalties were rarely severe. Ingenuity is seldom lacking in the criminal mind. It didn't take long for the gangs to have vehicles sprayed to look like ARP ambulances. They were kitted out with stretchers and blankets. So the loot could be brought out of bombed buildings disguised as a body.

The darkness and disruption allowed the young Billy Hill to pull off a series of daring jewellery heists. Successful crooks were making so much money they were finding it difficult to spend their ill-gotten gains. Whilst above them in the skies young men were risking their lives for the future of the country, the criminal dregs of society were only interested in lining their own pockets. For the most part, these were not men of great intelligence, rather of an animal cunning and a willingness to indulge in violence when provoked.

It was unusual for news of the war not to dominate the headlines. This changed for a time in February 1942. Suddenly, all the talk was of a mad killer on the loose. On 9 February, the body of forty-year-old Margaret Hamilton was found strangled in a surface air-raid shelter in Montague Place. The motive, seemingly, was theft. The following morning the mutilated body of Evelyn Oatley was found in her flat in Wardour Street. Reputedly a former Windmill girl (a fact refuted by her family), she had latterly turned to prostitution. Evelyn had been strangled but also defiled, supposedly with a tin opener. Piecing together evidence from the two crimes, the police deduced that the killer was probably left-handed. Three days later, another prostitute, Margaret Lowe, was discovered similarly strangled and mutilated. By now, the public were aware 'The Blackout Ripper' was on the prowl. The street girls of the West End were now thoroughly alarmed, particularly those newcomers as young as fourteen who were reported to be lining the streets around Shaftesbury Avenue. Away from Soho, the body of Doris Jonannet, a part-time prostitute, was discovered in a room in Sussex Gardens. Like the others, she had been strangled and horribly mutilated. The killer had been reckless, with the police finding clear fingerprints at each crime scene. Unfortunately, none matched those held in police records.

The killer now appeared to be out of control. A young woman, Greta Hayward, was attacked by a man who had picked her up and taken her for a drink at the Trocadero in Shaftesbury Avenue. On leaving, he dragged her down a darkened side street, where he attempted to strangle her. She struggled and her cries for help were answered by a delivery boy. Panicking, the assailant ran off leaving behind his gas mask, which had been issued by the air force and was marked with an identification number on the case. Undeterred, the killer now picked up Katherine King, another prostitute, in Regent Street. Back at her flat, just as he handed her £5, there was a power cut. At once he attempted to strangle her but again she fought him off. He was losing his touch. Alarmed by her screams, he pressed another £5 (£200 at today's values) into her hand and fled, this time leaving behind his service belt.

Now, with such conclusive evidence, it didn't take long for the police to trace twenty-nine-year-old officer cadet Gordon Cummins. He was a larger than life character. He claimed he was the illegitimate son of a member of the House of Lords. Although he had a lofty manner and was known to his fellow cadets as 'The

Duke', he was married and appeared perfectly normal. Initially, he appeared to have a solid alibi for the times of the murders. His billet passbook showed he had been in the barracks and his roommates confirmed they had seen him go to bed on each of the nights in question. He claimed someone must have picked up his belt by mistake and, anyway, gas masks were frequently and inadvertently exchanged. The enquiry had reached a dead end, but not for long. His fingerprints were found in two of the victims' flats. Then another girl reported that she too had been attacked by a punter. She too had been picked up in Regent Street outside Oddenino's. Back at her flat, Cummins attempted to strangle her with a row of beads she was wearing. Luckily for her, she had kept her high-heeled boots on. As they struggled, she gave him a hefty kick, knocking him off the bed. Suddenly, he had appeared embarrassed and, apologising, handed her £10 before making a speedy exit.

Back at the barracks, the police now learned that Cummins and a friend often used a fire escape to go out after lights out. His alibi was in tatters. He was picked out in an identity parade and he had also kept souvenirs taken from his victims. Despite the weight of damning evidence, Cummins pleaded not guilty. The jury took less than half an hour to find him guilty. On 25 June 1941, Cummins was hanged at Wandsworth, the only murderer recorded as having been despatched during an air raid.

Six months prior to Gordon Cummins's execution, a far more momentous event took place thousands of miles away. On 7 December 1941, Japanese planes attacked Pearl Harbor. Four days later, Italy and Germany declared war on the United States of America. With the possibility of a German invasion of Britain diminishing, the country still braced itself for an influx of Allied forces. Watch out Britain, watch out London, watch out Soho, the Yanks are coming!

8

Over-Paid, Over-Sexed
and Over Here!

11 November 1942 witnessed an invasion of London. Happily, it was not the one that had been feared. There were no Germans goose-stepping their way down Shaftesbury Avenue. It did, however, feature another foreign army, whose presence was to profoundly affect Londoners' lives for the next three years. It was centred on a club. Not a sophisticated nightclub or, indeed, one of the shady drinking or gambling joints that were so prevalent in the area. Rainbow Corner was a huge US Red Cross club situated on the corner of Denman Street and Shaftesbury Avenue. The five-storey building had previously housed the Café Monico, part of the giant Joe Lyons organisation. After months of reconstruction work, it was ready to form the focal point for the countless thousands of US troops who visited London during the remainder of the war.

Whilst obviously welcomed for their military might, the arrival of Americans en masse rather caught the British public off guard. Most Londoners had never been abroad and whilst Soho citizens were more cosmopolitan, their exposure to Americans had been mainly limited to trips to the cinema. Close up, the Yanks proved to be something of a culture shock. For a start, they looked different. They were generally taller, smarter, more confident. Their uniforms were well cut, so much so that British squaddies mistook American private soldiers for officers and saluted them. In contrast, Evelyn Waugh describes British soldiers in his diary entry for 15 May 1943 as 'horrible groups of soldiers in shabby battledress with their necks open, their caps off or at extravagant angles, hands in pockets, cigarettes in the sides of their mouths, lounging about with girls in trousers and high heels and film star coiffures'. He adds that he has never seen so many ugly girls making themselves so conspicuous. His attitude underlines how baffled the Americans were by our class system, which was particularly apparent in the distinction between officers and their men. This was even more pronounced in the exclusive cavalry regiments like the Royal Armoured Corps, described by an American counterpart as 'the most mentally inert, unprofessional and reactionary group in the British Army'.

Differences also loomed in attitudes to black GIs, who represented about 7 per cent of US forces in Britain. Most Londoners had never seen a black face before and showed little colour prejudice. The American units were still segregated and the black GIs found the British acceptance of them (however muted) a revelation when compared to the treatment they were accustomed to back in the States.

Pay was a major factor in the resentment felt by the British troops. On average, GIs were paid three times their British equivalent. It was difficult for the natives to compete for the attention of the prettiest girls. This was often the underlying cause of tension between the Allies. Although scuffles were common, the most serious outbreaks of violence were between white and black American troops – particularly those GIs from the American South who resented seeing black men escorting white girls. Restaurants and clubs started turning black soldiers away for fear of losing business. The famous West Indian cricketer Learie Constantine successfully sued when asked to leave a leading London hotel at the prompting of white Americans. The hotel was fined a derisory five guineas, although the judge deplored the fact that a legal technicality prevented him from imposing a more appropriate penalty.

It didn't take long for Rainbow Corner to become a magnet for crowds of good-time girls, many of whom were part-time prostitutes known as 'Piccadilly Commandos'. They were joined and jostled by spivs and barrow boys hoping to buy anything from the GIs which was in short supply in London. Stockings, perfume, watches and even items of food were sold only to appear hours later on Berwick Street market. Polish criminals and deserters were major players in black-market goods. Herman Schultz was convicted in 1943 for selling underwear and silk stockings on his stall in Berwick Street without coupons. He was found to have £3,000 in cash stashed away in his flat. He was sentenced to three months' hard labour and fined £500 for his trouble. The US authorities had created an Office of Price Administration in order to try and restrict activity but, although GIs were sent to jail for being involved, the trade continued unabated throughout the war.

The Rainbow Corner Club was huge and aimed to offer a slice of America for servicemen thousands of miles from home. There was a variety of cafés and restaurants where the food was more palatable than what was generally on offer in London. There was even a 'Dunker's Den' in the basement, where coffee and doughnuts were constantly available. There was also accommodation for those wishing to stay overnight. Valet and laundry services were appreciated, as were hot showers and a barber. The GI, now well rested and cosseted, could look forward to other important facilities on offer. Possibly the most important of these was the live music and dancing. Specially vetted English girls were employed as hostesses. Not the type available just around the corner in a range of dodgy clubs and dance halls. These girls were encouraged to try and bring a fleeting sense of homeliness and normality to young men, many of whom would shortly be risking their lives across the Channel. Here, warmth and companionship were on offer rather than sex.

There could be no dancing without music – and what music! The club rocked to Glenn Miller, who broadcast direct from the club, as did Artie Shaw's Naval Band. A young Petula Clark performed here for her rowdy audience. The Jitterbug was all the rage, which was totally unknown to most of the English hostesses. The exuberance of the GIs quite literally swept them off their feet. The dance captured the spirit of the times. Convention was cast aside. Life was for now, for tomorrow may never come.

Other famous personalities visited the club in an attempt to keep morale high. Fred Astaire's sister Adele (later Lady Cavendish) was often on hand to help with letters home to mothers and sweethearts. Irving Berlin visited, as did a succession of film stars, including George Raft and James Stewart. The club became so successful that 70,000 visited the premises to celebrate its first anniversary in 1943.

The arrival of the Americans resonated throughout the West End. Restaurant owners were frustrated by legislation that restricted them from charging more than 5s for a meal. There had to be a way for them to benefit from these welcome visitors looking for a good time and with money to burn. The price of wine spiralled, whilst rabbit was passed off as chicken and surcharges added. Hushed discussions with the waiter would sometimes prompt some black-market delicacy to be served (at a price). Somehow, famous Soho restaurants like Au Jardin de Gourmet and Kettner's managed to keep their demanding customers happy despite the constant shortages.

Most West End theatres, having survived the Blitz, now saw their attendances recover. Whilst many well-known actors joined the armed forces, the remainder of the 'luvvies' did their best to cocoon themselves in a bubble. One that banished as far as possible the horrid outside world and the effects of the ghastly war. Vivien Leigh was now Britain's brightest star after her triumph in the film *Gone with the Wind*. She, at least, was keen to volunteer to do some war work. She fancied driving an ambulance, or at least taking on fire-watch duty. Binkie Beaumont was horrified. He lectured her that her duty lay in entertaining the public, not putting herself in danger. Under his leadership, H. M. Tennant continued to thrive. His 1943 offerings of *Hamlet*, *A Midsummer Night's Dream* and *The Duchess of Malfi* hardly seemed to have a massive appeal for the thousands of forces personnel roaming the West End. He did lighten up slightly by reviving Somerset Maugham's *The Circle*. The previous year, Binkie acknowledged that there was a war going on with his production of Terence Rattigan's *Flare Path*, which opened at the Apollo in August 1942. Rattigan had volunteered for the RAF and saw action as a rear gunner, and the play offered a degree of authenticity. The production ran for 400 performances and shortly after it opened Winston Churchill made one of his rare visits to a theatre. He declared *Flare Path* to be a masterpiece. The RAF were so impressed with the endorsement that they released Rattigan from active service so he was free to write more patriotic plays.

Meanwhile, round at the Windmill, the queues lengthened. The slogan 'We never closed' was known to the troops as 'We never clothed' and they flocked to the theatre. Laura Henderson's relationship with Van Damm continued to be warm but questioning, as a note to him confirms. 'I wish you would give Hazel a little more covering in the last act. I'm afraid it might bring the Lord Chamberlain down on us.' No matter, the punters were not complaining. The American troops continued to bring a more raucous atmosphere to the shows, shouting out enthusiastically, 'Shake it, lady, shake it!' They were so rowdy that several performances had to be stopped until order was restored. One bewildered old lady who joined the wrong queue thought she was about to see *Blossom Time* at the neighbouring Lyric Theatre. Her only complaint on button-holing Van Damm was the absence of Richard Tauber.

Now troops from Holland, France, Poland and from the colonies were adding to the heady atmosphere at the theatre. There was more than a touch of the Wild West and the performers were buoyed by the unrestrained excitement generated. It was a time that they would never forget.

Laura Henderson continued to make regular visits to view the shows. Even during the height of the Blitz, her resolve never weakened. She showed no sign of nerves or concern for her personal safety, but her health was beginning to deteriorate. By the end of 1944 she was looking really frail. On a cold night in November she took her usual place in her personal box and appeared to enjoy the performance. That night her bronchitis worsened and without waking any of her staff she rang for an ambulance and was admitted to St George's Hospital on Hyde Park Corner. Van Damm rushed to the hospital on hearing the news, and found his millionaire partner lying in a public ward. She looked terribly vulnerable, with her grey wig lying on a bedside table. He had her moved to the comfort of the London Clinic. Sensing how ill she was, Laura Henderson had informed Van Damm that should she die, 'The show must not stop on my account.' She did die later that day. Like so many larger than life figures, it seemed unreal that she was no longer around. At eighty-one, her batteries had finally given up. Back at the Windmill, the show did indeed go on. Her last instructions were, 'Please, no sadness. No tears or sad music at my funeral. Carry on making people happy as I have been.' She had explained that she never felt old because 'I've spent so many years in the midst of youth and beauty.' A memorial service was held at St James's, Piccadilly. The whole cast and the rest of the company attended for, despite her quirky temperament, she was generally liked and admired. Months later, when her will was revealed, every member of the Windmill family found she had left them £10 (over £450 at today's value). More importantly, she bequeathed the theatre to Vivian Van Damm, ensuring that the company would carry on. A sometimes volatile relationship had mellowed over the years into one of mutual respect. She had, at least, lived to see the theatre become a commercial and financial success.

Established restaurants, the legitimate theatre and the Windmill represented the acceptable face of Soho. Swirling around them a murkier side lurked. Rows of prostitutes aged from fourteen to fifty lined the Soho streets and alleys. Admiral Sir Edward Evans lamented that 'Leicester Square is the resort of the worst type of women and girls consorting with both British and American troops.' The problem was so obvious that in August 1942 the *Sunday Pictorial* started a campaign to clean up Piccadilly and the surrounding area. Although the Messina brothers had control of many women, most girls still operated on a freelance basis, generally working for a ponce. Very little was done by the police to control the trade. Lust was allowed to flourish. Every available doorway was occupied, with the girls shining torches on themselves in an attempt to drum up trade. This was a golden time for prostitutes trying to service a tidal wave of potential punters. Gays, who for the most part had to act discreetly, congregated at the Byron in Greek Street or the Horseshoe nearby in Wardour Street.

The civilian and military police were far more diligent in their attempts to track down deserters. In May 1944 they, together with the US MPs (known as Snowdrops), conducted a massive swoop on the West End. They targeted hotels, bars, restaurants and amusement arcades. The Corner House in Coventry Street was raided and every customer was required to prove their identity. At the Astoria Dance Hall in Charing Cross Road, the band was stopped mid-number as identity cards and leave papers were checked. Fixed bayonets were even employed by the MPs when raiding particularly dubious premises. Despite all these vigorous interventions, the numbers of deserters captured were disappointing. The authorities had become particularly concerned about the increase in crime, much of which was attributed to deserters. By 1945, matters had deteriorated still further with kidnappings and a series of armed robberies taking place. Some 2,000 police flooded Soho, checking all premises for deserters. This time seventy-five people were detained.

One of the most worrying developments was the availability of guns. No longer was the pavement outside Rainbow Corner just a clearing house for stockings and watches. Now a whole selection of handguns was on offer. Hardened criminals and aspiring villains paid about £25 to get 'tooled up'. The prized Luger had the advantage of being functional, using Sten gun ammunition which was cheap and easy to obtain. Soon after the GIs' arrival in London, a Luger would cost £60 but its value fell as more were captured from the Germans.

As the war progressed, other Allied troops arrived in the area and tended to congregate in their own favoured pubs. There were over a dozen ancient hostelries in Soho dating back to the eighteenth century. Whilst 'De Hems' in Macclesfield Street attracted the Dutch, it is the French Pub in Dean Street that gained legendary status. On 16 June 1940, the French government collapsed and two days later Charles de Gaulle made a famous speech. In it he called for the Free French to fight on against the Germans and the Vichy government of Marshal Pétain. He had prepared the speech in a small room above the bar of the French Pub (the York Minster). Although the speech itself was not heard by many in France, its message was. Subsequent speeches gained a far wider audience and represented a rallying cry for the French to carry on the fight.

The French Pub had become a wine house in 1910 when it was owned by a German called Schmidt. He was ousted at the outbreak of war in 1914. The pub then came under the ownership of a Belgian, Victor Berlemont. Known already as The French, it drew in visiting personalities, including the boxer Georges Carpentier and the entertainer Maurice Chevalier, as well as a large number of French citizens who lived locally. It also became a favoured watering hole for the Bohemian set. Although the exterior of the building was badly damaged the night St Anne's church opposite was destroyed, the pub continued to be a meeting place for the exiled Free French.

As the war drew to a close, Great Windmill Street became the centre of unwanted publicity. Mae's Dance Hall was a popular venue for servicemen to meet women looking for a good time. Unfortunately, Gordon Johnson had not realised that his girlfriend was a part-time prostitute. On finding out that she had been sleeping with a GI he had caught her with, a fight broke out. A US private, Thomas Croft, intervened. Instead of trying to referee the dispute, Croft drew a dagger hidden in his boot and stabbed Johnson, who died almost immediately. The 'Snowdrops' were called and a month later Croft was sentenced to life imprisonment. This was surprising as the US authorities were normally severe in the punishment they meted out to their compatriots. Certainly the methods adopted by their military police had raised concerns with the British. They tended not to waste time on lengthy discussions with their suspects, often wading in wielding long truncheons and, on occasion, firing warning shots.

With the deployment of troops to mainland Europe, there were now far fewer Americans to be seen in the West End. They were missed by so many. By those who had fallen in love and longed to be reunited again. Also, by the girls who dispensed love of a sort, but for money. Certainly by the restaurateurs, club owners and spivs. By theatre managers, shopkeepers and cinemas. The Yanks had brought a vibrancy and excitement to staid old London. They were outgoing and friendly. Some found them brash, whilst others thought they were charming and polite. It is obviously impossible to sum up so many thousands of men living so far from their homes. One thing is certain, that without them we would all be living in a very different world today.

The news of the German surrender had long been anticipated. It was finally signed on 7 May and fighting stopped the following day. A flu bug was sweeping through London and many were declaring themselves too exhausted to enjoy the victory. Luckily, not everyone was so downbeat. Huge crowds swirled around the West End not quite knowing what to expect from the historic day. Many carried Union Jacks or were decked out in red, white and blue. There had been a thunderstorm in the night but now it was a perfect, warm, sunny, early summer's day. Loudspeakers relayed speeches by the King and by Prime Minister Winston Churchill. His wife, Clementine, was away in Russia at the invitation of the Soviet government on a goodwill tour. She sent a telegram from Moscow: 'All my thoughts are with you this supreme day, my darling. It could not have happened without you. All my love, Clemmie!'

Crowds spilled down Shaftesbury Avenue towards Piccadilly Circus, young girls in cotton dresses, children carried aloft on shoulders, old couples arm in arm. There were soldiers, sailors and airmen from across the globe. A member of the tank corps was the first who clambered to the top of the boarded-up Eros. He was joined by a paratrooper who, in turn, hauled up an attractive young blonde. The crowd cheered as two GIs joined them and soon the wooden pyramid was covered with young people. In the background, church bells rang out. Policemen stood by whilst bonfires were lit in the street and an effigy of Hitler was burnt to loud applause. US sailors formed a conga down Piccadilly, whilst

Londoners linked arms to do the Lambeth Walk. It was a heady day. A mass expression of thanks and relief that it was all over. Later, it would be a time to reflect on a conflict that left very few families untouched.

That night, Vivian Van Damm allowed members of the armed forces into the Windmill free of charge. As was to be expected, the atmosphere that night was even more uninhibited than usual. To help restrain the audience, wire netting was erected to protect the performers, whose songs were drowned out by shouting and wolf whistles. Champagne and prized vintage wines which had been saved throughout the war were served in Soho restaurants. For the moment, London celebrated. It had endured possibly the most difficult years in its long history. Later there would be time enough to reflect and even look forward. The clock finally turned full circle when Eleanor Roosevelt came to close Rainbow Corner. The building was sold and became an office block, indistinguishable from hundreds of others. It had been an oasis for thousands of homesick GIs, a source of wealth for spivs and crooks but, most importantly, it had introduced Americans en masse to a wide-eyed London.

9

Tough Times

Once more, the West End was out of step with the rest of the country. Whilst Piccadilly and the streets of Soho had been packed with crowds of revellers, elsewhere in London the victory celebrations had been muted. The population was scarred and exhausted by five years of war. A new Labour government was elected, Churchill discarded, and a new future beckoned. Some future! The country was virtually bankrupt. The government was forced to go 'cap in hand' to America to borrow an eye-watering $3.5 billion on none too generous terms. The balance of power had shifted. The future looked bleak, and it was.

In Soho, life was gradually regaining some form of normality. Most of the Italians who had been interned had returned and were busy trying to re-establish their businesses. Servicemen were also starting to get demobbed and finding their homecoming something of an anticlimax. Life was obviously going to be tough. Most in Soho were living in crowded, rundown rooms offering little in the way of comfort. There was no central heating, no washing machines or fridges. Most flats had no toilets and residents were forced to share with neighbours out on a chilly landing. Few flats had bathrooms either. It was down to a strip wash or a trip to Marshall Street baths. Kitchen comforts were confined to a sink, draining board and a mangle. True, the conditions were unchanged from before the war, but now rationing and perpetual shortages made life for most really miserable and, in reality, differed little from that experienced in Victorian times. The gloom was intensified by a sulphurous atmosphere and the smell of coal. Smoke belched out from a sea of chimneys and, as winter set in, Londoners had to endure days of unhealthy pea-souper fogs. Gas lamps mounted on short posts were still lit in several Soho streets, adding to the impression of an area set in the past.

The mood was lightened for a few days by the Victory Parade in June 1946. British and Allied troops were greeted by huge crowds. Many stayed in the West End that night to watch the sky lit up by a spectacular firework display. Just as they spluttered, faded and finally disappeared, so did the temporary feeling of optimism.

This did not apply to the local musicians. They were a special breed who refused to be cast down for too long. They brought enjoyment and they certainly sought it for themselves. In November 1946, a feature in *What's On in London* underlined their determination to have fun. The article gave details of a new type of club being formed at Chez Auguste in Frith Street:

A word of praise for the committee of the Rose Room Sunday Club – latest attempt to enliven the city's Sabbath – which opened for business a couple of weeks back in the banqueting rooms of Chez Auguste in Frith Street, W.1.

Recently demobbed Warwick Hurst-Barnes, lately Squadron Leader on General Eisenhower's air staff and pre-war drummer man with Debroy Summers' band, has taken on the job of secretary-manager of the new venture and has gathered around him on the provisional committee such stalwarts of show business as Ted Heath, guitarist Ivor Mairants and Pat Dodds (pianist of the Skyrockets).

Object of the club is to provide a rendezvous for musicians, show folk and those interested in the entertainment world, where they can meet and entertain their friends. On the evidence of the first two Sundays in operation, the object can be taken as gained.

Playing for dancing and background music at the Rose Room is the Hamish Menzies Quartet, but visitors can be assured of plenty of guest artistes getting up to strut their stuff in just the atmosphere to bring out the best in them. Last week, for instance, George Shearing – confidentially the best black and white artist in the land – took the stand to beat out those tantalising tenths on Menzies' piano. George promised to show up again this week with more of the same.

For the more mundane details, the annual subscription to the club is one dollar per person, with an extra five bob to be paid at the door for each visit. The Rose Room is open from 7 till 11.30 p.m. – and, of course, it's Sundays only. You can get dinner (à la carte), cold buffet and drinks (the cuisine and cellar of Chez Auguste, naturally, needs no recommendation to readers who have previously taken our advice in these matters).

Whilst the musicians were enjoying themselves, outside on the street the Messina girls were working diligently as usual. The loss of the Americans had seen a drop in the prices the girls could charge. Despite this, it was reckoned that the Messinas were pocketing an amazing £10,000 a week. Each girl was earning about £100 a night, but being paid only £50 per week. Today, girls tend to take to the streets to feed a drug habit. Back in the 1940s, they were either inveigled into it or chose selling themselves as a career option. Even working for the Maltese, the girls were earning ten times what they could get in a shop or factory. Most thought they could make some quick money and retire to a life of respectability. Few did.

After the war, there was an uneasy alliance attempting to control Soho crime. The White brothers joined up for a time with a group of Italians back from internment. Trouble arrived in the shape of Jack Spot. Sensing a weakness, he orchestrated a number of violent confrontations. The Whites retreated to their King's Cross stronghold. Spot was joined by Billy Hill, who, at the time, was slightly in awe of the older man. From 1947, and for another seven years, their hold on Soho was complete. This, in spite of Hill being sentenced to three years for armed robbery. Showing great loyalty to his younger colleague, Spot was on hand at the prison gates to greet Hill on his release. For the time being their uneasy partnership remained intact. Their skills complemented each other. Hill was urbane and pleasant enough to meet. He kept a firm discipline over his followers; although not as violent as Spot, he was generally feared and inflicted terrible damage with a razor on anyone who seriously crossed him. Spot was the enforcer, a violent, mentally disturbed thug. There were few who cared to argue with them, including the police, who were on their payroll. Although not directly involved in prostitution, it was reckoned that Hill and Spot took a regular cut from the Messinas.

In March 1947, Carmelo Vassello and four fellow Maltese made the mistake of trying to muscle in on the Messinas' business. They went around Soho threatening the girls and demanding one pound a day in protection money. Eugenio Messina was not amused. Acting without his normal caution, he sliced off two of Vassello's fingertips. Messina was sent down for three years for this indiscretion, at his trial at the Old Bailey. The police caught the Vassello gang demanding money with menaces from girls in Burlington Gardens. They were given four years' penal servitude. Alfredo, Salvatore and the other Messina brothers were left free to continue their trade unchallenged. However, they were now the subject of public interest and questions were raised in Parliament. It was time to resume a low profile.

Whilst the criminals of Soho were keeping warm taking slices out of each other, the rest of the country shivered and scratched at their chilblains. January 1947 witnessed the onset of the worst winter in living memory. Borne off an easterly wind, it threw a deep blanket of snow across the capital. Traffic in the West End ground to a halt. There were constant power cuts, despite the fact that electric fires were banned from use for a total of five hours a day. Moaning became a national pastime but still the snow fell. Coal was stuck at the pits and London was virtually cut off for a time. It was a case of wrap up and go to bed early. Vegetables were frozen in the fields and Berwick Street market had little to sell. For a time the streets turned to slush, only for overnight frosts to turn the roads into rutted skating rinks. Then came the next heavy snowfall. Between 2 February and 22 February the sun didn't penetrate the leaden skies once. Restaurants and shops were almost brought to their knees by the weather, which finally relented after three long months. The restaurant owners were already unhappy that they were still restricted by law to charging a maximum of 5s for a meal. Many were now adding a surcharge for service and the mark-up on wines helped them keep afloat. The choice of cuisines was still as varied as ever. Spanish restaurants were prominent, with the Argentina in Denman Street and Barcelona in Beak Street. There were also any number of French, Italian, Chinese, Danish and Kosher outlets to choose from. Old favourites had somehow survived from before the war despite the chronic lack of supplies.

Whilst London shivered, over in Paris a young Christian Dior was about to produce a collection which was to sweep across the

Channel. The 'New Look' was to prove a lifeline for Soho's rag trade. In was, in effect, a reworking and updating of the fashion of the 1930s. To young women it was truly liberating after years of make do and mend. The look was soft and feminine. Busts were back, as were tiny waists (with the help of corsets). To the outrage of some politicians, the outfits used as much as fifteen yards of material. No matter, there was a yearning for a return to colour and style, evoking pre-war days. The workrooms and sweatshops of Soho worked overtime to keep up with demand. Office girls and shop assistants reached for their Singer sewing machines. Windmill girls preened themselves in their cramped dressing rooms whilst streets girls paraded like models on the catwalk. The 'New Look' offered, perhaps, the first glimpse of better times to come.

Later in 1947, there was further reason to cheer up: the marriage of Princess Elizabeth to Lieutenant Philip Mountbatten. The crowds returned to the West End, and the clubs and restaurants of Soho were fully booked. No doubt the Messina boys became ardent royalists as their girls strove to satisfy the increased demand. Whilst the Maltese brothers lined their pockets, the happy royal couple were forced to honeymoon in Hampshire due to the draconian currency regulations instituted by the government. Evelyn Waugh, writing in his diary, was feeling distinctly grumpy: 'I intended a morning in the second-hand bookshops [in Charing Cross Road] but found them all closed for Princess Elizabeth's wedding. Also, great difficulty in finding a glass of beer!'

Vivian Van Damm and the Windmill Theatre emerged from the war years in good shape and the outlook was encouraging. The financial position was much improved, helped greatly by Van Damm inheriting the bulk of the company's shares from Laura Henderson. He was now in total control. He was able to invest in much-needed restoration to the theatre. All the seats were replaced, having been severely damaged by the constant steeple chase, as legions of randy servicemen tried to get a closer look at the girls. Van Damm helped pay for the improvements by increasing the number of daily performances to six. Entrance prices for the stalls were also hiked to 12s 6d (over £25 at today's prices).

The Windmill had survived, overcoming a disastrous beginning and, subsequently, producing many talented entertainers.

Few, though, had gone on to achieve stardom. John Tilley had become well known nationally, but his career was tragically short. Eric Barker had been associated with the Windmill since 1933. Although a talented comedian and scriptwriter, he rarely made the headlines. How strange that the Windmill's first real star should be a bird and animal impersonator. Amazingly, Percy Edwards remained popular with the public right through to the 1980s. The female artistes who made it into the big time were also something of a rarity. Jean Kent, under her stage name of Jean Carr, was fired by Van Damm for lacking sufficient personality before moving on to star in wartime films such as *Waterloo Road*. Charmian Innes also went on to appear in films after being sacked from the Windmill for being too fat. Not easily discouraged, she returned and, apart from films, appeared in the West End, in theatre and on radio. Why so few of the attractive and talented young women never blossomed professionally outside the tight-knit atmosphere of the Windmill remains a mystery. They had to be all-round entertainers who exuded personality, and had to be tough to survive the rigours of the Windmill. It seems possible that they enjoyed their time and the camaraderie so much that this lessened their ambition. Also, many fell for the charms of the stage-door johnnies and went and got married.

All was about to change. The end of the war unleashed a tide of incredibly talented comics who were to soar to national and international fame. Once demobbed, they headed off for auditions at the Windmill. The first to arrive was Jimmy Edwards. He had been awarded the DFC after being shot down in the disastrous attack on Arnhem in 1944. He suffered severe facial injuries and covered much of the damage by growing his trademark handlebar moustache. A graduate of St John's College, Cambridge, later in his professional career he became known as 'Professor' Jimmy Edwards. Appearing in front of a Windmill audience only interested in the girls was a daunting experience. He grabbed their attention by insulting them, much as a schoolteacher would a classroom of naughty boys. It worked. They loved him. Alfred Marks was another performer who took on the audience. Sheila Van Damm quoted him as starting his act by saying, 'I've never seen such a bunch of men all looking as if they have a guilt complex.' Edwards stayed at the Windmill for eighteen months before falling out with Vivian Van Damm, who had insisted that all members of the company sign in at least thirty minutes prior to the evening's performance. Edwards, who had never missed an entrance, refused and was sacked by the autocratic Van Damm. During the rest of the 1940s, a number of top-class comedians continued to cut their teeth at the Windmill. Tony Hancock maintained that any comic who could survive for more than six weeks at the theatre was destined to succeed in their career. The talent drawn to Great Windmill Street was astonishing. Although Sheila Van Damm recalled that most of those seeking auditions were embarrassingly bad, real gems continued to surface. The crazily inventive Michael Bentine, on leaving the Windmill, went on to be a founder of the Goons, along with Harry Secombe, Peter Sellers and Spike Milligan. Secombe and Sellers also started on their road to stardom at the theatre. Secombe, like Alfred Marks, had pretensions about becoming an opera singer but for the time being it was his ability to make people laugh that set him apart. Together, this small group were about to redefine British comedy. The Goons acquired a cult status that lives on today.

Perhaps the most talented, and yet difficult, personality was Peter Sellers. It is not surprising that it was he who went on to achieve international stardom. Sheila Van Damm recalls in her book *We Never Closed* that Sellers was spotted by BBC producer Denis Main Wilson. He promised Sellers he would recommend him for a new radio programme being planned. Days passed and Sellers had heard nothing. Never one to give in easily, he rang the producer and demanded to know 'Why hasn't this Sellers fellow been given the chance to broadcast?' imitating the voice of well-known comic Richard 'Stinker' Murdoch. He then broke into impersonations of Kenneth Horne and Sam Costa in quick succession. 'What on earth...?' the producer queried. Peter Sellers quickly explained himself. For him, the BBC was to be just the beginning.

There were other comedy partnerships that could trace their roots back to the Windmill. Bill Kerr was to team up with Tony Hancock in the popular radio programme *Hancock's Half Hour*. Kerr was an Australian who perfected a pessimistic routine and the catchphrase 'I'm only here for four minutes', spoken as if he had just received some ghastly news.

Arthur English came to represent the archetypal spiv. In 1949 he was working as a painter and decorator. He came up to London with his wife to attend the Ideal Home Exhibition. He decided to call in at the Windmill, having heard they held regular morning auditions. Dressed in a loud suit and an outrageous, four-foot-long tie, he launched into a constant stream of Cockney patter. Van Damm realised at once that here was another potential star – a likeable spiv, shooting out punchlines timed at 300 words a minute. Arthur was able to put his paintbrushes away. He started at the Windmill that afternoon. The 'Prince of the Wideboys' had arrived. Robert Moreton centred his act around his muddled gags, where he frequently forgot the punchline. Being naturally shy and studious-looking made his chaotic act all the funnier, and he went on to be a favourite radio star during the 1950s.

The Windmill helped launch the career of another performer who was neither a comedian, singer nor dancer. Leslie Welch became known as 'The Memory Man'. He was able to recall the minutest detail of sporting events dating back into the distant past. He had worked in ENSA during the war and his act managed to keep the audiences' minds off the girls for at least a few minutes. During his time at the theatre, it was reckoned he answered about 5,000 questions, only failing on very rare occasions. Later, Welch went on to become a leading star appearing in eight Royal Command performances and thousands of radio broadcasts.

Although Vivian Van Damm had a unique knack of spotting star potential, even he was not infallible. A double act appearing as 'Bartholomew and Wiseman' bombed. For three days their attempts to engage with their audience were met with total silence. Van Damm called them into his office on the Wednesday and told the disappointed pair that they could leave at the end of the week. Eric Morecambe and Ernie Wise must have cut forlorn figures as they left the Windmill's stage door. For them it was back to the drawing board.

Soho had its own little separate whirlpools of activity. Just around the corner from Archer Street, Binkie Beaumont and H. M. Tennant were thriving. He was feeding the theatre-going public a diet of undemanding plays. By the end of 1946 *Crime and Punishment* was showing at the Globe. Down the road at the Lyric *The Winslow Boy* starring Emlyn Williams and Angela Baddeley was getting rave reviews. But Binkie's stranglehold on Shaftesbury Avenue was challenged by

Emile Littler presenting Ruth Draper, America's 'Queen of Monologues', at the Apollo.

Beaumont now exhibited a rare talent that kept him so far ahead of his rivals. He was able to sense talent, sniff it out, often even before the person concerned understood it themselves. He had been introduced to a rough, monosyllabic Welshman with amazing eyes and a pockmarked face. The young Richard Burton wasn't even sure he wanted a career on the stage, or to be involved with this strange, camp little man. He had been warned that Binkie was manipulative, devious and dangerous to cross if he wanted a future in the profession. Grudgingly, he was persuaded. He appeared in a number of walk-on and small parts, without seemingly raising much interest, but Binkie was convinced that the young man from the valleys had an aura about him that would eventually transmit itself on stage. He was right, of course, but not just yet. It was Burton's voice that first came to the public's notice when he appeared in a radio play by fellow Welshman Emlyn Williams in 1947. Next, he was seen on stage in John Gielgud's production of *The Lady's Not for Turning* by Christopher Fry. Sitting in the auditorium, Binkie realised that although Burton was only playing a minor role, he had become the centre of the audience's attention when on stage. He seemed to generate a base, animal appeal. At a party held after the opening night, Binkie described it as 'hypnosis at its crudest and fiercest'. How right he was. By 1950, Richard Burton was taking leading roles in the West End. Audiences loved him, so did a succession of leading ladies. Binkie wasn't alone in liking a bit of rough.

Beaumont's talents were by no means confined to discovering new stars. As Burton had been warned, Binkie was manipulative, devious and dangerous. He was also quite ruthless – qualities that seemed totally divorced from his physical make-up. Many of the methods he employed would have been admired by the Messinas and Billy Hill, although he had no need to resort to physical violence. His influence over the West End stage was so great that by 1949 his competitors, in desperation, formed themselves into a committee in an attempt to limit his control. Leading West End managers Tom Arnold, Emile Littler, Jack Hylton and Lee Ephraim set out in an attempt to cut out what they maintained was unfair competition. Binkie remained sanguine. He attributed their hostility to jealousy. The new

committee complained that H. M. Tennant had accumulated
huge capital reserves by manipulating tax laws. By doing so,
Beaumont was in a position to outbid other organisations in
landing the rights to all the most important plays being created
in Britain and the States. He was currently running half a dozen
Broadway hits, including *Death of a Salesman* and *A Streetcar
Named Desire*. Thanks to his financial reserves, he was able to
pay royalties well above the norm. Sometimes he would pay
double the going rate and further nail down the deal by making
a substantial down payment. He was also known for his lavish
entertainment and extravagant gifts to those who could, in any
way, influence a deal.

Emile Littler and his partners continued to lobby those with
influence and Binkie was asked to appear before a Parliamentary
sub-committee to explain his seeming monopoly. He was
damning in his criticism of his rivals, saying it was they who
were forcing him to pay inflated royalties. He maintained that
leading producers came to H. M. Tennant for the prestige and
professionalism that the organisation represented. A member
of the sub-committee, Sir Ernest Pooley, commented tetchily,
'Everything you touch seems to turn to gold.' Smiling demurely,
Binkie replied, 'Yes, one does seem to be on the crest of a wave,
but it hasn't always been like this. One's had a number of notable
failures …' He may have been ruling the world of London
theatre, but now he was even beginning to talk like royalty!

Binkie remained relaxed as the complaints about him rumbled
on. In his own mind, he had nothing to worry about. Both he
and George Watkin, his financial adviser, had been meticulous
in their running of H. M. Tennant. They had broken no laws but
had actually used the existing laws to their own benefit. It was
time for his competitors to play catch-up, get smarter. No empire
lasts forever and with the approach of a new decade it wasn't just
the theatrical world in Soho that was going to witness change. A
golden era for this vibrant square mile was waiting impatiently
in the wings.

37. The Palace Theatre in the 1950s.

38. The beautiful Penny Calvert, who married fellow Windmill performer
Bruce Forsyth.

39. There was a huge variety of restaurants in and around Soho to choose from.

40. A 1950s view of Old Compton Street, clogged with traffic. Finding a parking spot was a real problem.

41. The corner of Frith Street and Old Compton Street, pictured in 1952, later the site for the infamous fight between Jack Spot and Albert Dimes.

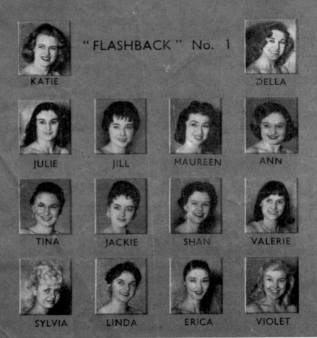

42. An Irving Theatre programme. The Irving produced the first show in London where the nude models moved about the stage.

the Irving girls
in your pocket!
Exciting! Novel! Intriguing!

VISTASCREEN

3-D VIEWS

5/- per set of ten pictures

You have never seen anything quite like this. The girls come to life in 3-dimentional relief in the most alluring way.

Obtainable only from the Irving Theatre, Leicester Square

43. The Irving was the brainchild of lawyer and owner Dhurjati Chaudhuri.

IRVING THEATRE
(Set One)

JUST ON

ARTISTIC

MISSION

VISTASCREEN
TRADE MARK

SERIES C.86

44. The girls performing at the Irving Theatre were wholesome, rather than sexy.

45. Paul Raymond, whose hugely successful Revue Bar was to lure customers away from the Windmill and help point it to its demise.

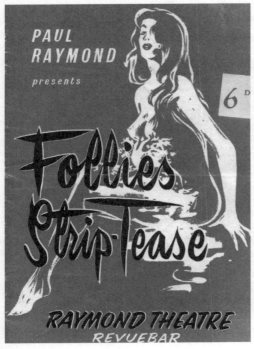

46. A programme for Raymond's Revue Bar.

47. The Panama Theatre Club was one of the many Raymond imitators which flourished for a time.

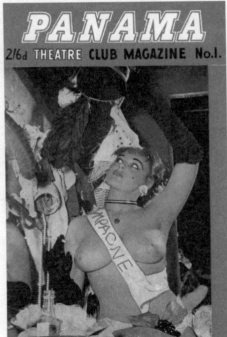

48. The Panama Theatre was at least professional, introducing its own magazine, but the premises were too small to mount a significant challenge to Paul Raymond.

49. The sexy Pamela Green, co-founder with George Harrison Marks of their glamour empire.

50. Pam Green with George Harrison Marks, pictured in business mode.

This page: 51 & 52. Two copies of the staggeringly successful *Kamera* magazine, in which explicit photographs within the law were pushed to their limits.

This page: 53 & 54.
The gorgeous film-star
looks of model Jean Sporle
were complemented by
her ability to type and
help run the office for
Harrison Marks.

55. The Apollo Theatre in Shaftesbury Avenue, where *Seagulls Over Sorrento* was a huge success for Binkie Beaumont, encouraging him to stage shows with mass appeal.

56. Jean Mara (Winkie Winkfield) makes the coveted front cover of the programme for the 287th edition of Revudeville.

57. The team that helped Van Damm to run the Windmill like a well-oiled machine.

Left: 58. The cute and cheeky Jean Mara (Winkie Winkfield) bares all.

Below left: 59. Billy Hill, the suave, self-appointed 'king of the underworld'. A meticulous planner, he was the brains in his partnership with Jack Spot.

Below right: 60. Jack Spot, the tough guy in an increasingly uneasy alliance that, for a time, controlled Soho.

PART 3

THE FIFTIES

10

Peering Through the Gloom

Sex, drugs and rock 'n' roll are often reckoned to encapsulate London in the 1960s. Add huge excesses of alcohol and you have the backdrop to Soho in the preceding decade. As usual, Soho was slightly out of step with the mainstream, although for the first couple of years of the decade the difference was less pronounced. These fundamental changes lurked in the background waiting to be unleashed.

Since the end of the war, the Labour government had launched many far-reaching initiatives. Despite the introduction of the National Health Service and the nationalisation of major industries, many felt short-changed. Life continued to be a struggle against a background of constant shortages and the realisation that Britain's influence throughout the world was in decline. The public punished the Socialists by electing the Tories in October 1951. Somehow the re-emergence of Winston Churchill at the age of seventy-seven hardly pointed the way to a forward-looking Britain. It seemed much of the country remained Conservative, even if it was only with a small 'c'. With clothes rationing ending in 1949, at least women were looking less dowdy. A sense of style was returning with innovative variations of the 'New Look'. Young men took to wearing duffle coats and corduroy trousers. The duffle coat was a variation on wartime naval issue. Some also cut a dash wearing a belted gabardine raincoat much favoured by stars of the silver screen.

As if to underline the sense of conservatism, the theatres along the length of Shaftesbury Avenue continued to offer a diet of unchallenging productions. In September 1950, Tommy Trinder and Rose Murphy topped the bill at the Palladium.

King's Rhapsody, a musical by Ivor Novello, was showing at the Palace Theatre, offering sumptuous sets, dazzling costumes and memorable songs, including 'Someday My Heart Will Awake'. Sadly, Novello's heart did the opposite. The show outlived the composer, who died in 1951 aged fifty-eight. Countless matrons throughout the country mourned his passing, unaware that he was gay – a fact that had been generally screened from view due to the continuing criminalisation of homosexuality. The Casino in Old Compton Street offered a Robert Nesbit production of *Latin Quarter*, a revue starring Vic Oliver and Sylvia St Clair. Any hint of plays with a harder edge was totally lacking. One of the huge hits at the time was *Seagulls Over Sorrento*, a comedy showing at the Apollo with Ronald Shiner and William Hartnell (later to become TV's first Doctor Who) as a bullying petty officer. Comedy was also on offer at the Lyric, with Nancy Mitford's adaptation of a French play, *The Little Hut*, starring Robert Morley. The escapist and undemanding fare was continued at the Globe with another French play translated by Christopher Fry. *Ring Round the Moon* had a heavyweight cast led by Paul Scofield and Margaret Rutherford. Lavish American musicals *Brigadoon* and *Carousel* were also being shown in the West End. The public was seeking escapism from the continuing grind of austerity. It was the only way theatre producers could compete with the continuing popularity of the cinema.

Another competitor was also beginning to stir, although so far only 350,000 licences had been taken out on television sets and most of the programmes, for the time being, ranged from amateurish to outright embarrassing. Easy on the eye viewing was continuing at the Windmill and still the public flocked to the shows; their continuing success was underlined by a healthy bank balance of over £25,000 (almost £1 million at today's value).

Whilst nobody went hungry in early 1950s Britain, the standard of food served, particularly in hotels and restaurants, was dire. Soho alone was the exception, apart from the Joe Lyons Corner Houses which at least made an effort. Home cooking tended to be stodgy and certainly unadventurous. Brits generally were very wary of foreign food. My mother rather scoffed at the cooking of a young French neighbour, whilst I marvelled at the smells coming from her kitchen. Watching Suzanne prepare a salad was a revelation. Not for her tinned pilchards, a few lettuce leaves and a tomato cut into quarters.

In 1950, a book on Mediterranean food by Elizabeth David shone a light, explaining that eating should be one of life's real pleasures. With a dust jacket illustrated by Soho devotee, John Minton, it opened up a world of unfamiliar spices and olive oil. The following year she published *French Country Cooking*. She had succeeded in awakening a real interest in food, a bridgehead for others to develop and refine. Her efforts were helped by the many returning servicemen who had served all over the world and had developed a taste for different cuisines. In addition, the Chinese were beginning to arrive in London, escaping from the war between the Red Army and the Nationalists under Chiang Kai-Shek. They started opening restaurants which found immediate favour as they were for most people new, exciting and cheap.

In the spring of 1951, the journalist and writer Raymond Postgate launched the *Good Food Guide*. Like Elizabeth David, he was horrified at the generally vile standard of food on offer in British hotels and restaurants – even worse, he reckoned, than what was served back in Edwardian days. The standard of food in Britain had become a laughing stock. It had to change. Postgate's idea was for members of the general public to submit their honest views on the restaurant meals they had eaten. The book sold some 5,000 copies, proving there was a ready market to be tapped. The vast majority of the restaurants listed were in London (mostly in Soho) and almost all of them served foreign food. The contributing comments were short and pithy but gave enough information for the prospective diner. The following were featured in the first edition.

The Hungarian Csarda in Dean Street served 'Food in the peasant mode, but not at peasant prices.' Table d'hôte 7s 6d, carafe wine 11s 6d, but the finest Tokays knocking you back 27s 6d.

Choys in Frith Street had wines at 16s, but the guide suggested drinking tea. Set dinner was 5s. If French cuisine took your fancy Père Auguste in Gerrard Street listed main courses at 3s 6d to 5s and wines ranging from 10s to 30s, which would get you a bottle of '37 Clos du Roi. The guide also informed readers that Monsieur Auguste would always be there in person.

Père Auguste was obviously something of a local character and his service with the Free French during the war was rewarded with the Croix de Guerre. An article in a 1951 guide to Soho described him as having:

a shiny bald head, a defiantly distinguished beard and merry
eyes that snap like castanets at the sight of a pretty girl. He
looks like a diplomat in a morning coat and striped trousers
and his business has made him diplomatic. He knows all
London's celebrities, winks at their weaknesses and has a
card index mind about their divorces and co-respondents ...
Sprightly and gay, he has always found champagne more fun
than cocoa.

The article ends with Père Auguste's recipe for Omelette Quarter
Latin, which will be light, piquant and easily digested:

Reduce in oil a pound of tomatoes, four ounces of onions, one
shell of garlic, some tarragon, parsley and minced basilica. In
another frying pan, prepare the omelette as usual with six eggs.
Pour in the mixture as you begin to cook your omelette. Stir
well and serve frothy and, above all, very hot. Bon Appétit!

Other restaurants in the guide included simple Greek food at
the Blue Windmill. Since when was Escalope of Veal a Greek
speciality? Never mind, it would have cost you 3s 6d. Chez Victor
in Wardour Street, which had been in the area for over twenty
years, was, strangely, closed on Saturday evenings. Kettner's
was described as luxurious. It claimed to be the cheapest of dear
places with Lobster Newbury at 8s 6d, whilst a whole capon or
duck served at your table was 60s. It boasted a choice of over
150 wines from 14s, and excellent service. Here, then, were the
first rumblings of a slow-burning food revolution. By 1951 it was
reckoned there were over 400 restaurants in Soho. Whilst French
and Italian predominated, cuisines from across Europe and the
Far East were well represented. The Taj Mahal in Romilly Street
was a standard bearer for the Indian invasion still to come.

The *Soho Guide* informed its readers that, in addition to the
amazing choice of restaurants, the Soho of 1951 had much else
to offer. There were 'bakeries, patisseries, delicatessens, garlic,
aubergines, artichokes and canteloupes available from the
markets'. Further local colour is graphically described: 'pimps,
pansies and prostitutes – the latter posted in doorways and on
street corners are earthier, less handsome than the fashionable
demi-mondaines of Soho's long ago!' The article describes
Americans on Charing Cross Road wearing drape suits with

padded shoulders (known as Jewish muscles), suede shoes, pointed collars and jazzy ties. It describes what it calls the hoi polloi of the stage talking in superlatives about their contracts and bookings and of their much-needed rests. There were also:

> agents, publishers, song-pluggers, crooners and band leaders talking about picking up royalties for broadcasts on air. There are barrow boys with wads of cabbage and the Greyhound Express, movie men from Wardour Street with loud ties and cigars, small time prize fighters with their managers, racecourse touts, waiters, beggars, drinking clubs, rehearsal rooms and the sound of Le Jazz Hot ... bookshops with thinly veneered pornography, postcards in windows that somehow manage to hint at immorality and perversion in the most innocent of phrases. This is the Latin Quarter of London, vice ridden, glamorous, dirty and yet romantic, where the streets are shady on both sides of the road.

The shady side of Soho's underworld continued to fascinate. The uneasy alliance between Billy Hill and Jack Spot ensured a surface calm, but the balance of power was shifting. Enter a new character who was to have a huge influence. Duncan Webb was an investigative journalist for *The People* newspaper and he was responsible for the break-up and downfall of the Messina brothers. His articles adopted a high moral tone, yet his background might suggest a tendency to hypocrisy. Webb was invalided out of the Army in 1944 after serving in West Africa. He returned to take up his career in journalism, working on the *Daily Express* before joining *The People*. His zeal to expose criminal activity was rather compromised by his closeness to Billy Hill. He was later involved in the ghostwriting of Hill's biography *Boss of Britain's Underworld*. Webb also had form. In 1944 he appeared at Marlborough Street on charges of grievous bodily harm and impersonating a police officer. It was alleged that having had sex with a prostitute called Joan Grewes he refused to pay her the £2 agreed. Strangely, he hung on at her flat whilst she went for help. She telephoned the police and asked a friend, the actor Herbert Wadham, to come back to the flat with her until the law arrived. Webb flashed his press card, which he tried to pass off as a warrant card and, after hitting Wadham, fled the scene. When the police caught up with him, Webb denied that he had ever seen Wadham, and the charge of impersonating a policeman was eventually dropped. He was, however, fined two guineas and bound over. Years later, he wrote with seemingly no sense of irony, 'On the night of 30 June 1950 I performed one of the most distasteful duties I have ever carried out in my career as a crime reporter. Something I would never want to do again. I went to the West End of London and picked up a woman of the streets.'

On 3 September, Webb wrote an article that had the Messina brothers scurrying for cover:

'ARREST THESE FOUR MEN, THEY ARE THE KINGS OF VICE IN THE HEART OF LONDON.'
THE MESSINA GANG EXPOSED by Duncan Webb

The article was illustrated with photographs of the brothers, some of the girls and flats they operated from. Webb's style was so sanctimonious that it seems ludicrous today. He began:

Today I offer Scotland Yard a dossier I have compiled which uncovers a monstrous vice gang that is operating in the West End of London. This is an unsavoury story which will appal every decent citizen. It is, however, one which this paper feels bound to reveal, so that immediate action can be taken. I intend, over the coming weeks, to expose in detail the way these sordid men operate and profit from their shameful trade.

He went on to name the brothers and the aliases they were using. He explained their Maltese and Egyptian background and their legal activities as merchants and dealers. 'There are dozens of women who are completely in their power ... This is a state of affairs that would disgrace the most licentious ports of the Middle East.' Webb maintained that 'the Messinas controlled well over half the prostitutes operating in Soho'. Damningly, he queries why it was that 'the Messinas have been talked about in high places for years, yet nothing has been done to close down their operation which defames the name of our capital'. Listing the addresses of the flats owned and rented by the gang provided further damning evidence, but Duncan Webb had other juicy facts for his readers:

Why do these women submit themselves to such a tawdry life?
A comfortable flat is provided together with first class meals
served in their own room. They have no need to worry about
clothes, as these are all taken care of. The Messinas even run
their own clothing exchanges here.

Rather than a condemnation, the article is beginning to sound
like a recruitment campaign. Webb continues:

In addition to generous holidays, the women are all offered
protection by the Messinas and their henchmen. Any freelance
who dares encroach on their territory is soon warned off. In
exchange for their generosity the brothers expect a frightening
level of productivity. My survey logs an average time spent
with a client is eight and a half minutes. It is not unusual for
them to entertain five clients in an hour … I have made it my
duty to check on the prices charged. I found that two pounds
was the absolute minimum. Later investigations revealed that
certain women indulged in the most ghastly perversions. These
practices encouraged clients to pay up to twenty pounds for a
half hour session.

Webb then went on to report that 'each girl has a trusted maid
who is responsible for handing over the money to the Messinas'.
He also mentioned savage beatings handed out to any girl
suspected of cheating.

Other articles followed. It was time for the Messina boys to go to
ground. Eugenio and Carmelo climbed into their Rolls-Royce and
departed for France, to be followed by Salvatore and Attilio. Alfredo
decided to take a chance and stayed. It was a poor decision and in
March 1951 he was sentenced to two years following a trial at the
Old Bailey. It appeared that the Messinas were a broken flush, but
their tentacles ran deep. It was left to French-born Martha Watts,
who was controlled by Eugenio, to organise the increasingly young
girls he was sending over from the Continent.

Meanwhile, Duncan Webb basked in glory and, claiming now
to be a devout Roman Catholic, placed an advertisement in *The
Times* offering thanks to St Jude as patron saint to hopeless cases
(of which, in many ways, he was one).

At the end of 1952 the whole of Soho and Greater London
ground to a halt. Businesses were closed, theatre performances

cancelled. People struggled for breath and, alarmingly, the death rate throughout the capital soared. London was about to witness four of the most frightening days in its long history. Fog had increasingly been a part of London's life since the industrial revolution, but this was different. On Friday 5 December an all-encompassing fog descended, reducing visibility to a few feet. It was dry, acrid and smoky and attacked the lungs. It permeated through closed windows, forming a ghostly mist in living rooms. Traffic ground to a standstill. Theatregoers sitting at the back of the auditorium couldn't even see the stage. People huddled round their fires in an attempt to get warm. The belching chimneys added to the problem and the fog worsened. By Sunday the papers were referring to smog and still the atmosphere and visibility worsened. It was possible to get lost within yards of stepping outside. I remember it being impossible to see a hand in front of your face or glancing down to see your feet. The smoke from chimneys, which would normally have been dispersed in the atmosphere, was being trapped by an anticyclone hanging over London. Thousands died from its cloying effects and huge numbers were made ill. By the end of the year the skies had cleared again. Steps would be taken to introduce smokeless fuel, but not until 1956. Fogs did return, but never with such devastating effects. Lessons were learnt. It was as if the dispersing of the smog pointed a way forward to a brighter future. Soho was about to turn its back on austerity.

11

Everyday Soho

Popular belief has it that the Soho of the mid-1950s was inhabited solely by famous writers, artists, musicians, drunks, whores and razor-slashing thugs. They were all there, of course, but there was a more mundane side populated by ordinary people trying to make a living.

At the time I was able to view this at first hand. A school friend's father was an electrical contractor and for eight weeks during my summer holiday I worked in Wardour Street as an electrician's mate's mate. This, in the hands of someone who struggles to change a light bulb, was bound to lead to trouble. Over the coming weeks I managed to plunge not just the building, but the whole block into darkness on several occasions. The Sabrina Coffee Bar was situated on the ground floor of 15 Wardour Street. It advertised itself as London's only espresso coffee and cocktail lounge and was open from 10 a.m. to midnight with an extension on Friday and Saturday to 1 p.m. The venue was named after a curvaceous, blonde bombshell, reckoned to be Britain's answer to Jayne Mansfield. Sabrina was a Welsh girl whose real name was Norma Sykes. She claimed she could neither sing, dance nor act, yet she had become a household name in the days before the current obsession with celebrities. Described by an elderly workmate as a 'bonny girl', she arrived one afternoon to see how work was progressing. Certainly, it seemed that wherever she went she was preceded by her riveting 42-inch bust. Her dramatic hourglass figure rather detracted from what was a really pretty face with a radiant smile that I was convinced was directed solely at me, and then she was gone and it was back to trying to make sense of an incomprehensible jungle of wires.

Soho, over fifty years ago, was a very different place. Sure, there were fashionable restaurants and clubs. From mid-afternoon battalions of working girls lined the streets. There was an occasional glimpse of a famous face and any number of dodgy-looking characters, and yet the chances of finding any trouble were seemingly far less than in any major town centre throughout the country.

My working day started with a fry-up at a greasy spoon café just round the corner from the Sabrina. There were several basic working men's cafés nearby, a type that scarcely exists in the West End today. Sitting at Formica tables, it was impossible to see outside onto the street for the clouds of smoke belching out of a gigantic tea urn. There was not a single foreign dish on offer. They served massive helpings of fried eggs, beans and rashers of bacon, all served on a bed of bread fried in lard. Thick hunks of bread covered in margarine were plonked on the plate and the whole lot was washed down with mugs of steaming, sweet tea. Two heaped teaspoons were statutory. Requests for no sugar were ignored.

It was during my lunch breaks and after work that I was able to begin my discovery of the real Soho, as lived by the majority of people who had little money to spend. With supermarkets still to make much impact in the area and few households having fridges, daily food shopping was the norm. Soho probably offered the greatest choice in the whole of London. The number of delicatessens matched that of Soho's pubs, weighing in at about fifty. Once any early morning mist cleared, it was a sense of smell that dominated the crowded streets. Best known of the delis were Fratelli Camisa in Berwick Street and Parmigiani's, who had several outlets, including one on Old Compton Street. They displayed shelves of cheeses, freshly baked pizza and a huge range of sausages, swaying from hooks. There were jars of olives, anchovies and raffia-clad bottles of Chianti. There were Jewish delis with long sticks of Polish dried sausage and Kiben stuffed with chopped meats. There were also shops specialising in Greek, Indian and Chinese food. Just down the road from Parmigiani's, the smell of freshly ground coffee beans dominated. The Algerian Coffee Shop still trades today in Old Compton Street. Early risers would be engulfed by, perhaps, the most wonderful smell of all – freshly baked bread that was on sale at Grodzinki's in Brewer Street, whilst, arguably, the best croissants outside France were available from Maison Bertaux. If you fancied a cake or pastry, Patisserie Valerie was probably the best.

The mid-1950s were on a cusp where individual service in shops held sway over the arrival of supermarkets and checkouts. Each transaction involved talking to the person serving you and watching as your purchase was carefully weighed and packed. It was noticeable that, whilst everywhere else in the West End people appeared to be in a rush, in Soho the pace was more measured. There was time to pause, to amble and take in all that was going on around you. The difference also seemed to apply to the Soho street markets. It would be unusual today to find a stallholder selling only one product, and yet I remember barrows devoted to just potatoes or bananas. Most of the pitches in the markets were controlled by a small number of families who had traded locally for generations. Some had progressed to owning shop premises but they still pitched a barrow outside their front door. In winter the markets stayed open after dark, creating a slightly eerie atmosphere with lanterns hanging from the overhanging canopies. At Christmas, they stayed open late and canny shoppers left their buying until the last minute in the hope of purchasing an unsold turkey at a bargain price.

The other smell it was impossible to escape from at the time was cigarette smoke. It appeared everyone was puffing away. Tobacconists were plentiful in the 1950s. Real tobacconists that sold nothing else. There was a dedicated specialist on the corner of Frith Street and Old Compton Street that sold everything from Woodbines to Gauloises and cigarettes customised for individuals. They also stocked pipes, tobacco and fat Havanas, as well as a selection of snuff which was still quite popular. Although people were becoming aware of the health risks, it had yet to cause a significant decline in sales. From the roll-your-own market trader to the cigar-wielding businessman and the callow youth sucking on a half-empty pipe, smoke and smoking were impossible to avoid. It hung heavily in pubs and clubs, it clung to clothes, and yet the cigarette was seen as a romantic accessory, constantly promoted in the cinema.

Romance didn't feature much in the sprouting numbers of 'dirty bookshops' in Soho. What was on show at the front of the shops during the early 1950s offered nothing more shocking than energetic naturists playing volleyball as featured in *Health and*

Efficiency, and a variety of coy pin-up magazines. Behind a tacky bead curtain much stronger stuff was on offer from the Continent and the States. Pornography was to become hugely profitable, as we will discover.

Traditional trades that had existed in Soho streets for generations still flickered during the first half of the 1950s. Most had been forced to adapt. Watchmakers had become mere repairers, whilst the leading dealers had decamped to Clerkenwell Road, likewise the jewellers to Hatton Garden. Those remaining in Soho were involved in costume jewellery. Windows were lined with trays of glass beads, Marcasite brooches and imitation pearls on offer at 39s a dozen. The Jewish tailors were still trading, particularly around Berwick Street, many still speaking in Yiddish. Above their shops were cutters, pressers and button-holers, all working in hot, crowded conditions which would be outlawed today. Cyril Stein had a hairdresser's in Wardour Street. He set out to appeal to men in the theatrical profession, no doubt being aware that his boys wouldn't accept the short back and sides still favoured by many. He offered permanent waving, blow waving and tinting. As ever, the luvvies were ahead of the game.

For those of us with little money at the time, there were a few places where we could take a girlfriend out to eat without breaking the bank. The Omelette Bar at 18 Lisle Street was a great alternative to the Quality Inns and Wimpy Bars which were appearing all over the West End. You could choose from a wide range of omelettes which were cooked in front of you with a great flourish by a white-clad chef. From memory, you helped yourself to salad and then a choice of fruit pies for pudding. Red gingham tablecloths gave the place a Continental feel and it stayed open to the early hours and was very popular with late-night cinema-goers. If you needed to stay in Soho overnight, it was sometimes possible to get a bed at the Interval Club in Dean Street. This had been formed in 1926 for Roman Catholics in the theatrical profession, but by the 1950s they had relaxed their requirements. Providing you accepted the small bedrooms and were prepared to share the bathroom and toilet, it saved many the trauma of walking the streets at night or dossing down on a bench in Soho Square.

Watching mugs fall for the 'three card trick' was one of the great spectator sports that I remember from the summer holidays all those years ago. Three men were normally involved: a lookout

to warn if the law was in the area, the stooge (who played the
punter that appeared to win) and the card sharp. The trickster
set up shop often using a briefcase as a makeshift table. With a
flourish he would place three cards face up. One was a queen.
Usually, it was a diamond or heart as, presumably, this appealed
psychologically more than the rather sinister black queens. With
a little chat the sharp would gather a small crowd of inquisitive
onlookers. Allowing his audience a good look, he would turn
the cards face down. Then came the moving of the cards that
was done so quickly it was difficult for the onlookers to keep up.
Enter the stooge, who was the first to bet, placing a ten-bob note
on a card that he told everybody he knew was the queen. Surprise,
surprise, he won. The crowd shifted forward, anxious now to get
a close look. A couple of punters followed the stooge where he
placed his money and they won too. So, it was possible to win.
'Folding money only,' the sharp shouted, as if offended by the
sight of coins, and the notes were slammed down. Nobody had
noticed that by now the stooge had disappeared into the crowd.
The confidence of the punters faded as the sharp palmed the
queen for three successive bets with no winners. As the crowd's
mood changed to anger, the lookout shouted 'Quick, the law!'
The three disappeared in different directions, leaving the punters
feeling stupid and aggrieved. It wasn't only the Billy Hills and
Jack Spots of this world who earned their money from crime;
there had to be room for the small man too and there were plenty
of them. 'Put me in the swindle' was a popular catchphrase then.
Bookies' runners and card sharps were as much a part of the
Soho scene as the working girls that lined the streets. Soon those
girls were going to have to operate differently as new legislation
removed them from view. Whilst this may have indicated a move
towards more restrictive times, in fact the mood of the public and
those in power was to loosen the grip on sexual expression. What
had started in 1934 with the opening of the Windmill Theatre
was now about to result in an initial breaching of floodgates and
the dawning of the permissive society.

12

Stripping Away
the 1950s

For twenty-five years, attractive young women had appeared nude on the London stage unmoving, as if frozen in time. What had started at the Windmill had been imitated, but constrained by the Lord Chamberlain, and unchallenged except in a few illegal backstreet clubs. Trust a lawyer to be the one to find a way round the law. Dhurjati Chaudhuri, a bespectacled Bengali barrister, was an unlikely candidate to become the owner of London's first non-stop striptease club. He took advantage of a loophole that had previously been used by theatre clubs and which allowed them to produce plays formerly banned by the Lord Chamberlain. Chaudhuri had been using his premises in Irving Street just off Leicester Square to run his Asian Institute of Art and Theatre. Support from the great and good of the London arty scene had done little to stop the project haemorrhaging money. It suddenly seemed obvious that by converting the property into an intimate club, with one leap he could be free from the Lord Chamberlain's clutches. The door protecting Britain from the permissive society was creaking but not yet coming off its hinges.

Chaudhuri's move was helped by the changing moral and social climate. Memories of the war were beginning to fade. A new generation was beginning to challenge the status quo. Outwardly, the country continued to project a rather puritanical image. Sex, like cancer, was rarely discussed publicly but Chaudhuri, by his action, had opened up opportunities that others would pick up and run with. Sex equated to money and profit. To a couple of men in particular these attractions were irresistible, but they would wait awhile and observe. Chaudhuri's initial optimism was challenged by existing licensing regulations that required a 48-hour waiting period from the time a prospective member signed the application form. In addition, he required a public music and dancing licence, which the London County Council refused to sanction for a strip club. His pragmatic solution to this was to pay the regular £100 fine and cost it into his regular overheads. The summer of 1957 saw a line of men snaking their way down Irving Street, anxious to pay their 25s for membership which included one complimentary ticket, although subsequent visits would cost an extra 16s 6d. For those really ardent devotees of the female nude, a full membership of £26 5s would allow free admittance at any time provided seats were available (which was by no means certain as the little theatre only seated ninety-eight). Membership was, no doubt, encouraged by a large sign advertising 'Non-stop, continuous striptease 2.30 p.m. to 11 p.m. Licensed bar, members only.'

The Irving Theatre had a certain ring to it and Chaudhuri, from the beginning, sought to retain an air of respectability. In a nod to the legitimate theatre he issued programmes listing the acts and the artistes performing. The rather tacky eight-page programme also pointed out that photography in the theatre was forbidden and artificial aids to vision were not allowed. Whilst Chaudhuri claimed to have devised and directed the non-stop revue, he employed business, production and stage managers. There was also a choreographer and assistant producer, together with seven people devoted to the music and lyrics performed. Given the level of organisation it is possible to imagine a slick, professional show. No such luck. The performances were so amateurish as to be embarrassing, but few cared – there were acres of moving, bare flesh to be ogled. Strippers of all shapes, sizes and ages pranced around the small stage wearing just a G-string. The routines were poorly rehearsed and the music provided by a single pianist and lone drummer, more suited to a village hall. In an effort to copy the Windmill, Chaudhuri introduced a couple of male dancers and a comedian. For a time a young Victor Spinetti appeared doing impersonations of film stars. Never mind the quality, the little theatre was playing to full houses, and well-known celebrities were well represented along with a curious, repressed public.

By 1958 the quality of the shows and the artistes had improved. Business continued to boom. Chaudhuri now offered his customers *Vues from Revues*, a quarterly magazine featuring articles that nobody read and lots of nude ladies. The summer edition for 1958 included an article by Wolf Mankowitz, who had written *A Kid for Two Farthings* which had been made into a film directed by Carol Reed in 1955. Was he feeling sorry for Chaudhuri? Surely he wasn't hard up as 1958 was the year he published the bestseller *Expresso Bongo*.

Chaudhuri was now able to inform his readers that in eighteen months of non-stop revue at the Irving, his company had completed over 2,500 performances. He boasts of adapting productions 'to take advantage of the small stage to create a true sense of intimacy'. It is striking how unsexy the featured girls appear. It is as if they have been recruited for their wholesome looks. It appears that even though another barrier had been broken down, British prudishness towards nudity and sex had to be maintained. The first hint of a change of direction was the appearance of Julie Mendez in the Irving cast. She was later to become a star performer at Raymond's Revue Bar, where the heat would be turned up a couple of notches.

By 1959 the Irving was claiming a membership of 50,000 which was, doubtless, vastly inflated. *Vues from Revues* was proving popular and was unique in as much as the girls pictured could be seen in the flesh on stage. The summer edition for 1959 offered the opportunity for the repressed men of Britain to view the girls in 3D. A set of ten pictures cost 10s with a free viewer provided. The editorial in the same edition spelt out the trouble the Irving was going to encounter. Chaudhuri mentions several competitors moving into the market. Although they too would base their shows on the Windmill format of employing two companies (albeit with far less artistes) who would appear on alternate days, these new operators were prepared to offer sexier and more explicit entertainment.

The first strip club to open in the heart of Soho in 1957 was the Nell Gwynne in Meard Street. Formerly the fashionable Gargoyle Club where the rich and famous had congregated, it was acquired by Michael Klinger and Jimmy Jacobs. They managed to turn this iconic building into a tatty, smelly strip club. Illegal clubs like Vicki's Studio in Old Compton Street were also springing up. Nudity was in great demand. A variation on a theme was available to red-blooded (or sad) aspiring photographers at the Visual Arts Club. Hence, they could pretend or actually snap away whilst staring blankly at the nude models.

Two future major players were watching and planning, aware that a more ambitious form of strip club needed to be developed. They both realised that there was serious money to be made. Paul Raymond had the massive advantage of having staged shows all over the provinces. He also had a wife who was a proven professional choreographer. In addition, he had built up a healthy bank balance. All he needed were suitable premises. Murray Goldstein had no experience or money, but a single-minded determination to get into the strip club business. He had pretensions about his ability to create shows and write lyrics, and about becoming an impresario. What these two men really had in common was the love of money, and they could smell it. Both had visited the Irving and they knew they could do so much better in both the quality of the shows and the profits to be made.

Paul Raymond was a complex personality, as was fully explored by Paul Willetts in his biography *Members Only*. Whilst he craved acceptance as a respectable and successful businessman, his appearance in those early days bore more than a passing resemblance to Arthur English, the archetypal spiv. In effect, that is how Raymond established himself after the war before turning to stage management. The suits were dark and conservative, but the hairstyle and pencil moustache conveyed his true provenance. He had already put in a great deal of hard work and learnt his trade. He was adept at negotiating deals and handling staff. He just needed suitable premises. Despite being warned about intimidation from criminals such as Jack Spot, he was set on locating his club in Soho. The building that attracted his attention was not an obvious choice. He showed the ability to look beyond the dismal façade and the tacky interior. Walkers Court, which connected Brewer and Berwick streets, was itself little more than a dingy alley but Raymond was excited by the building's potential.

It had previously housed the grand-sounding Doric Ballroom. There were two sides to the building connected by an enclosed footbridge. The only nod to the erotic in Walkers Court was a scruffy bookshop selling under-the-counter pornography. Small rundown shops dominated except for Isow's, a restaurant that attracted celebrities intent on a little slumming. In the basement below the restaurant was a nightclub, the Jack of Clubs, also run by Jack Isow. This ray of glamour amongst a sea of neglect added to Raymond's interest and he approached Isow about taking over the lease of the former ballroom. Isow was a Polish Jew, born Joseph Isowitski. He was a man in his mid-fifties, round, avuncular and shrewd. Like Raymond he had been involved in the black market but on a grander scale. Despite having that in common, it never served to improve their relationship, which continued to decline as the years passed. In any project there are always people warning of difficulties. In addition to the area's reputation of harbouring organised criminals, Raymond was now advised that trying to run a club other than at ground level was inviting disaster. He ignored the soothsayers and entered into negotiations with Isow. Eventually, early in 1958, Paul Raymond signed a twenty-one-year lease on the premises at a seemingly hefty rent of £5,000 a year. Isow, for all his business nous, made a vital error in not including any provision for a rent review. He had grown complacent. Historically, few tenants of his Soho properties stayed in business long enough for rent reviews to apply. He had reckoned wrongly that Raymond's venture would fold. It was to cost him dearly and it rankled.

Through years of organising provincial shows, Raymond had built up a substantial war chest to enable him to refurbish the down-at-heel property. He knew he was taking an enormous risk, but he remained confident of success. His ability and vision served him well through his life. The risks he took were always thought out and calculated. Isow would not be the last to underestimate him. He now set about organising the opening of the club. He obtained licences that enabled him to register the Raymond Theatre Revue Club and to sell alcohol. Together with his wife Jean, they interviewed staff for front-of-house jobs and sat through hours of auditions for potential performers. He managed to get permission for a giant neon sign to be erected in Brewer Street and to move the front entrance for the club into Walkers Court. Raymond understood that many of his customers might prefer the relative anonymity of a backstreet. A late blast of winter held up auditions due to the freezing rehearsal rooms. They had been overwhelmed by the number of applicants for strippers and dancers. Over eighty girls entered a competition he arranged for amateurs, no doubt encouraged by the £2,000 prize money on offer. There were shades of Vivian Van Damm when Raymond informed the press that his club was going to

be utterly respectable, 'a place where a man can take his wife'.
The popular press that thrived on sex and scandal professed
hypocritical outrage. 'Stay dressed, girls,' demanded *The People*,
incensed by Raymond staging an amateur striptease competition.
'Let Mr Raymond catch a cold with this silly and scandalous
stunt.' Who were they kidding? The article was accompanied by
photographs of two of the young contestants.

As in many building projects, the refurbishment of the
property was falling well behind schedule. With only days to go
to the launch, carpenters and decorators were still hard at work.
Amidst the chaos Jean Raymond was drilling the performers
into shape. Her work as an experienced choreographer was key
and she was planning complex routines normally associated
with West End productions rather than a backstreet strip
club. This, the Raymonds hoped, would set them apart from
competitor clubs, of which there were three already open in the
area. They then learnt that another competitor, the Casino de
Paris in Denman Street, was scheduled to open the same night as
the Revue Bar. Although, along with the other clubs, the Casino
de Paris was much smaller than Raymond's Club, there were
rumours that their show was to be much more risqué, really
pushing at the boundaries of current public acceptability. The
club was run by Ray Jackson and Eric Lindsay, who had earlier
opened the very popular Heaven & Hell Coffee Bar. Once more
their publicity blurb promised the club would have 'an emphasis
on good taste'. This, apparently, included performers stripping
off stage in amongst the punters, to the accompaniment of the
song 'Love for Sale'. They also offered the supposedly Viennese
sex symbol Alma Caddilac and, from Hungary, the Volcanic
Lola Stromboli.

Paul Raymond's worries about competition were eased
during the first week of the box office opening. Over a thousand
signed up as members, generating revenue of over £10,000. The
members were encouraged to have their annual subscription
automatically renewed through their bank, thereby removing
any embarrassment of having to confront bank staff or their
wives (who probably didn't understand them!). The garish
signage heightened the curiosity of the passing public prior to
the official opening. Adjacent to the box office it was possible to
make out the sweeping staircase, a fountain and a thick crimson
carpet. The venue had every appearance of kitsch luxury, far

removed from the normal perception of a grubby, squalid strip club.

There was a 'soft' launch for the first public show at the Revue Bar. The matinee started at 2.30 p.m. on 21 April 1958. As the first customers shuffled in, they passed posters of alluring nudes that lined the staircase to the upper floor. Here they discovered a sweeping bar, illuminated by deeply glowing red bulbs. Despite well-upholstered chairs and settees, the effect was more Las Vegas than Claridges. The lack of class was augmented by an intrusive, giant television. Despite the brashness of the decor, most people's abiding memories on entering the club for the first time were of girls in skimpy uniforms, high heels and fishnet tights, dispensing drinks and selling cigarettes from a tray situated just below an inviting cleavage. The opening act featured Ted and Renée Lastair, who were covered all over in gold paint. Once more it was nudity presented as an art form. True, Ted had performed on stage with Markova and Anton Dolin but the audience, as ever, were only interested in gawping at the girls. Forget the bloke prancing about, however talented he was!

From the very beginning, Raymond was pursued by the police, who appeared intent on closing him down. Either Raymond had not offered any form of bribe or Superintendent Strath and his team were actually straight. Raymond was aware that the police were present at almost all performances and looking for him to slip up. He was relaxed. He realised from the first day, when takings were over £500, that he had discovered a winning formula. On the first Sunday after the opening he pushed his luck by staging *Call Me Mister*, an all-male revue aimed at the local gay community. It included drag striptease. Superintendent Strath was not impressed and neither was the public, and the attendance and takings were disappointing. Raymond was antagonising the police and a full-scale raid took place early in May. A couple of dozen plain clothes detectives and a posse of uniformed women officers rushed in. They discovered customers who had been served drinks but were not members, or had not been properly proposed and seconded. Raymond had invited trouble and now he had found it. He set about ensuring in future that all members were correctly processed. Too late. Raymond and his manager, George Richardson, were required to appear at Marlborough Street Magistrates' Court. Following a degree of horse-trading between the prosecution and defence teams, it was agreed that the charges against Richardson would be dropped, but Raymond would change his plea to guilty for breaking the law relating to licensing and unauthorised public dancing. He was fined on both counts and had to pay police costs in addition to his own. He reckoned it was money well spent. He would now concentrate on his burgeoning business, which was taking in excess of £5,000 a week and boasted a membership of over 30,000.

By the summer of 1958 another competitor arrived with the opening of the Panama Theatre, almost opposite the Windmill Theatre. Here was a different form of threat. The Panama was being run by Len Mitelle, who had acquired years of experience working at the Windmill, where his sister Anne was still so influential. Len Mitelle knew how to produce shows to a similar standard to the Revue Bar but, again, Raymond remained relaxed. The venue was too small to make an impact on his business. Mitelle had recruited one performer that Paul Raymond was interested in. Julie Mendez had worked at the Irving and was being promoted as the star attraction at the Panama. It didn't take long to lure her away. Many who subsequently visited the Revue Bar have fond memories of the dark-haired beauty doing some very bizarre gyrations with a live snake. It was all too much for the theatre critic of *What's On in London* when he lamented, 'The face of our town's West End is disfigured by an eczema of crude club shows known collectively as a multitude of skins.' It appears most of his male readership disagreed.

Watching the success of the Revue Bar was an impatient Murray Goldstein. Whilst outwardly harbouring theatrical ambitions, he had realised early on, following visits to the Irving, the potential for strip clubs. Frustratingly, he had no capital so he decided to learn his trade by working for Freddy Irani, a smooth Iranian Jew. He would make his mistakes at Irani's expense, but the Iranian wanted a lot for the £30 a week he was paid. He was expected to write some of the sketches, the songs, recruit the artistes and produce the show. Initially, he was worried about recruiting girls who were prepared to strip off. His advertisements in *The Stage* brought in a deluge of young and not so young women prepared to bare all. Although a quarter of a century had passed since the first *Revudeville*, the format laid down by Van Damm was still being adhered to by the clubs. Based on the legitimate theatre formula, there continued to be a set number of acts, each with a corny theme like Salome, Delilah and Jezebel, or Maracas in Caracas. Basically, however outlandish the themes, it was just an excuse for girls to get their clothes off so they could cavort around the stage wearing just the obligatory G-string.

The Tropicana in Greek Street opened in May 1959. Goldstein enlarged the existing stage and installed improved lighting and a sound system. In a routine that would probably be banned today, the opening number at the club was 'School for Strip'! With gymslips and blue knickers, Goldstein was out to shock. He followed it up with a routine that involved hula hoops and mountains of wobbling flesh as the girls twirled away. In his book *Naked Jungle* Goldstein laughingly congratulates himself on making a great artistic breakthrough. Sanctimonious hypocrisy continued to be voiced by all those making money from the canter towards pornography. Although much smaller and less plush than the Revue Bar, the riskier shows being produced at the Tropicana were proving to be a great success. Irani converted Freddy's, his former jazz club, into Peeperama. Hot girls rather than hot jazz! There were now over a dozen strip clubs in Soho and it was only a matter of time until the hardened criminals got in on the act. It was reckoned that the combined membership of the clubs was around a staggering 200,000 and annual box office takings were in excess of £2.5 million. Astonishingly, this dwarfed the takings of blockbuster films: the profit margins were immense.

Suddenly, the newspapers were endorsing the interest in striptease by claiming it was 'the most fantastic evolution in British entertainment since the talkies'. Paul Raymond was on hand to give a catchy quote: 'The female form is one of God's most beautiful creations.' Quite, and he was making sure that he was going to cash in on it. Murray Goldstein was scheming and dreaming, intent on starting his own clubs as a new decade beckoned. By the end of 1959, Raymond was putting on three shows a day plus a late-night cabaret. Profits had soared to over £2,000 a week. He was no longer worried about competition. He knew he had devised a winning formula. He was being helped by changing perceptions driven by the young. They queried and challenged everything. Satire was in vogue, poking fun at the establishment. They congregated in coffee bars and listened to skiffle, jazz and rock 'n' roll. Raymond sensed, correctly, a change in the moral tide and a chance to cash in. Not far away in Gerrard Street, a photographer had also set about redefining the boundaries of decency.

13

The Bare Facts

Fifties Britain was publicly uncomfortable with displays of nudity. Outwardly prudish and sanctimonious, it was also in large part hypocritical. Sexually repressed Victorians had helped to create armies of prostitutes (many of them children) engulfing the West End of London. Whilst our Continental neighbours had a generally relaxed attitude to sex, their British counterparts sought to indulge their excesses guiltily and hopefully out of the public's gaze. This was a fertile market that Vivian Van Damm had recognised and Paul Raymond was to refine, whilst still clinging to an outward air of respectability.

From the moment the camera had been invented, photographers sought models prepared to strip off. They claimed it was in the cause of creating art. What had been good for generations of painters now applied to their modern equivalent. Here were the historical roots of the glamour market. The requirement to only publish work with artistic merit was still in effect at the outbreak of the Second World War. In 1938 Roye, a modern exponent of nude photography, still managed to outrage public opinion with a photograph of a nude nailed to a cross wearing a gas mask. Profane and sacrilegious was the verdict. Roye (Horace Roye-Narbeth), during a long life, continued to argue for free expression and no censorship. He wrote *Nude Ego*, a rather wordy, self-justifying book to publicise his views. Jean Straker formed the Visual Arts Club in Soho Square in 1951. He was a controversial character. His parents had both been dancers in the Paris Bergère, and this no doubt influenced his interest in nude photography. Being a conscientious objector, his wartime output was largely confined to photographing operations being carried out at London hospitals.

Like Roye, he campaigned for complete freedom of expression. Whilst considering himself a true artist, his commercial senses were also well developed. He advertised his *Femina* collection of over 4,000 nude studies. He operated a collectors' plan whereby members or visitors to the club would purchase a minimum of twelve 5-inch by 4-inch prints for 4s each copy, provided a 10s registration fee was paid. Any unwanted image could be returned for an exchange fee of 1s 6d. Straker took himself very seriously, giving daily lectures and demonstrations. He informed his clients that all his studies were 'produced with the maximum technical skill and utmost artistic merit, and sincerely express the author's appreciation of the truth, beauty, power and purpose of the human form'. The Jean Straker collection is now housed at Cymiarth Bwlchllan, Lampeter, Dyfed.

It was left to another photographer to fully exploit the glamour market. Although his photographs were technically excellent, he had no artistic pretensions (although he too played the game for a time). Harrison Marks and Paul Raymond were the two most influential figures in breaking down previously held taboos. Later the two men became friends and made fortunes. There the similarities ended. Paul Raymond continued to invest and expand, whilst Marks drank to excess and sprayed his money around with the recklessness of a man intent on living every day to the full.

In 1951 George Harrison Marks was down on his luck, living in a squalid one-room flat. He was existing with virtually no money and not even a regular job. He had been working previously by photographing holidaymakers on the front at Brighton. A chance meeting led him to accept similar work, but this time in Trafalgar Square. With his 'gift of the gab', there was reasonable money to be made during the summer, but the colder autumn weather saw his income fade away. He realised there had to be a more lucrative way to exploit his limited photographic talent. He fancied becoming a theatrical and showbiz photographer. To help himself gain credibility, he became a member of the Royal Photographic Society. A photograph taken of him at that time depicts a rather satanic figure. A very stylised shot shows him with hair slicked straight back, a goatee beard and a cigarette complete with holder. He looks older than mid-twenties, unsmiling with dark, intense eyes. Doubtless, like all young men, he was trying to create an impression, but it is not an altogether comfortable one.

Early in 1952 George rented a first-floor flat at 4 Gerrard Street. This was a perfect location, being in the heart of London's theatreland. Back in the 1950s, Gerrard Street was very different from today's pedestrianised and Chinese-dominated thoroughfare. My parents used to take the family each year to the Restaurant de Boulogne at 27 Gerrard Street prior to a visit to the theatre. A mosaic doorstep remains today listing Hotel de Boulogne, which had been in existence since 1874 before becoming a restaurant only in 1917. Marks's flat was at the scruffier Newport Place end of the street. The basement was occupied by a dingy, after-hours drinking club that seemed to attract criminals from across Soho. Although not ideal, the flat doubled up as a photographic studio. He had business cards printed and started trekking round theatres and agents in search of work. It was a slog but he had some success photographing well-known entertainment figures, including Max Miller and Michael Bentine. Being a one-man band was very difficult as he was often out touting for business and therefore not able to deal with any telephone enquiries. For a time his wife Diana helped him. He had married very young and they were already living separate lives.

Early in 1952 Bernard Delfont was about to produce a show based loosely on the Folies Bergère. The star was to be Norman Wisdom, whom George had photographed when he was appearing in Brighton. Using that connection George was able to obtain the commission to take the publicity photographs and those to be displayed in the foyer of the theatre. This included head and shoulder shots of all of the chorus girls. Although he didn't realise it at the time, one of these girls was going to change his life.

Pamela Green was in her early twenties, a beautiful and creative young woman who had come up to London in 1947 to study at St Martin's School of Art on Charing Cross Road. It was a three-year course based on fashion drawing and design. Family financial problems made it essential for her to earn money to enable her to continue. She began by modelling at the school for fashion classes but soon realised that modelling in the nude paid better. Once she overcame the embarrassment of posing for her fellow students, she enjoyed the work. She was extremely pretty with a flawless figure and also found she was able to hold memorable poses without moving. She was rightly proud of her looks and she quickly obtained work at other art schools. A natural progression was to model for professional photographers. In 1949 she went to the

Greek Street studio of Douglas Webb, an ex-RAF pilot complete
with a handlebar moustache. Having asked her to strip off, it
didn't take him long to realise that she would be worth promoting.
He paid her two guineas an hour and soon he was distributing
sets of her poses to shops throughout Soho and down Charing
Cross Road. They were both happy. Pam was still attending art
school but demands on her time were making studying difficult.
She had some of her own art studies accepted by the Royal
Academy in 1950 and she received a small grant to encourage her
to continue at St Martin's, Money was still tight, but she joined a
sun club in order to get an overall tan that looked so much better
in photographs. She started sitting for other photographers and
registered with a leading agency. Doing underwear shots, she was
also paid two guineas an hour. She was being weaned away from
art school by the earning potential. Life was frantic and exciting.
She had started getting stage work dancing and also appearing as
a static nude at the London Casino.

She posed for Hungarian photographer Zoltan Glass and
for Philip Gotlop for his book *Figure Photography*. During this
whirlwind period she also married Guy Hillier in September
1951. She continued to be busy appearing in a feature in the now
defunct magazine *Lilliput*. Within months her marriage was in
trouble. The charming Mr Hillier was, it seems, an overbearing
drunk. Although they split up after eighteen months he told her
divorce was out of the question as he was a Roman Catholic. Not
long after the break-up Pam was walking along Gerrard Street
when she remembered the attractive theatrical photographer who
had snapped the giggling collection of chorus girls.

Harrison Marks, now separated from his wife, was still lounging
about in his pyjamas. 'I don't suppose you remember me?' she
asked, holding out her hand. 'I'm Pamela Green.' 'I do,' George
replied, 'and you know what, green is my favourite colour.' It
was too. Those who remember him from that time picture him
forever dressed in green corduroy with matching shirt and tie.
It was Pam who suggested that he should try his hand at nude
photography. He didn't need to be asked a second time. She was
a shrewd girl and could see the potential for a joint enterprise, all
the more so as the couple had become lovers soon after meeting.
There was a snag, though. George, as ever short of cash, had
gone into partnership with businessman Harry Kweller, who was
getting increasingly tetchy at seeing no return on his investment

in the young photographer. Pam, unlike George, had always been careful with money and her offer of £100 to buy out Kweller was gratefully received. Remembering the success Douglas Webb had enjoyed with the sale of the nude studies, they decided to repeat the recipe. For a time life was extremely tough, with little to eat and a trip to Endell Street baths considered a treat. They survived on one ration book as Pam had left hers with her husband. Horsemeat steaks bought on Berwick Street were an affordable delicacy, shared with George's Alsatian and their two cats. Things were so tight financially that even their bed was repossessed by the bailiffs, but their luck was about to change.

Life is so unfair in the attributes each of us is dealt. The gods obviously looked kindly on Pamela Green. Sure, she was beautiful, but also creative and intelligent with a friendly, engaging personality. Much shorter than she appears in photographs, she was only 5 feet 2 inches in height. Her hourglass figure of 38–24–36 was perfect for a generation of men who appreciated feminine curves rather than the anorexic models who tend to dominate today. Having only one model was obviously going to restrict the new venture, despite the use of wigs and make-up to add variety. They set about trying to recruit new models, but in the early 1950s finding girls willing to appear in the nude or even topless was difficult. They also had to be well endowed. Marks soon found out that shots of scrawny girls didn't sell. Gradually, more girls came forward from agencies, 'resting' showgirls and even a couple of enterprising street girls. Lorraine Burnett became one of the studio's most sought-after models. She had a blue-chip pedigree, having graduated from the Windmill and the Panama Club. Later she became a star attraction at Raymond's Revue Bar.

The introduction of new models saw the postcard sets fly off the shelves. The images, whilst sexy and suggestive, were of a high standard. George had learnt his trade. The lighting was used to clever effect and the stage sets were imaginative. Pam was now not just modelling, but had taken charge of make-up and directing the shots. She had an ability to relax the models who had no previous experience and who would have felt uncomfortable being alone with George. In those early days he seemed not at all interested in the other attractive girls he was to photograph, and was obviously still very smitten with Pam. He claimed that for seven years he was completely faithful to her. This is unlikely but, for the moment, the pair were concentrating on developing their burgeoning business.

Another very popular model arrived in the very shapely form of Pat Sutcliffe. She was renamed as the alluring Marie Devereau and it was she who was photographed in double shots with Pam. Although very tame by today's standards, this was a radical departure. Another brick taken from the morality wall. The naturist magazine *Health and Efficiency* often featured groups of girls frolicking together on sun-drenched beaches, which was absolutely acceptable, but the Harrison Marks photos had an underlying sexual tone.

With their financial situation improving, George and Pam had little reason to travel outside Soho for all their needs. Fruit and vegetables were bought from market stalls, whilst meat, now off ration, was purchased from the Belgian butchers in Old Compton Street. Even props and material required as backdrops for photographic sessions could all be obtained within a stone's throw of the studio, whilst any sexy underwear came from Weiss in Shaftesbury Avenue. This was also a favourite haunt of the working girls and Pam became friendly with several who rather intrigued her. The going rate was two pounds in Gerrard Street, thirty bob down the road in Newport Court, and Lisle Street was the bargain basement where the business could be completed for a quid. Pam was particularly fascinated by Phyllis, who paraded the streets as if she was on her way to church, all tweeds, twin set and pearls.

It is surprising that it took the couple so long to appreciate the potential of magazine publishing. A book devoted to Pam released by the Luxor Press in 1955 prompted the idea. Although she was never paid for the project, it encouraged them to transform what was essentially a cottage industry into a bona fide profitable business. The project required an injection of capital, finding a reliable printer and taking one enormous gamble. Whilst they schemed and planned the new venture, their income was supplemented by George obtaining a regular monthly commission from a showbiz magazine to photograph British and visiting American stars. By now they were enjoying a hectic social life in and around Soho.

Finally, in 1957 they took the plunge and launched *Kamera*, a 32-page pocket magazine. They located a good-quality South London printer who was desperate for work. Their competition was limited to magazines featuring pin-ups, like *Lilliput* and *Tit-Bits*. *Spick and Span* had pushed the boundaries a little further but fell short of showing nudity. *Kamera* was a leap in the dark, launched in

June, just a few months before the opening of Raymond's Revue Bar. They took a substantial risk by ordering an initial print run of 15,000 at a cost of £500. The first edition featured sixteen different models and cost 2s 6d, double the price of *Spick and Span*. Despite the printing and distribution costs, they stood to make a healthy profit providing they could sell out the print run. Their worries were short-lived. Within days it became obvious they were on to a winner. The first edition sold in excess of 100,000. The format was simple, a colour front cover followed by a bevy of alluring nudes. Each shot had to be retouched to avoid the attention of the authorities. This skilful work was again undertaken by Pamela Green, who was the driving force behind the company. Views of pubic hair were still prohibited and a generation of schoolboys grew up confused about the make-up of the female body. The models were like mermaids with legs! Cashing in on the initial success, the magazine advertised 10-inch by 8-inch prints of the readers' favourites. Shots could be ordered for a fee of 5s 6d.

Business was booming, but now they were confronted with a new problem. The basement of No. 4 was being let as a drinking club owned by a large, bearded man known solely as Hamlet. He had a prison pallor and a wild look. During the weekdays there was little trouble but Saturdays seemed to attract groups of Irishmen who tended to be drunk and intimidating. Pam and George were pleased to have Silver, their Alsatian, to create a path through the crowds blocking the way to their flat. A criminal element had traditionally congregated around Gerrard Street and one night the couple were wakened to find two men wielding knives, standing over them. The intruders had assumed they were raiding a club and were demanding the takings. George threw them his wallet which only contained a few pounds and, appealing to their better nature, informed them that his wife was pregnant. Cursing, they stumbled down the stairs leaving £300 in cash that was safely locked in a bedside cupboard.

Most of the buildings in Gerrard Street dated back to the Georgian period. At that time they would have been sizeable properties but, subsequently, had been split into separate units. Doors had been bricked up, staircases blocked off. Lack of space was fast becoming a problem as the business expanded. They took up the lease on the basement of No. 5. This was converted into a darkroom, workrooms and a bathroom. This expansion was short-lived as the front part of the basement was let as another drinking club. There were continual fights and then some crook threatened George at knife point, mistaking him for Hamlet. Luckily, they were now offered the upper floor of No. 5 and so they left the basement gangs to sort themselves out.

They only went to Hamlet's club once. Pam described meeting the most frightening character she had ever encountered. She said he was like 'a slab of cement. Hard, with a lined and scarred grey face, narrow eyes and a slit of a mouth.' Neither tall nor well-muscled, he had huge hands. He had been in prison for most of his adult life and had been given the 'cat' twice. Taking a liking to Pam and George, he became an asset, someone they could turn to if any other crooks started to bother them.

Despite this, gangsters continued to inhibit their lives. Now the police warned them of impending trouble, which normally was still mainly restricted to Saturday nights. They were advised to stay in and lock the doors when a disturbance was predicted. Sure enough, the gangs arrived on cue armed with chivs, razors and bottles. The local lads were there to welcome them. Eventually, the police arrived to carry off the unconscious and the injured. A few weeks later they saw a body lying in the street and the assailant crouching behind dustbins in their backyard. They kept their own counsel; to tip off the police would have led to reprisals. Over the years many have attempted to downplay Soho's criminal connections and yet, in the 1950s, Gerrard Street could be a really frightening place. It was time for Pam and George to move on.

The money was now rolling in. Loads of it. G. Harrison Marks Ltd was proving to be a phenomenal success. The publications, whilst undoubtedly sexy, were not pornographic and yet their existence tapped into a changing public mood. The British sense of decorum was still evident in 1958 when Pam changed her name to Pamela Marks. Although unable to marry, she obviously felt more comfortable appearing to be George's wife. They now had enough money to use Gerrard Street as a studio only and move to a desirable property in Hampstead overlooking the Heath.

With success came problems. George, being a social animal, had always enjoyed a drink. He now went on regular benders. Money also burned a hole in his pocket and he swapped his modest Hillman Husky for an outrageous multi-toned Oldsmobile. He belonged to the 'if you've got it, flaunt it' brigade. He did everything to excess, particularly the booze and, increasingly, the use of the casting couch. Harrison Marks had become a name, a brand. This was acknowledged when a Rediffusion crew arrived to film for the popular *The Week* television programme. The studio had been expanded to include the upper floor of Gerrard Street and George was filmed with Pam during a photographic session, although it was never shown due to the untimely death of the Pope. Away from the glamour shots, George, an animal lover, produced a book, *Cats' Company*, in conjunction with the author Compton Mackenzie.

Now their operation extended to the basement, finally vacated by the warring drinking clubs. The extra studio space allowed Pam to develop ever more extravagant and realistic sets. To assist her they employed Tony Roberts, a young man, to help with the increasingly physical work. It was during one of their exhibitions open to the public that the film director Michael Powell walked in. There was a large photograph of Pam pictured naked except for high heels, thigh-length stockings and a fur wrap. She was seen on a mocked-up street scene set, standing beneath a street lamp. She was wearing a wig and smoking a cigarette. The inference was obvious. Here was a provocative nude streetwalker. Powell turned to a colleague and said, 'That's the girl I want for the film.' Pamela Green had never had any acting experience but she was offered a part of a nude model in *Peeping Tom* provided she passed muster at an audition, which she did.

Michael Powell was already into his fifties when he started shooting *Peeping Tom* in the autumn of 1959. He had enjoyed a long and distinguished career in the industry and had formed a successful collaboration with Emeric Pressburger, a Hungarian-born director, producer and screenwriter. They worked together on over twenty films before going their separate ways after the war, but were remembered for successes like *The Red Shoes* and *Black Narcissus*. *Peeping Tom* follows Mark Lewis (played by Carl Boehm), a shy, reclusive serial killer who films his victims' terror in close-up as he kills them. It stars a young Anna Massey and Moira Shearer. Pam found Powell cold and frightening. They fell out when he demanded she strip for her major scene. She informed him she was not a stripper and she only ever appeared in the nude when photographed by her husband. They reached a compromise by her being filmed protected from the gaze of most of the crew by erecting black velvet curtains. She was the first nude to appear in a major British film. Despite most of the film crew being hidden from view, Pam was amazed to see two young boys sitting on the floor in front of the cameras. They were Powell's own sons, a strange action from a hugely talented yet strange man.

The film has retrospectively been hailed as a classic, but its release was met with a storm of protest. There is no doubt that it is very atmospheric, claustrophobic and downright creepy. It remains shocking and disturbing over fifty years after being made. Much success in life is to do with timing and Powell misjudged the public's mood. He was pilloried, although he did live long enough to see the film become something of a cult success during the 1970s.

Money was burning a hole in George's pocket. In 1959 he visited the Boat Show at Earls Court and splashed out on a 30-foot motor launch. Cracks were beginning to show in his relationship with Pam. He was totally unsympathetic when she was diagnosed with a duodenal ulcer. Selfishly, he still wanted a drinking partner and he ridiculed the fact that she was forced to drink milk. They had worked so hard to build up a viable and profitable business and yet, as a new decade beckoned, the magic that had existed between them was all but spent.

14

A Model Young Lady

What's a girl to do? Jean Sporle belonged to a generation whose parents didn't give praise lightly. Success was welcomed, but few youngsters were allowed to believe they were exceptionally gifted. Floweringly good looks were seldom commented on. It was important for youngsters not to get big-headed. So it was a genuine surprise when Jean's friends, whilst they were on holiday in Clacton, suggested she should enter the town's beauty competition. You can just hear her, 'What, me? You must be joking.' The thought of parading in that vast ballroom wearing just a swimming costume appalled her at first. All those dirty old men leering at her and the ribald comments and whistles of the young. Then she thought, why not? It could be fun, and it was. She won. She was approached to join the beauty parade circuit, but decided the life was not for her.

Jean, a Londoner, had been evacuated to the North during the war. Following her return home on leaving school, the type of jobs available for girls from relatively modest backgrounds were fairly restricted, despite full employment. There were plenty of opportunities in local factories, shop work, hairdressing, clerical jobs or the typing pool, which is what she opted for. Returning to office work after her brief flirtation with fame made her realise other more exciting opportunities beckoned. Soho drew her like a magnet during her lunch breaks. She started going to a café in Gerrard Street, favoured by resting actors and film extras. The street was rather shabby and rundown but different and exciting for a young girl. The Chinese influence was already making itself felt with a couple of restaurants together with other shops selling brocade pyjamas and slippers. The whiff of exotic herbs and spices lingered long after leaving the area. She decided that modelling could be the way forward and posed for some glamour shots featured in *Spick and Span*. She had often noticed a photographic studio at the really tacky end of Gerrard Street. The entrance hall was decorated with models in skimpy bikinis. Anxious to supplement her £3 10s weekly wage, she went in to be welcomed by a beautiful blonde who introduced herself as Pamela Green, the wife of the photographer. She was booked for a shoot. The going rate was £2 per hour – riches indeed! Her earliest memory of George Harrison Marks was of a kindly, sympathetic man who had the ability to put her at ease. After a couple of sessions she agreed to pose topless and it was at this point that George informed her that his business was based on nude photography. Pam was quietly persuasive, but Jean was incredibly nervous as she stripped off for her first session. The shoot was made more difficult by her having to pose on top of a vaulting horse. It was all too much for her. She was paralysed with fear, shaking and quite unable to smile despite constant pleading from Pam and George. Amazingly, the shots turned out really well and she felt her confidence returning. Despite her fears about what her parents' reaction would be to her appearing in the nude, it was initially her father who seemed to be more supportive than her mum, but time would win her over too.

Despite her good looks and fabulous figure, Jean had other attributes that appealed to George. She could type. She became a full-time member of staff just as *Kamera* was about to be launched. It was a worrying time for Pam and George, but fraught emotions turned to elation as the massive sales of this first edition became obvious. Not only was Jean doing secretarial work, serving in the shop and helping in the darkroom, she was also featured on the front cover of the second edition of *Kamera*. She didn't feel the shots were particularly flattering but she was now an important part of an expanding organisation. She became very friendly with Pam and the work was varied and enjoyable. George was a fairly benign boss, turning a blind eye to her constantly turning up late for work.

No two days at the studio were the same. One day modelling, the next in the shop serving lines of men nervously waiting to buy the latest edition of *Kamera*. These were always being bought for a friend, or perhaps by a bowler-hatted gentleman who was apparently studying figurative drawing. She smiled benignly as the unlikely excuses were trotted out. Increasingly, Pam asked for help in the darkroom with the airbrushing of offending pubic hair. Now very much part of the Harrison Marks family, Jean was included in their increasingly flamboyant lifestyle. There were trips to film premieres and dinners in fashionable restaurants, including Isow's and Le Caprice. She dated the young Anthony Newley, who was known at the time mainly as a pop vocalist. He had two number one hits during the early 1960s, including 'Do You Mind?' written by Lionel Bart. Jean also became friendly with Leslie Bricusse and his wife. Bricusse and Newley later combined in the huge stage musical hits, *Stop the World – I Want to Get Off* and *The Roar of the Greasepaint – The Smell of the Crowd*. She stayed at the studio long enough to witness George's increasing extravagance and vanity. He drove a huge, brightly coloured Oldsmobile and she was a passenger when, trying to negotiate his way out of the Lex Garage in Brewer Street, he came face to face with Diana Dors in her pink Cadillac. For a time the air was blue as neither was prepared to give way. George now reckoned he was as big a star as the famous blonde bombshell, but he did eventually reverse to allow her through.

Jean was approached by an agent who wanted to know if she would be prepared to appear topless in a film called *Serious Charge*. At £40 for a day's work, she was delighted to accept. Filmed at Elstree Studios, it featured the first cinema appearance of Cliff Richard in which he sang 'Living Doll'. Jean's scene was simple enough. She had to dive into a swimming pool, once dressed in a petticoat for the repressed American market, a bikini for the partially liberated Brits, and topless for the degenerate French! She even had a line of dialogue but her introduction to film was, unfortunately, not to lead to universal stardom. Jean had to be thankful for small mercies; the initial film was damaged, leading to a reshoot and an additional forty quid.

Life in Soho was never dull and Jean had acquired something of a celebrity status, certainly among the stallholders of Berwick Street. Larger than life characters were almost the norm. The working girls were a constant source of interest, including a particularly beautiful black girl who gave potential punters a preview by opening her fur coat, under which she was completely naked. George was a great lover of animals. He

owned an Alsatian and an assortment of cats. A prize tabby, who
was supposed to feature in a cat calendar George was shooting,
went missing. Jean was sent off to track down the missing
moggy. He often went next door to Brenda, one of many friendly
prostitutes working the street. Pushing the door to the flat open,
Jean spotted Uncle, the offending tabby, purring contentedly at
the end of the bed. On the bed an astonished client looked up
in alarm. 'Excuse me,' said Jean, demurely, gathering up the cat,
whilst the poor man did his best to cover his embarrassment.
Soon after, a mynah bird was added to the menagerie, squawking
out 'Hello George' and a selection of swear words that he was
quick to pick up.

Life remained enjoyable for Jean – from simple pleasures
like visiting the Nosh Bar in Windmill Street, or eating
delicious salt beef sandwiches at Phil Rabin's, to dancing in
the evenings at Whisky A-Go-Go. In 1960 Jean appeared with
Pam in *Artist's Model*. This was George's first attempt to enter
the film industry. Although he was a thoroughly professional
photographer, his films viewed today appear amateurish at
best. He fancied himself as an actor, director and producer,
but the results are embarrassing. Maybe an excuse can be
made for *Artist's Model* being his first attempt, but it is pretty
dire. Gorgeous though the girls look, the plot is contrived,
but nothing could convince George that his future didn't lie
in film-making. Although noticing a change in Marks, Jean
was convinced he was still deeply in love with Pam. She felt
that he had become bored with photography and the models
he photographed. He never made a pass at her, even on trips
together to his swanky new home on Reddington Road in
Hampstead. It was during this period that Jean's own marriage
broke up and both George and Pam were very supportive. She
continued modelling and featured in the 1961 Harrison Marks
calendar. The following year she felt it was time to move on.
Like many of us back then, she had flirted with fame and the
famous. If you look at the glamour shots of her at that time,
she looks every inch a star. Perhaps, had she been born back in
the war years she would have been. There is still something of
a look that belongs to that era. A touch of the girl next door,
a warmth that whilst so appealing is unthreatening. None of
the hardness that emerged in the sixties and is still alive today.
Jean saw dozens of the glamour girls who walked that fine

line before the open arrival of pornography. Like them, she endured the ghastly pancake make-up caked all over them to give the appearance of an even tan. She thought they were all truly beautiful. No Botox, no implants, all wonderfully toned and going in and out in all the right places. She says, 'I have never worried that any of it would come back to haunt me. I have nothing to be ashamed of.'

Jean continued to enjoy a life dedicated to promotional work and beauty consultancy. She remained friends and in contact with Pamela Green until the latter's death in 2010. Jean now lives in Spain with her husband Pete. If anything, she looks even better than when she was young. She still has the same measurements she had in 1956, although she concedes 'it all needs a good ironing'. It's true beauty is only skin deep, but for some it continues to shine.

15

Grist to the Mill

Although not infallible, and suffering the occasional setback, Binkie Beaumont's star continued to shine throughout the 1950s. Actors and agents deferred to him. He dispensed favours and expected loyalty in return. It was rumoured that he had a blacklist. Anyone refusing an offer never worked for him again. There were no unpleasant scenes or histrionics, just no work. He was ruthless and yet, to those he favoured, thoughtful and charming. He was, above all, a fearful snob. So much so that it almost cost him one of his greatest successes. He had long held the view that staging plays featuring the working classes in anything other than walk-on parts was doomed to failure. It was bad enough that one had to come into contact with them from time to time. John Osborne was going to put a spoke in that particular wheel, but for the moment Binkie chose to ignore the threat.

Binkie had no hesitation in turning down *Seagulls Over Sorrento*. He reckoned that if the play had been about the officer class rather than ratings, it might have been amusing. He was not alone; other producers turned down Hugh Hastings's play, but his agent, Eric Glass, was persistent. Two years after his initial rejection, Binkie was persuaded to give it a go. The play, staged at the Apollo, was a runaway success, playing to over 1,500 performances. It served as a wake-up call as Binkie, seated in his eyrie looking down on Shaftesbury Avenue, plotted and schemed for the production of two shows which defined the late 1950s. It was as if his conversion to popular entertainment was complete with his entry into musicals. *Irma La Douce* had been a hit on the Paris stage, with music by Marguerite Monnot, in 1956. Binkie took the actress Elizabeth Seal to see it with him and duly secured the London rights. Once again, he was perceptive in his choice of leading lady. She had come to the public's attention when appearing in *The Pyjama Game*, but there was still some horse-trading to do regarding pay. Binkie offered Seal £120 a week but made it clear that he expected her to dress like a star, not a beatnik (she liked jeans and sloppy sweaters). Not unreasonably, her agent said that to enable her to dress like a star she needed to be paid like one. Eventually £200 a week was agreed, although it is not clear that Elizabeth Seal was converted to haute couture, long white gloves and all, so admired by Binkie.

The plot, whilst somewhat far-fetched, was appropriate for a Soho theatre where young and not so young working girls continued to ply their trade. It concerned a young law student who falls hopelessly in love with a prostitute and disguises himself as Oscar, a rich older man, in order to keep in contact. Unable to keep up the pretence, he 'kills off' Oscar and is sent to Devil's Island, having been convicted of his murder. Escaping, he proves his innocence and is reunited with Irma. The audiences loved it and the opening night in July 1958 was a triumph. Binkie had another hit on his hands, with glowing notices. The great and the good flocked to the Apollo and Elizabeth Seal went on to repeat her success on Broadway. The London production ran to 1,512 performances, but it was to be trumped by Binkie's ultimate triumph in the same year.

My Fair Lady opened on Broadway in March 1956 to huge acclaim. A posse of British producers beat a path to New York thinking they were in the running to obtain the London rights. The confidence of Littler, Grade, Hylton and Parnell was high, as up to that point Binkie had shown no interest in producing musicals. They were all to be desperately disappointed, for Beaumont had weaved his magic again. What they didn't know was that he had secured the rights some eighteen months previously and kept it a secret. It involved an element of luck and the ability to seize the moment.

Originally, it was Michael Redgrave who was offered the leading role of Henry Higgins, not Rex Harrison. He had the looks, the bearing and he could sing. He seemed the perfect choice, but there was a snag. He was very concerned about being typecast and was alarmed at being asked to sign a two-year contract. Even tying him down for a year was too much. Six months was his maximum and he wouldn't budge. In January 1955 the American production team arrived in London to offer Rex Harrison the part. He and his wife Lilli Palmer were appearing for Binkie in *Bell, Book and Candle* at the Phoenix theatre. At the time, Harrison had started an affair with the lovely Kay Kendall, and playing love scenes with his wife was testing their professionalism to the limit. Harrison agreed in principle to play Henry Higgins and Binkie informed the Americans that he would be withdrawing *Bell, Book and Candle* in the spring. However, just when attendances were thought to fall off, the play started to perform to full houses again. The advance bookings right through to Christmas were buoyant. Good news for Binkie, potential disaster for the Yanks. Rex Harrison was still contracted to Binkie for a further eighteen months. They had already booked the theatre on Broadway and the cast had been finalised. A postponement was impossible. Binkie was holding all the cards. Had he led them into a trap? Harrison had been practising the songs for months. He was perfect. It was too late to find a substitute. Binkie appeared so polite and civilised as he turned the screws. How could he help? He would be delighted to release Rex but in return he needed some compensation. Surely that was reasonable? He struck a hard bargain, probably the best in a lifetime of deals. He required the British and Continental rights to *My Fair Lady* and 1.5 per cent gross of the Broadway and touring shows, plus a small matter of £25,000 in cash. Herman Levin, the Broadway producer, recognised a pro when he saw one. The deal was settled over a spot of lunch at Scott's, Binkie's favourite restaurant. There was much rejoicing and celebration high above the Globe Theatre. Rex Harrison went on to star in the Broadway production for two years, so it wasn't until the spring of 1957 that plans were finalised for the London opening. Publicity stoked public interest to fever pitch. Still Binkie sought to maximise his investment by persuading the Society of Authors, who looked after George Bernard Shaw's estate, to ban all productions of *Pygmalion* in Great Britain for a ten-year period. Being paid 10 per cent of the gross helped calm any of the Society's qualms that they may have felt. Binkie also imposed a ban on any of the songs being broadcast until after the opening, but here even he was thwarted by imports of long-playing records of the show coming in from the States.

The countdown to the opening night was hysterical. Seats were changing hands for record prices. The audience for the opening night had been carefully screened. Joe Public hardly got a look in. The great and the good and the not so good, but filthy rich, jostled for a place at the bar. The social editor of the *Tatler* was overwhelmed. Leading lights from Debrett's rubbed shoulders with the stars of stage and film. Rich Americans had flown over in such numbers that listening to the shouted conversation you felt for a moment you were in New York. Because of the crush the curtain went up fifteen minutes late. On cue, the show was a triumph. The curtain calls were endless, lasting almost half an hour. The reviews were overwhelmingly positive. *My Fair Lady* ran for over 2,000 performances and was the high point of Binkie Beaumont's career – a far cry from his humble beginnings but earned by a unique mixture of charm, single-minded devotion to his work and an ability to win people over by whatever means.

The old saying that 'you can climb Everest, but you can't live there' could now be applied to Binkie. His gradual decline had yet to set in, but around the corner in Great Windmill Street the process was already under way. Vivian Van Damm had been a lifelong sufferer of asthma but the development of Parkinson's disease formed a debilitating cocktail. Despite periods of remission, it had an invasive effect. He realised that it was time for his daughter Sheila to be brought into the business full time. She had worked at the Mill previously, dealing mostly with publicity, but now it was important for her to learn how to run the theatre. It was not going to be easy to tempt her back. She had been enjoying international success as a rally driver. She was the women's European Touring Champion in 1954 and won the Coupe de Dames in the 1955 Monte Carlo Rally. She already sensed that her reign was coming to an end and it was time for rival Pat Moss to have her day. The timing was good. Now that she was aware of her father's health problems, he seemed willing to share the knowledge that he had built up over his lifetime in show business. No longer showing his autocratic side, he encouraged her to just watch and observe so that she could gradually come to terms with all aspects of the job.

The years following the war had continued to be successful, with the theatre playing to full houses. They had built up a substantial balance at the bank so the outlook appeared even brighter when, in the 1957 Budget, the Chancellor, Peter

Thorneycroft, abolished the entertainment tax. At that precise moment audiences started to stay away. It was as if someone had turned the lights down. Whilst the backstreet strip clubs had made little impact on the theatre, the arrival of Raymond's Revue Bar certainly did. A younger Van Damm would have sensed the danger and adapted but, set in his ways, he continued with the tried and tested format that was beginning to look somewhat tired and dated. The girls were still as pretty and vivacious, the shows as well staged, but they lacked edge. What had seemed dangerous and daring twenty years previously was caught in a time warp.

As the audiences declined, albeit slowly, so the overheads grew. Over fifty live performers were matched in number by backstage staff. Although a tough boss, Van Damm attracted tremendous loyalty, with many of the staff having been with him since the start. A modern manager would have made substantial staff cuts but Van Damm belonged to the old school of British management. Tough, autocratic and yet paternalistic. Loyalty was given as well as received. Anne Mitelle, his general manager and assistant, was a permanent fixture. There were others: Johnny Gale, the stage director; Ernest Horton, the house manager; and even Violet Goodall, the bar manageress. Maisie Cryer was the long-time dance producer, and Keith Lester the veteran ballet choreographer. From stage doorkeeper to box office cashier, the staff rarely changed. The Windmill was often referred to as a happy family, the oxygen being supplied by the changing artistes and newly staged productions. Perhaps the management had become too inward-looking. Ignoring the changing public mood was fatal, but not just yet.

The theatre, with its open-house policy of granting auditions to almost anyone who walked in from the street, still managed to attract an amazing pool of comic talent. Amongst those who cut their teeth on the uniquely demanding audiences were Tommy Cooper, Terry Scott, George Martin, Arthur Haynes and Des O'Connor. Barry Cryer recalled attending his audition with Van Damm buried in the darkness of the stalls. He told his jokes and sang a song. A voice asked if he knew any more jokes? You bet he did. He ran through another routine, which was met with silence. Then the voice from the deep enquired, 'Would you like to work here?' 'Yes,' replied Barry, eagerly. Another lengthy pause. He was led off stage to meet Johnny Gale, the stage manager, described as a mountainous man with his trousers pulled up to his armpits. To his amazement, Cryer was told by Gale that he was due to start that very afternoon. The theatre was fairly full but quiet and off-putting. The only effect his jokes had on the audience was for a couple of them to open newspapers and start reading. Later, he was called in to see Van Damm, who, not unkindly, dissected his act. Cryer was to spend a happy seven months at the Windmill learning his trade. Top of the bill during his time was Bruce Forsyth, a really talented, all-round performer. He danced, mimed, did impressions and even told jokes that actually raised a laugh. Barry Cryer was impressed. So was Van Damm. Forsyth was the only comedian to get his name on the honours board whilst still appearing at the theatre. Bruce Forsyth appeared at the Windmill for over two years, no doubt encouraged by meeting Penny Calvert, a fellow artiste, who became his first wife. It was Forsyth's agent who advised him to give up impersonating others and to develop an act that would make others impersonate him. He came back in 1957 to appear in the twenty-fifth anniversary show at the Mill. His demented performance of 'The Galloping Major' was a show-stopper and within a year he had been chosen by Val Parnell to compère the hit television show *Sunday Night at the London Palladium*.

Despite Van Damm having a great track record for discovering comedians who went on to be stars, Morecambe and Wise were not the only ones to elude him. Over the years he turned down Spike Milligan, Benny Hill, Norman Wisdom and Roy Castle. Whilst most of those who worked at the Windmill looked back at their time with nostalgia, Nicholas Parsons was less impressed: 'What I learned was how to make a very odd, unbalanced audience of men laugh.'

The celebrated critic Kenneth Tynan described *Revudeville* in his usual dismissive way as 'ninety minutes of pallid concert party'. This was probably true. A very British way of presenting wholesome glamour. This was endorsed by an article written by William Fisher for *Illustrated Magazine*. He describes eighteen-year-old dancer Susan Denny as 'demure and modest. Her clean fresh beauty is very English. Yes, she looks lovely – even in clothes!' He was writing to commemorate the theatre's coming of age. He continues, 'The Windmill is twenty-one years old – older than most of its performers, a group of superbly shaped, expertly selected, brilliantly coached, talented, but otherwise typically home bred British girls.' Fisher had obviously been allowed access backstage as he states, 'After a few days in the company of these girls, I have come to the conclusion that there is more to the Windmill's success than meets the eye. Naked virtue is more attractive than vice – however ingeniously disguised!' In that very phrase Fisher explains the strength, but also a vital weakness, of the Windmill in a changing market. The girls were lovely, talented and genteel, but the British public now wanted their women to be raunchy, sexy and dangerous, but there was life in the old dog yet. The fall-off in British attendance was partially offset by the Windmill becoming a major tourist attraction for foreign visitors. Sheila Van Damm quoted many favourable comments from around the world: 'The best show I have ever seen,' wrote a South African. A Pakistani visitor requested 'more lights, and brighter when the nudists are on stage'. The best quote must go to an Iranian who said, 'Your girls are great. Please, I wish I could have one.'

William Fisher went on in his article to say how few people could appreciate the work that preceded the appearance of the chorus line. Hour after hour he watched 'the girls going through the Mill preparing for the next show. The old fashioned rabbit-warren of a theatre ... reverberates with the strumming of never silent pianos and tapping feet. Downstairs on the stage there is a coming and going of elfin figures clad in transparent nothings.'

Vivian Van Damm was a great publicist and rarely a week went by without a story concerning the Windmill appearing in the national press. No publication was too obscure. In 1959, *Scooter News* reported on problems the Windmill girls were experiencing getting home each night after the last performance. Traffic had increased, as had rents which precluded most of the girls from living in central London. Enter the trendy Lambretta. Scooters had become very popular, allowing the rider to weave through the clogged up traffic. Wendy Clarke and Rita Hammerton lived out in Dartford and they managed to cut their journey time to and from the theatre by half. They are pictured fresh-faced and wholesome beneath statutory crash helmets.

Today, it is often technology that overtakes and consumes companies and brands that, for generations, had been market leaders. By the end of the decade, the Windmill 'brand' was looking tired and out of step with accelerating modern trends. Although Van Damm fought his illness bravely, his family were informed he had developed cancer. Either he was never told or he just never acknowledged it. He continued to drag himself into the theatre each day – like many in old age, unable or unwilling to embrace the changes going on all around. These would be left to his daughter Sheila to fight. Perhaps she would have a solution to reverse the decline.

16

Winkie Winkfield

With a name like Winkie Winkfield, a young fifteen-year-old girl heading for her first professional audition had every reason to hope she was about to become a star. Over sixty years later she was, but not in the way she longed for that dank, drizzly morning in 1949.

Turning left from Leicester Square underground station, she headed in what she thought was the general direction of Gerrard Street. Like so many entering Soho for the first time, she was struck by a strangeness, a difference from the streets just a few hundred yards away. Even at a time of food rationing there were lingering in the air exotic reminders of meals served the previous evening, or of those being prepared for the lunchtime rush. With the confidence of a girl brought up in the East End, she stopped to ask the way to Richardson's Rehearsal Rooms. She was directed to a dingy door at the far end of Gerrard Street. A worn staircase descended into darkness. Mildew lined the walls and the smell of damp was overpowering.

Winkie had received almost no formal education. Her mother had died when she was young and her father was rarely at home. During the war he was driving petrol tankers to airfields throughout the country. In 1946 he set up his own band and was seldom around. So Winkie was brought up by her grandmother. What with bomb damage, which caused numerous changes of home, and a generally chaotic upbringing, she reckoned she only had a few months of formal schooling. So whilst school lessons had a low priority, those for tap dancing were never missed. She knew where her future lay. She was stage-struck.

Descending further into the gloom, even the stairs became slippery with mildew. On the first landing, lit by a single light bulb, was an office no bigger than a cupboard. A man with a pencilled moustache and a trilby tilted back on his head sat behind a rickety desk. His sole office equipment amounted to a single Bakelite telephone. It didn't ring. Life as a theatrical agent was obviously proving to be tough. He glanced at the attractive young blonde as she continued her descent before gazing once more at the telephone, willing it to ring.

Finally, she reached the bare rehearsal rooms and sat waiting her turn to perform. She went through her routine and felt she had done well. No joy. 'Sorry love,' she was told. Rather dejected, she climbed her way towards the street. On the way she was stopped by a stout, middle-aged woman. 'How did you get on, dear?' Winkie told her the bad news. They walked up the stairs onto Gerrard Street. The stranger looked her up and down and asked her a few questions. 'How would you like to join my company as a dancer?' Presumably, hidden from view, Marie De Vere had watched Winkie's audition. A contract was produced and there on the street, bustling with pedestrians, Winkie signed to be a part of the De Vere Dance Troupe.

Unusually, her father was at home that night and 'he blew a gasket' when he heard his daughter's news. By the next morning he would have realised that Winkie was not going to listen to his reasoned arguments. He did, however, insist on going up to the West End with her to meet Madame De Vere and reluctantly gave his blessing. The next day Winkie woke up in Skipton as one of the dancers in the Roberts Brothers' Travelling Circus. This was to be the start of a five-year period in which the young girl became a true, all-round pro. She performed across the country and in America, appearing in revues, variety shows and pantomime. She could sing, dance and act. She had a cute, cheeky, almost childish face and a body she describes as being more like Diana Dors than Twiggy. Quite a potent combination!

The spring of 1955 found her 'resting'. With no immediate prospect of work she trawled the advertisements in *The Stage*. There were regular inserts for the Windmill Theatre. In those relatively repressed days of post-war Britain, appearing in the nude on stage was a risk for a young performer. Aware that her future career could be compromised, she decided to take a chance and apply for an audition. These normally took place on a Monday but she rang too late to take her place and was told to attend the following morning, having given details of her career to date.

That bright, sunny Tuesday, a pretty blonde dressed in a smart grey suit and sporting very high heels made her way to the stage door in Archer Street. Picking her way through lines of musicians hoping to be signed up, she ignored their wolf whistles and was told by the doorman to go on up to the rehearsal room. Climbing the six flights of stairs, she arrived slightly breathless to find a large, empty room with, marooned in isolation, just a piano and a worn settee. Nervously she sat down and waited for someone to appear. She was beginning to have second thoughts when after twenty minutes no one had shown any interest in her.

It was just as she was thinking of leaving that a formidable woman dressed in black appeared and asked what she was waiting for. Stammering slightly, Winkie explained she had an appointment to attend an audition. The woman, who was in her forties, turned out to be Anne Mitelle. Of Jewish background, she had once been secretary to Vivian Van Damm and was now his casting director and co-producer. Mumbling that she had no knowledge of any such appointment, Mitelle seemed to have taken an instant, irrational dislike to Winkie. She was told that at twenty she was too old for the job as many of the Windmill girls started as young as fifteen. With that little gem of information Anne Mitelle stomped off, leaving a disappointed and angry Winkie to gather up her vanity case containing her leotard and dancing shoes. Whilst she was collecting her belongings Winkie sensed another figure who perched herself on the arm of the settee. This was a younger woman who, obviously, by her build was not part of the dance company. Winkie was asked about her background and experience. After a few minutes of chatting she was asked to wait. Now enter an even grumpier Anne Mitelle, who informed Winkie that despite her misgivings, she had a job. Without knowing it, Winkie had been interviewed by Sheila Van Damm. The fact that Mitelle had been overruled led to constant friction between her and Winkie during Winkie's stay with the company. She must have been one of the few girls to be appointed without even having to audition. Mitelle was determined to salvage something from what she saw as her humiliation. She declared that Winkie Winkfield was a stupid, ludicrous name. No amount of pleading was going to have any effect and one of the great stage names was lost to the world. Enter Jean Mara.

The antidote to a memorable name. Once more, a contract was signed on the spot. London had a new Windmill girl.

The following Monday the newly named Jean turned up for intensive rehearsals, which were to last for weeks. There were two companies, A and B. Jean joined B Company and the rehearsals were carried out in the cold audition room accompanied by a single pianist. The work was hard and physically draining. Shows ran daily from noon to eleven at night, during which time six performances were given. Each company alternated daily, giving live performances which were followed the next day by rehearsals. As a new show approached rehearsals were increased in intensity. Nothing was left to chance. The dances, songs and costume changes had to be of the highest standard under the ever-watchful eye of Vivian Van Damm. Dress rehearsals were always held on a Sunday. Friends and relatives of the cast were all welcome and it became something of a tradition that those performing in other West End theatres would also attend.

Jean was paid £10 a week when she joined, which rose to a heady £16 a week by the time she left the Windmill some three years later. She came into daily contact with both Vivian Van Damm and his daughter. Although already suffering from declining health with the onset of Parkinson's disease, nothing seemed to escape his attention. He was very approachable and took a real interest in the welfare of his girls. He was keen that they appeared to be ladylike at all times. Swearing was banned and romantic relationships within the company were not encouraged, unless marriage seemed likely. Stage-door johnnies tolerated during the thirties and war years were actively discouraged. According to Jean, the girls worked so hard that most were only interested in getting the first tube home at night. Sometimes on their day off they would have supper together at one of their modest flats. Most of the girls were on friendly terms with the prostitutes who lined the surrounding streets. After all, many of the Windmill's audience would subsequently become clients of the street girls, having had their appetites whetted, albeit in the best possible taste.

Coffee breaks were often taken at the Dairy in Great Windmill Street. Mostly, though, the cast ate at the subsidised canteen on the top floor of the Windmill building. The food, which had to be ordered the day before, was plain but wholesome. Eating in the canteen had an added attraction. Van Damm would frequently

entertain leading figures from the film and theatre world at his
permanently reserved table. Jean remembers sitting at the next
table to Peter Sellers and Dickie Henderson senior.

Being a Windmill girl was incredibly demanding. Appearing
in six shows a day could have easily led to boredom and this
was overcome to a large extent by the girls alternating their
routines. A roster was posted each day listing each girl's required
performances, ranging from lavishly produced routines including
solos, to nude appearances as the central attraction in the next
show as a single spotlight beamed down. As each show finished
and some of the audience left, it was time for the Windmill Grand
National as punters leapfrogged the seats to get a ringside view.
This was really only necessary for the seriously short-sighted as
the theatre was tiny by West End standards, seating only just over
300.

The Windmill was already famous for producing a string of
star comedians. Jean became friendly with the young Bruce
Forsyth and his wife to be, Penny Calvert, who was also a
Windmill girl. Dickie Henderson, Harry Secombe and Michael
Bentine were all contemporaries. Although outwardly friendly,
they were encouraged not to become too close to the girls by
the ever-watchful Van Damm. The only false note was struck by
Kenneth Williams, who, although not part of the company, was a
regular visitor to the canteen. He was appearing next door at the
Comedy Theatre in *Share My Lettuce* with Maggie Smith. The
girls thought he was weird and aloof in contrast to the overall
camaraderie which permeated through the company. The family
atmosphere so encouraged by Van Damm was still much in
evidence during the 1950s.

Music formed an important part of the Windmill's shows. By
Jean's time the orchestra had been reduced to a trio of piano,
drums and bass. There were two conductors and arrangers. The
duties were shared by Ronnie Bridges and Dennis Hodges. He
had served in the RAF during the war and sported a huge 'Flying
Officer Kite' moustache.

The choreography was organised by Maisie Cryer. She had
joined the Windmill in 1935 expecting to stay for just one show
but was still there over twenty years later. An amazing character,
she had appeared in the Folies Bergère at the age of thirteen. Four
years later saw her on Broadway as one of the famous Ziegfeld
Girls, where she was taught to tap dance by Gilda Gray. Back

in Britain she was signed on by C. B. Cochran at the same time as another chorus girl, Margery Robertson (later to become Anna Neagle). It was Cochran who gave Cryer a real break into choreography, appointing her ballet mistress for the production of *The White Horse Inn*.

Romances within the company, although gently discouraged, were inevitable. Jean started going out with fellow dancer Alan Wren and they were married in 1958. Whilst the warmth of a family atmosphere within the Windmill was well known, this didn't seem to extend to generosity where wedding gifts were concerned. A telegram of congratulations was all Alan and Jean received from the Van Damms. The generosity of Laura Henderson was obviously a tradition that was not always carried on. It is possible that Anne Mitelle had influenced events. Amazingly, she never seemed to forget the slight she felt following Jean's appointment. Increasingly, she introduced a work schedule that was physically impossible for Jean to complete. Times for costume changes were shortened and required stage appearances increased. Sheila Van Damm appeared not to realise the snub she had inflicted on Mitelle or later to understand that Jean was beginning to feel somewhat victimised.

All of this was happening when the Windmill was coming under threat with the arrival of Raymond's Revue Bar in April 1958. Increasingly, it appeared that the Windmill's extravagant, well-staged shows were outdated. They were too tame for a public demanding change. Inevitably, the Windmill productions were forced to become slightly more explicit. This, together with the pressure being put on her by Anne Mitelle, led Jean to think it was time to quit. She was now a married woman and it was time to be conventional and settle down. She didn't. Well, not really. After having two children she applied for a job at Raymond's Revue Bar as a Bunny Girl. This really just involved looking glamorous and serving drinks. She had worked for Raymond in one of his touring shows, *Las Vegas*, in 1953. She had lied about her age to get the job and was worried when Raymond spotted her one night and said he was sure he had seen her somewhere before but couldn't place her. She just smiled back and the moment passed.

A client at the Revue Bar suggested she could better herself and arranged an interview for her at Murray's Club in Beak Street. On the surface suave and sophisticated, the club in those days was little better than an upmarket escort agency. Many of the hostesses would take their clients home after the lavish cabaret ended. That was not for Jean and she soon realised there was equally good money to be earned without compromising herself. She latched onto the corporate parties, who were big spenders. She was entitled to 20 per cent of the take. She left after six months with enough money to buy a house in Spain. The champagne must have been quite expensive.

It was then time to go back to her showbiz routes and over the next few years she appeared regularly in America on Joey Adams's TV show *Coast to Coast*. Back home she was a star in the holiday camp comedy *Hi-di-Hi* and was seen for a period in *Eastenders*. Time for another change of direction. Her marriage to Alan Wren had drifted and they were divorced. She married again to Brian and also took up painting seriously. She enrolled as a mature student at St Martin's School of Art in Charing Cross Road, where she received her diploma. She then obtained a BA Honours degree in fine art from the University of Hertfordshire. Today the remarkable ex-Windmill girl, now Jean Picton, exhibits all over the country and her paintings are reproduced as prints worldwide.

Vivian Van Damm was always looking for personality, beauty and talent in his performers. Well, this girl had all three attributes and still does. They don't make them like Winkie Winkfield any more!

17

A Spot of Bother

For generations there had been an undercurrent of criminal activity in Soho, which increasingly broke cover in the 1950s and erupted onto the streets. Rival gangs fought each other and old scores were settled. The uneasy truce between Billy Hill and Jack Spot had broken down. Like a doomed love affair, jealousy lay at the heart of the problem. Spot, the older man, was widely thought to be a spent force and he took exception to Hill proclaiming himself to be 'King of the Underworld'. More fundamental to the breakdown in their relationship was their method of operating. Hill was a strategist. All his successful heists were down to detailed planning. He was widely admired within the criminal community and boasted that so many wanted to work for him that he had to introduce a rota system. Hill invested his money in a string of clubs and property. Although described by 'Nipper' Read as a typical 1950s spiv, he did present a veneer of sophistication, hair slicked back and expensively suited. Increasingly, a comfortable retirement appealed to him.

Jack Spot was unaware of his former friend's aspirations. Spot was the counterpoint to Hill, which initially worked in both their interests. He was impulsive, volatile and sensitive to criticism. He was, in truth, a thug with a degree of animal cunning. An old fashioned hoodlum who was looking increasingly vulnerable. In the autumn of 1954 he made the first of a series of damaging mistakes. He had become increasingly irritated with Duncan Webb, the journalist who had exposed the Messina gang. Webb had been retained by Billy Hill to ghostwrite his autobiography. He had been prying into Spot's private life and at a meeting at the Horseshoe pub in Tottenham Court Road Webb had insulted him by boasting that Hill was 'the sole governor now'. That was bad enough, but Webb followed this up with a deeply offensive anti-Semitic remark. Squealing, the journalist was dragged outside and given a couple of right-handers. Unfortunately, Webb fell, breaking his wrist. Spot was charged with GBH, but some hefty handouts ensured he was not jailed and only fined £50.

Hill's success continued in September 1954 with another bullion raid planned with military precision, which netted a cool £45,000. Meanwhile, Spot was reduced to handling stolen goods and even on the racetracks his dominance was being challenged. It appeared that Albert Dimes, who was an enforcer for Billy Hill, was causing the trouble. Spot felt threatened and, for a time, employed the young Kray twins to protect him. They realised his influence was in decline but they took his money and bided their time. Matters came to a head in August 1955 and confirmed Jack Spot's demise as a feared and respected figure in Soho. He was enjoying a drink in the Galahad Club when a messenger arrived to inform him that Albert Dimes wanted a word. The cheek of it! Spot rushed out in pursuit.

Dimes, who was in his late forties, was a well-built Anglo-Italian gangster who had been brought up in Clerkenwell. He had originally been charged with the murder of Harry 'Scarface' Distleman back in 1941, although it was 'Babe' Mancini who was eventually hanged for the offence. Spot caught up with 'Big Albert' on the corner of Frith Street, traditionally Italian territory. Recollections vary but it appears Spot launched himself at Dimes, brandishing a knife. Dimes turned and ran away. If Spot had left it at that, his street cred would have been restored. The big Italian seen running in fear of his life would have been judged a total humiliation. It was not to be; Spot was out for blood and he got it. Unfortunately, most of it was his own. He caught up with the Italian and they grappled and fought, watched by a bemused crowd of onlookers. Each seeking the advantage, they staggered through the door of the Continental Fruit Stores. With blood flowing, the large and redoubtable Bertha Hyams, the shop owner, smacked Spot a cracking blow with a brass weighing pan. A bystander reckoned that Spot was just about 'to do Dimes' when the pan descended. Instead, 'Big Albert' grabbed the knife and went to work on Spot. Crashing wildly through the door, Dimes was gathered up by Bert Marsh and thrown in a taxi to take him to Charing Cross Hospital. Bleeding profusely,

Jack Spot fell headlong into a neighbouring hairdresser's and demanded that the barber 'fix him up'. Having fainted, he was carted off to Middlesex Hospital.

Here, I am able to give a personal twist to the story. The young houseman on duty that day is a friend of mine, a retired GP now in his eighties. 'What have you been up to?' he enquired. The classic response was, 'I fell down the stairs, guv.' Never an oil painting, Spot now sported a deep gash running from his hairline down to his eyebrow. His cheek and left ear didn't look too good either and he had also been stabbed in the chest and arm. Back at Charing Cross Hospital, Dimes also wasn't looking too chipper. He had slashes to his head requiring twenty stitches, and wounds to his stomach and thigh.

The fight dominated the front pages of the national press. There was talk of unrestricted gang warfare breaking out. Eleven days later, patched up and on the mend, the men appeared at Marlborough Street Magistrates' Court and were committed for trial at the Old Bailey. Initially, it was to be a joint trial but the judge changed his mind, informing the jury that 'it was not for Dimes to prove that he was acting in self-defence, it is for the Prosecution to prove that he was not'. The jury were not convinced and the judge directed that Dimes be acquitted of possessing an offensive weapon. He was given bail whilst Spot was remanded in custody and had to appear at a separate trial fixed for later in the week. As the trial proceeded, it became clear that the dispute related to Dimes trying to break up Spot's monopoly on allocating racecourse pitches. Spot informed the court that 'Big Albert' had told him, 'This is your final warning.' Spot was indignant. He had paid £300 for the pitches. Dimes told him, 'I don't want you to go racing no more.' He reckoned it was time that someone else got a look in.

As always, there was sharply conflicting evidence, but the case turned on a surprise witness. Enter the Reverend Basil Andrews, an eighty-eight-year-old retired vicar. Frail, shabby but strangely dignified, it appeared he had been in Frith Street the day of the affray. It was a time when authority, the professions and certainly men of the cloth were respected. Evidence from the well-modulated voice of a cleric was valued rather more than the Cockney slang uttered by the other witnesses. Andrews assured the court it was Dimes who had been the aggressor. Surely it was obvious from his evidence that Spot was innocent? With arms aloft, like a triumphant boxer, Jack Spot was discharged. His elation didn't last long. Duncan Webb was on the case. He found that Andrews was a discharged bankrupt who continued to be pursued by bookies for unpaid bets. Tackled by the press, Andrews reminded them that he was 'a cleric in holy orders. My harmless flutters in the sporting world were only temporary.' Debts would be repaid. These revelations threw huge doubt on Spot's acquittal and it was decided not to proceed against Dimes. Andrews had, of course, been paid to give false evidence. He finally admitted that he had been very wicked and asked God to forgive him.

Events rumbled on with Rita, Spot's wife, being fined £50 for her part in getting the old vicar to perjure himself. Three of the others involved were given prison sentences for perverting the course of justice. Rumours spread through the underworld that Spot was 'a grass'. He felt humiliated and, true to form, he had one last desperate throw of the dice by hiring a hitman to take a pop at Billy Hill and Dimes. Getting a tip off, they arranged a welcoming party. A gang led by Frankie Fraser set about refashioning poor old Jack's face again. Despite being badly wounded, Spot told the police he didn't recognise his attackers. Rita had other ideas. Naming his attackers resulted in them being sent down for seven years. Still Spot was pursued and his remaining clubs were smashed up. By 1958 Spot was evicted from Hyde Park Mansions and declared bankrupt. For a time he went to live in Ireland but returned to work in a meat-processing factory. It is strange that, in common with many of his contemporary criminals, although making huge amounts of money he had apparently lived quite modestly. Despite this, his downward spiral continued when Rita left him. He died penniless in 1995.

Soho was in for a change. Having seen Jack Spot off the scene, Billy Hill decided he had made enough money to retire. He had acquired a taste for mixing with people who didn't have to rob or terrorise to make a living. He wanted to be fêted and respected outside of criminal circles. There has always been a mutual attraction between the minor aristocracy, celebrities and high-profile gangsters. A fair selection gathered at Gennaro's in Dean Street, a property currently occupied by the Groucho Club, for his book launch. What a ragbag lot they were. The crooks all smartly suited trying to look respectable and failing, the others uneasy but intrigued. Duncan Webb, amongst them, had become a national figure since exposing the Messinas, but he was a complex, possibly unbalanced, character. Ostensibly, he was on a mission to expose crime with an almost religious zeal. Somewhere along the way he appears to have got his wires crossed. Through his close association with criminals he was defending the very people he had set out to expose. He refers to Billy Hill as 'a genius and a kind and tolerant man'. A clue to Webb's character is illustrated by his marriage to Cynthia Hume. For a supposedly religious man to marry a former nightclub hostess is slightly strange. For her to have been previously married to a man convicted of murder is also intriguing. Donald Hume, a small-time crook and car dealer, had been convicted of murdering his boss Stanley Setty, back in 1949. Was Webb trying to rescue her from a sordid background or did he have an unhealthy obsession with crime and criminals? Previously he had courted the girlfriend of the acid bath murderer John Haig. Webb was undoubtedly a rather weird character, but he had certainly pleased Billy Hill with his contribution to the book *Boss of Britain's Underworld*.

Webb was not the only journalist present at Gennaro's. Hannen Swaffer, known as 'the pope of Fleet Street', and a gaggle of other hacks drank to Billy's health. Swaffer, a socialist and spiritualist, gave a speech in which he informed the gathering that if he had come from the same environment as Billy Hill he could have easily entered a life of crime. Everyone applauded politely. Fake telegrams were read out, the one causing the greatest laugh being 'sorry, can't be with you, but I'm in a spot'.

The highest profile guests were Sir Bernard and Lady Docker, a couple known for their profligate spending in an era of austerity. He was chairman of the Daimler Motor Company. He married Norah Turner, a former dancer at the Café de Paris. Sir Bernard's company made the money and she spent it. They would have fitted perfectly in today's world of conspicuous consumption. Massive yachts, gold-plated cars upholstered in zebra skin, mink coats and buckets of champagne represented her style of living. Initially, even she was nervous attending such a louche gathering but she was quoted in the *Daily Mirror* as saying, 'I didn't know Mr Hill before, but now I think he is a charming person.' Frankie Fraser verified her appreciation by suggesting he discovered Billy 'giving her one' whilst the party was still in full swing. Later she claimed that she had been misled into attending the launch and issued proceedings against Webb and his employers, Odhams Press. Her cause was not helped by photographs of her being kissed by Hill, with Sir Bernard smiling benignly in the background.

Having enjoyed the champagne that flowed, the journalists from the nationals then presented their readers with columns of self-righteous indignation. William Hickey, writing in the *Daily Express*, summed up the general mood. Referring to the assembled 'rogues gallery', he stated, 'They are not heroic characters. They are sad, little men who have lost their way.' An interesting footnote occurred later in 1959, when Lady Docker had her jewellery collection, valued at £150,000, stolen from her home. She contacted Hill to see if he could help. He vowed to retrieve the jewels, but seemingly failed. Several years later, having just announced my engagement, I was approached by a man in a pub in Islington, assuring me he could offer a ring containing a reset diamond from the Docker robbery. I wonder how many gauche young men had fallen for that pitch? Luckily, I was not quite that gullible.

With Billy Hill now running his interests from Spain, there was something of a hiatus in those seeking control of Soho. Albert Dimes appeared more interested in the influence he exerted on the racetracks, although rumours persisted that he was the American Mafia's representative in Britain. Certainly he continued to be treated with respect. He was careful with his money, but in Soho most of what he wanted was free. Meals, suits, even manicures for his shovel-like hands. Others reckoned Bert Marsh, a quietly spoken Frith Street bookie, was the Mafia's top man. The fact was the West End's organised crime scene remained fragmented. There was still plenty of scope for all types of crooks to make a dishonest living.

18

One for the Road

By the end of the 1950s, prostitutes had been banished from the streets and replaced by hordes of teenagers hanging about outside coffee bars. Old-timers and well-known 'Soho faces' didn't know what to make of it all. The street girls had helped create the area's unique character. Peering red-eyed through their latest hangover, the boozers, who later would become household names, rather resented the intrusion. Undeterred for long, they carried on cementing their reputation for hedonistic living. To become accepted by this loosely knit group, the one essential was to have a capacity to drink to excess. Drug-taking was optional but sexual indulgence actively welcomed. Homosexuality represented no hindrance to joining this exclusive club and some talent in the arts was considered desirable. Being boring, conventional or plain ugly were judged to be cardinal sins. Such unfortunates were derided by this louche crowd, who have come to represent the Soho of the 1950s. Like an endangered species, they tended to congregate together, arguing, bitching, loving and shagging in ever-changing combinations. Their favoured watering holes have become synonymous with Jeffrey Bernard, Daniel Farson, Francis Bacon and the rest of the gang. Serious drinkers generally have an active dislike of luxurious surroundings for their sessions. They are drawn to bars where the decor is secondary to the company and the conversation, although this is largely forgotten in a blur by the time they break up.

Fitting the criteria for a perfect bar was the Colony Room in Dean Street, known to regulars as Muriel's. It was a dingy, one-room drinking club which had opened in 1948 and was run by

Muriel Belcher, a woman of Portuguese and Jewish extraction. It was necessary to negotiate a line of dustbins before climbing the foul-smelling staircase to the first floor. You were likely to encounter a client of one of Muriel's prostitute neighbours making a dash for the anonymity of the street. Inside the club, the dark green walls gave the place a rather gloomy atmosphere. Belcher was thought by many to be a lesbian, but was actually a bi-sexual who had a string of lovers from both sides of the fence. By middle age, her aggressive personality was mirrored by her crow-like looks and even pictured as a younger woman she appeared wary and hard. An early customer at the club was a struggling young artist. She took a liking to Francis Bacon and for a time paid him a weekly wage to bring in new punters. The Colony soon became a favourite with the Bohemian set and those who were amused by being verbally abused. Her language was foul and her manner camp. Being referred to as 'cunty' bestowed acceptance. A dropping of the 'y' indicated that you were not welcome. She despised boring and frugal bastards, prompted no doubt by her own known love of money. She referred to her male friends as her daughters and her own sexuality encouraged a dedicated following of gays.

I remember being taken to the Colony as a young man and it was an intimidating experience. Through a fug of smoke and boozy fumes, I was propositioned by men and women, all to my mind old enough to be my parents. I have no idea who any of them were but I was acutely uncomfortable and out of my depth amidst a clever, bitchy stream of conversation. George Melly, who was a regular at the Colony, described Muriel Belcher as 'a handsome Jewish dyke ... A benevolent witch who managed to draw all London's talent up those filthy stairs. She was like a great cook working with ingredients and drink.' She featured in a number of seemingly tortured paintings by Francis Bacon. Horrible at first glance, they have the capacity to draw you in as he bares her soul for all to see.

She was also photographed by John Deakin, whom she loathed for his meanness. 'Get your bean bag out!' was her welcoming cry. Although a regular drinking companion of Bacon, he was not popular but was, undoubtedly, a talented photographer. Again, it was George Melly who described him as a 'vicious little drunk of such inventive malice and implacable bitchiness that it's surprising he didn't choke on his own venom'. Deakin captured the leading celebrities of the time, including Yul Brynner and Yves Montand, but the outstanding body of his work was of Soho characters. Daniel Farson, no mean photographer himself, described Deakin's work as 'prison mug-shots taken by a real artist'. Farson's photograph of Deakin is, by contrast, rather stylised and it was left to Lucien Freud to expose the inner sadness of the man in a revealing portrait.

Often barred from the Colony, Deakin would decamp next door to another favourite drinking den. Les Caves de France was also patronised by other well-known 'Soho faces', even tempting Julian MacLaren-Ross to venture now and again from Fitzrovia. Generally, it attracted a gaggle of Bohemian wannabes. Described by writer Elaine Dundy as a place 'possessing an atmosphere almost solid with failure', it drew in budding poets, writers, artists and dancers, joined by prostitutes of both sexes. They sat around for hours nursing their drinks, putting the world to rights and talking pseudo-intellectual babble, whilst the true Soho-ites drank solidly before departing for their next watering hole.

Their choice had been diminished since the sale of the Gargoyle in 1952. Once, it had attracted the rich and famous but by the late 1950s it had reinvented itself as a seedy drinking and strip club known as the Nell Gwynne, who was rumoured to have lived in the original house. So, for the regulars of the Colony or Caves de France, it was a quick totter down Dean Street to the French Pub, known then as York Minster. The pub has come to represent the essence of 1950s Soho with its cast of larger than life characters. A place where ordering a pint of beer established you as a tourist. A home to good, strong Belgian beer and a house red wine superior to many served at much higher prices in surrounding restaurants. Visiting Hollywood stars were seen there, as was Salvador Dali and well-to-do socialites, but it is for its hardcore seasoned drinkers that we remember it most. We picture Dylan Thomas and Brendan Behan holding forth, together with a supporting cast of regulars including Jeffrey Bernard, Daniel Farson and the artists Francis Bacon and Lucien Freud.

Gerry's, in Shaftesbury Avenue, was the favourite haunt of those involved in show business and the theatrical world. It was owned by Gerald Campion, who found fame playing Billy Bunter in the 1952 TV series *Billy Bunter of Greyfriars School*. A love of gourmet food and good companionship encouraged him to open the Buckstone, a club situated opposite the stage door of the Theatre Royal. This established a following from those working in the entertainment industry who loyally followed him to his next venture, the Key Club. Situated close to the London Palladium, it issued members with their own individual keys to obtain entrance. It was Gerry's that really established itself as the place to go to ogle the stars, as well as lines of resting actors. Situated in the heart of theatreland, it provided a congenial meeting place for the luvvies and their kindred spirits. Campion was a figure regarded with affection, particularly by those down on their luck. A tab behind the bar was seldom refused and many referred to Campion's generosity and kindness.

Freddie Mills was another leading personality entering the club scene. A brave and successful boxer, he was Light Heavyweight Champion of the World from 1948 to 1950. Upon retirement he opened Freddie Mills' Chinese Restaurant on Charing Cross Road. Although charming to meet, he mixed in dubious company. Having taken some fearful punishment during his career, he was subject to blinding headaches which, together with his lack of business knowledge, led to growing financial problems. He converted the restaurant into a nightclub which attracted many of London's criminal elite, including the Krays. Mills' is a story of seedy decline from the days when he was fêted for his feats in the ring and for his engaging personality that made him one of Britain's favourite sports stars. Many wild rumours circulated following the discovery of his body in a yard at the back of his club. It was rumoured that he committed suicide having become a suspect in the murder of eight prostitutes. Other theories abounded. Had he refused to pay protection money to the Triads or fallen out with the Krays? It was also suggested that there had been a police cover-up. The mystery remains unsolved.

Historically, most clubs in Soho were shabby and sleazy and only existed to fuel the demand for out-of-hours drinking. Some were gambling dens, others clip joints, but there were a few who attempted to offer a veneer of respectability. Murray's Cabaret Club in Beak Street was opened in 1933 by Percival Murray. It had a reputation for producing elaborate floor shows and attracting the louche and those hovering on the fringes of acceptable society. It was described as discreetly risqué. By the 1950s it was being run by Percival's son, David. The younger Murray had enjoyed 'a good war' serving with the SOE. The club

was to gain notoriety in the 1960s with club hostess Christine
Keeler being at the centre of the Profumo scandal. Previously
referred to as 'a virtual brothel', it still attracted heads of state,
leading politicians and Princess Margaret. Increasingly, gangsters
seeking an aura of respectability were added to the mix. In
hindsight, this volatile brew was always likely to explode into
the general public's consciousness – but not just yet.

Today, Old Compton Street is the centre of gay London.
The street is lined with gay bars, which mushroomed from the
1980s onwards. In the 1950s, homosexuality was still illegal and
generally condemned except in theatrical circles. Even within
Soho, normally so accepting of minorities, gay men had to be
relatively discreet. Many even resorted to speaking Polari, a type
of slang named after the Italian word *palare* – to talk. Formerly
popular with sailors and East End dockers, it allowed gays to
talk and make contact with like-minded men without the fear of
exposure. Attitudes towards gays were savage and homosexual
acts continued to be known as 'the abominable crime'. Some, like
Daniel Farsen and Francis Bacon, chose to flout the law in their
blatant approach. Their choice was often for a bit of 'the rough
trade'. There was seldom a shortage of willing working-class
men to go along with their masochistic desires in exchange for a
bed for the night and a few quid. There was a widely held belief
that these ghastly queers could corrupt the youth of Britain and
convert them to their deviant ways. Strangely, it was never illegal
to be gay, just as long as no sexual activity was undertaken.
Generations of British men were, therefore, either forced to deny
their natural instincts or to live a lie, constantly worried about
arrest or blackmail.

The Swiss Tavern in Old Compton Street was described as
being 'not entirely straight' and was one of a number of pubs in
Soho where gay men could happily meet in the 1950s. Originally
known as the Swiss Hotel, it was built in 1890 to accommodate
numbers of Swiss nationals visiting relatives who had settled in
the area. Later known as the Swiss Tavern, it has now become
Compton's, one of the most popular gay pubs in Soho. Round the
corner in Dean Street, the Crown & Two Chairmen also offered
a relatively safe retreat for homosexuals, as did the Golden Lion,
also situated in Dean Street. Quentin Crisp, who for a time
was Britain's best-known gay man, always felt safer in Soho.
Customers who made fun of him in the Coach & Horses were

sent on their way by the landlord. Crisp, who had been rejected by the British Army as suffering from 'sexual perversion' when attempting to join up, came to embody the archetypal gay man of the post-war years. Caked in make-up, mincing and witty, he found refuge in Soho, as countless other minorities had before him. All strands of humanity could thrive or destroy themselves in Soho.

Sadly, many chose the latter, competing in a macabre procession towards a tawdry ending. Most of this boozy, talented group of companions who drank epic quantities defied logic by surviving well into the 1960s and beyond. They included the Bernard Brothers. Jeffrey, who later found fame with his 'Low Life' column in the *Spectator*, was also captured in the Keith Waterhouse play *Jeffrey Bernard is Unwell*. His brothers Oliver, a respected poet, and picture editor Bruce were also very much part of the scene. Artists were well represented in this group, who not only enjoyed a good drinking session but also engaging conversation punctuated by some really outlandish behaviour. The group included, as ever, Francis Bacon, but also Robert Colquhoun, Rodrigo Moynihan, Frank Averbach and Lucien Freud. Actor Norman Bowler, writer Colin MacInnes, George Melly and Frank Norman (who wrote the musical play *Fings Ain't Wot They Used T'Be*) were also frequently on hand.

There were, of course, women who joined the group – some fleetingly, either because they couldn't stand the pace, or due to a love interest that had faded, making it time to move on. Two women, Nina Hamnett and Henrietta Moraes, came to represent the dangers and ultimate tragedy of a decline into alcoholism. It was as if Henrietta Moraes used Hamnett as a role model to signal her spiralling decline, although she survived into her sixties, dying in 1999. Both were beautiful when young and became models for famous artists. Nina Hamnett, who was born in 1890, had gone off to Paris seeking a Bohemian lifestyle after studying at the London School of Art. Before leaving she had already had an affair with Henri Gaudier-Brzeska, who had completed a series of nude bronzes of her. Bedding the artists she modelled for appeared a statutory requirement, as world-famous names from the arts were added to her list of conquests, including Modigliani, who declared she had the best tits in Europe. She adopted a lifestyle which was considered flamboyantly outrageous. Already drinking heavily, she was bi-sexual and promiscuous. Back in London, Hamnett became known as 'the queen of Bohemia' drinking alongside Augustus John, who had also been born in her home town, Tenby. Dylan Thomas was also a constant drinking companion, before Nina moved south into Soho, which became her boozing base. Now in her sixties, raddled and her beauty gone, she was banned from the Colony for peeing all over her barstool. Reduced to cadging drinks next door in the Caves or at the French Pub, she cut a sorry picture. A drunken fall in 1953 left her lame. In 1955 her second biography, *Is She a Lady?*, was published. The following year a radio play portrayed her life in 1930s Fitzrovia. Some days after the broadcast she was found impaled on railings having fallen from her room in Westbourne Terrace. She was reckoned to have committed suicide, but in a final kind gesture towards her the coroner recorded a verdict of accidental death.

By the time Hamnett died, Henrietta Moraes was already the toast of Soho. Dark-haired with still darker eyes, she exuded sexual magnetism and danger. Her introduction to Soho, like many of her era, was the 100 Club, before moving a few hundred yards south into Soho proper. By nineteen, she was married to Michael Law, a documentary film-maker. She became a model posing for Francis Bacon and Lucien Freud, who we are told had his wicked way with her over his kitchen sink. She threw herself into a self-indulgent Bohemian lifestyle, joining the premier division drinking circuit of the French, Café Torino and the Colony. Her love of artists was transferred to John Minton, a kind and generous man. Unfortunately, she was wasting her time. Minton was a confirmed homosexual who, in turn, was in love with Norman Bowler (who went on to play Sergeant Hawkins in the TV production of *Z-Cars*). Having divorced Law, she married Bowler. Was it out of spite that she married him or was it the closest she could get to Minton? After giving birth to two children, she was eventually married a third time to poet Dom Moraes. Alexandra Pringle, her literary agent in later life, concluded that 'her great loves were for gay men or women'.

Unrequited love always leads to unhappiness but Henrietta's passion for John Minton was to end in tragedy. It appears that Minton was known for his generosity, a trait not always on show amongst the Soho boozers. He made friends easily and was something of an exhibitionist and given to clowning about. He was reckless when in love and made many often intense, short-lived gay relationships. Unfortunately, he also had a deep-rooted preoccupation with death. A painter, poster artist and book illustrator, he was described as a lyrical, neo-romantic artist. He is remembered for his illustrations for Elizabeth David's *Mediterranean Food* and *French Country Cooking*, his landscapes and rather haunting portraits. His family was connected to the famous Minton ceramics business and he lived in some style. None the less, it was a huge surprise, but little consolation, to Henrietta Moraes when she learned that Minton had left her his valuable property in Chelsea following his suicide. Not content with drinking herself into oblivion, drugs now became her new obsession. Following the path laid down by Nina Hamnett, she charted a similar downward spiral. Her relationship with Moraes was tempestuous and doomed. Soon the house was gone, the proceeds drunk and injected. She is quoted as saying, 'I picked up bad habits like a magnet does iron filings.' She started writing articles about her addictions in the national press. She, at various times, attempted suicide and lived as a gypsy for years before becoming a PA to the singer Marianne Faithfull. She published her memoirs, *Henrietta*, in 1994. Though she was beautiful and talented, it was, in truth, a life ruined by drink and drugs.

The fifties is lauded as the great age for Soho but, in looking back, we must ask, has the era been romanticised? Is it possible that, like glancing back at our childhood, we only remember what we want to? All those sunny, warm summers stretching into autumn. Was it really so wonderful? Do the few survivors from those drunken lunches, stretching into evening sessions and mammoth hangovers really seem so attractive in retrospect? Certainly, the 'live now, pay later' lifestyle took its toll on the gallant band of brothers who bestrode the bars of Dean Street. It was not just alcoholism that took its toll. Suicide, accidents and early death all featured. David Archer, who ran a bookshop in Greek Street and whose Poetry Press was the first to publish Dylan Thomas, was a member of the boozing tribe. He took an overdose in his sixties, having gone through a sizeable inheritance. The outstanding Scottish artist Robert Colquhoun died an alcoholic, whilst his long-time partner, Robert MacBryde, was killed in a street accident four years later. The unloved photographer John Deakin was sixty when he died, but the life he had led made him look far older. So beware – Soho, a place made famous for enjoyment and having fun, has a malign side. An ability to draw even the wary into temptation. It always has. Doubtless, it always will.

19

The Beat Goes On

Visitors to Soho often have a specific reason in mind. Maybe a trip to the theatre, followed by a meal at a favourite restaurant. The street markets draw foodies from across London, as do the pubs and clubs. Some come in search of love, although what is on offer tends to be expensive and does not last long. Added to the list in the 1950s was music. Some came to listen earnestly to every note, others to dance and jive. Traditional jazz, blues, folk, skiffle and rock 'n' roll – each had their own enthusiastic following. On occasions they would merge, becoming indistinguishable from each other. Only the sombre-suited modern jazz exponents stood aloof, convinced that their virtuosity set them apart from the armies of amateur strummers and wailers. Soho was alive with the sounds of music, but also witness to a social revolution.

Popular music after the war was dominated by American recording artists. The airwaves featured the likes of Bing Crosby and Doris Day, punctuated by British favourites such as Ronny Hilton, Donald Peers and the strangled tones of David Whitfield. Vera Lynn's 'Auf Wiedersehen Sweetheart' peaked just too soon to become the first number one hit in the newly launched *New Musical Express* Top Twelve Chart in 1952. That honour went to Al Martino with 'Here in My Heart'. In the same year Radio Luxembourg introduced *Top of the Pops*. A young, developing audience wasn't going to put up with the cascading strings of Mantovani or inane songs like 'How Much Is That Doggie in the Window' for long. Something had to change and it did. 1955 saw the arrival of Elvis Presley, Bill Haley and the jukebox, which transformed the youth culture of the country. Big bands, previously so popular, were dealt a mortal blow. High-quality recordings were now available on demand. Within two years, 8,000 jukeboxes were thumping out their beat across the country.

This was the era that saw the emergence of the teenager as a social and economic force. There was full employment and the young, generally, had a disposable income not enjoyed by previous generations. No longer were they willing to be clones of their parents. Dress was now the cause of many family rows. Duffle coats were allowed but jeans or American drape jackets were frowned upon. So was long hair, and yet shorn-headed crew cuts were also criticised. There was no pleasing square, middle-class parents. No working-class lad would be seen dead wearing a flat cap. For the first time it was difficult to pick out a youngster's background by the clothes they wore. John Stephen, a young Glaswegian, was the first to recognise the pent-up demand for men's teenage fashion when he opened His Clothes in Carnaby Street in 1958, a street that would become a symbol of the Swinging Sixties.

In Soho it was dress that indicated the type of music you favoured rather than your social background. At the hot and sweaty 100 Club on Tottenham Court Road, crowds of young women surrounded the bandstand wearing tight sweaters or cardigans over circular skirts puffed out by layers of nylon petticoats. They gazed longingly at a tall, elegant trumpeter, their boyfriends banished to the outer reaches of the room, all beards, sloppy sweaters and open sandals. No competition, really. Humphrey Lyttleton, an ex-Etonian Guards Officer, was at the forefront in the revival of traditional jazz in Great Britain. Jazz musicians and their followers tended to take themselves rather seriously at the time and the fact that the catchy 'Bad Penny Blues' soared to the top of the hit parade actually offended some followers. Jazz musicians were an argumentative lot. It was as difficult to get them to agree as reconciling an Irish Republican and an Orangeman. The modernists, great admirers of Miles Davis and Charlie Parker, were viewed as zealots by the revivalists who favoured the authentic sounds of New Orleans.

The first jazz club to open in Soho after the war was Club Eleven in Great Windmill Street. The club featured two bands, one led by Ronnie Scott and the other by Johnny Dankworth. The club had acquired a somewhat dubious reputation and was closed following a police raid in 1950. Scott, a superb saxophonist, subsequently went on to play in Jack Parnell's orchestra before teaming up with Tubby Hayes. He is best remembered for his jazz club at 47 Frith Street which continues to be a Soho institution today after transferring from Gerrard Street in 1965.

Another early arrival on the club scene was opened by Cy Laurie in 1951. The entrance was in scruffy Ham Yard. Members arriving had to pick their way through lines of barrows parked overnight by Berwick Street traders. Inside, the club was dark and sweaty and featured threadbare settees and filthy toilets. At least the music was great and the joint rocked most nights with line-ups that often included the likes of Chris Barber, Diz Disley and George Melly. Laurie, despite his generally Bohemian clientele, didn't fit into the normal jazz musician's profile. A non-drinker, who had little regard for commercial success, he retired from the scene in 1960 to pursue his interest in philosophy and meditation.

A major influence in the British jazz scene was Ken Colyer, a superb trumpeter. Back in the 1950s it was reckoned that 'Humph was for tourists, Ken Colyer for purists and Cy for jiving and raving'. In 1951 Colyer opened Club 51 in Great Newport Street. Although he continued to play in the New Orleans tradition and despite internal disputes, there was an inevitable crossover in styles. The divisions between traditional jazz, blues and folk were often difficult to identify and from this mixture came the birth of British skiffle, originally the offshoot from Ken Colyer's revivalist New Orleans jazz band. Skiffle was catchy and, importantly, only required rudimentary instruments. It became a sensation almost overnight among armies of youngsters. Initially, its success was largely due to one man. Lonnie Donegan was a guitarist and banjo player in Colyer's band. Whilst other members of the band took a well-earned rest, Donegan began performing skiffle numbers during the intervals. Soon crowds were going to the club to hear Donegan rather than the resident band. He cut his first LP with Chris Barber's jazz band and sales exceeded all expectations. The record producers sniffed success. One of the numbers on the LP *Rock Island Line* hit a chord with the public and was released as a single. It soared to number one in the charts, selling over 3 million copies. It also became the first British record to feature in the US Billboard Chart. This record set off a craze. Throughout the country thousands of youngsters formed skiffle groups. There was a boom in the sale of cheap guitars. Tea chests were like gold dust and hardware stores reported a surge in the sales of broom handles. Within days it was possible, with the additional help of a washboard and kazoo, for a group to make a reasonable sound. Skiffle clubs in Soho were erupting like spots on a teenager's face. They provided a crossover for the folk enthusiasts to join a younger, more catholic, audience.

Chas McDevitt, like Lonnie Donegan, hailed from Scotland. He was often seen busking in Soho before teaming up with folk singer Nancy Whisky. Their recording of 'Freight Train' was a massive hit and helped to establish skiffle at the forefront of British popular musical taste, despite the grumblings of more serious jazzmen. Donegan, who was to influence a generation of emerging pop stars, followed up with another smash hit, 'Cumberland Gap', in 1957. Aware of continual carping from some of his peers, Donegan insisted he was out 'to widen his audience beyond the artsy-craftsy crowd and pseudo intellectuals'. The centre of popular music was shifting from the dance halls to outlets where the young congregated as never before. The first coffee bar to open in Britain was Moka at 29 Frith Street. Soho was the natural home for London's prime outlets as the Italian Gaggia Company's UK headquarters was in Dean Street. Frothy coffee produced from snarling stainless steel machines was a revolution. Coffee in Britain had largely been confined to a bitter-tasting essence extracted from bottles similar to those containing HP sauce. Moka was opened in 1953 by the Italian film star Gina Lollobrigida. Neither she nor Gaggia could have foreseen the growth or influence the coffee bar was to have on a generation of British youth. Old Compton Street became 'Espresso Alley' sporting Act One, Scene One; Amalfi; The Pollo; and Heaven & Hell. Soon almost every street in Soho supported a coffee bar, the most unusual being Le Macabre at 22 Meard Street where you sat on black wooden coffins amongst hanging skeletons.

Most of the coffee bars featured simple Formica tables and plastic chairs. Almost anything foreign was now considered worthwhile after years of austerity and little consumer choice. This even extended to a liking for Danish pastries and apple strudel. Music formed the cornerstone of most coffee bars, with a jukebox blaring out the latest hits, whilst in the evenings room was made for a live band and a dance floor. Some Soho favourites featured live music. The 2i's at 59 Old Compton Street was a major launching pad for British rock 'n' roll. The venue was named by the two Iranian brothers who leased the property to Paul Lincoln, an Australian wrestler who fought under the name of Doctor Death. Initially, the business was losing money on a dramatic scale. Its change of fortune was down to chance. Wally Whyton was part of the Vipers skiffle group. In July 1956 they took shelter from a shower whilst attending the Soho Fair, starting an impromptu session. Lincoln was amazed at how quickly a crowd gathered. He offered the group a regular opportunity to play and in doing so stumbled on a winning formula. Other groups queued up for the chance to play, together with crowds of teenagers who wanted to listen. He opened up the cellar that had previously been used for storage. I remember going there soon after it opened. It was a small, dark room with a tiny platform at the back that acted as a stage. It had been decorated by Lionel Bart, a former art student at St Martin's. It had a black ceiling which drew the room in further, with strange painted eyes on the walls. Hundreds crammed into this suffocating space each night, where heavy, clinging perfume fought a losing battle with cigarette smoke and sweat. It wasn't long before a new sign outside the front door proclaimed 'The world famous 2i's coffee bar, home of the stars'. On the ground floor the overall appearance was tacky, but no one seemed to mind. There was the mandatory coffee machine, orange juice dispenser and a display counter with tired, curled-up sandwiches.

The 2i's, in common with other trendy Soho coffee bars, was booming. The real fortunes being made were initially largely confined to the managers of the budding stars. Larry Parnes was a young, not particularly successful, fashion retailer. Whilst the old-time musical agents were convinced that the new musical fad would be dead within weeks, Parnes and his partner, John Kennedy, thought differently. There was a sense of liberation amongst the young. Parnes felt it, understood it and smelt money. He was right. He was to become the archetypal rock 'n' roll manager. He cruised the coffee bars looking for talent. He combined charm, opportunity, persuasion and an ability for hard-headed negotiation. Parnes and Kennedy's first major signing was Tommy Hicks, a nineteen-year-old from Bermondsey. Hicks had initially been offered a recording contract by a producer who had seen him at the 2i's. Given a tip off, Parnes went to see him perform at the Stork Room in Regent Street. He persuaded Hicks to appoint him as his manager. Tommy Hicks promptly became Tommy Steele, Britain's first rock 'n' roll star. His first number, 'Rocking with the Caveman', stalled at number thirteen in the hit parade, but his follow up, a cover version of Guy Mitchell's 'Singing the Blues', soared to number one. George Melly reckoned that Steele's gyrations on stage were 'not so much a sexual courtship dance as a suggestion that he had wet himself'.

Parnes's next major discovery was scheduled to be made at the Condor Club, situated beneath the Sabrina Coffee Bar in Wardour Street. He had been alerted to the raw talent of a tall, well-built teenager by his friend, Lionel Bart. Parnes arrived late at the club and missed the performance. Undeterred, he tracked Reg Smith back to the house in Essex where he lived with his parents. Here was someone whom he felt could be Britain's answer to Elvis Presley. He looked every inch a pop star and he had a really strong, likeable voice. The young man had been performing as Reg Patterson. Marginally better than Reg Smith, but hardly memorable. Exotic names came easily to Parnes. He suggested Marty Wilde. It was manly, even suggesting a whiff of danger. Reg liked his Christian name and suggested Reg Wilde. Eventually, Parnes prevailed and Marty Wilde was launched onto the excited, excitable pop scene.

Wilde appeared much brighter and streetwise than many of his peers who were seeking fame at any price. He only used the 2i's for afternoon rehearsals, having realised that the clientele at the Condor were more likely to provide him with a breakthrough. The club attracted celebrities of the day like racing driver Sterling Moss. Marty Wilde also appeared at the upmarket Blue Angel. Many of Parnes's young discoveries were only paid a derisory wage, but Marty negotiated a deal that left him with 60 per cent of his earnings. The 40 per cent retained by Larry Parnes seems monstrous but Marty still maintains that he was perfectly happy with the arrangement. Although Parnes's reputation has taken a battering over the years, Marty Wilde still remembers him with affection. Once he had brushed off his manager's rather half-hearted sexual advances, they got on fine. Years later they went to Monte Carlo together, where Marty watched as Larry Parnes indulged his other weakness of gambling away much of his new-found wealth. Wilde's first record didn't chart, but by 1958 he was one of Britain's top rock 'n' roll stars alongside Cliff Richard. His popularity soared with regular appearances on *Six-Five Special* and ITV's *Oh Boy*. The two programmes were fighting over a teenage viewing audience estimated at 15 million. His courtship of Vernon girl Joyce Baker was followed avidly by the popular press, but their marriage heralded a decline in his popularity. The couple have had the last laugh, though, as they remain happily married and formed something of a rock dynasty with the success of their daughters Kim and Roxanne.

Parnes was now building up a stable of home-grown stars, most of whom he discovered in the coffee bars of Soho. He gave them crazy names and groomed them to appeal to an affluent teenage market. The singers had to be good-looking and have a half-decent voice. Parnes had good connections at all the major record companies and unleashed the likes of Johnny Gentle, Rory Storm, Dickie Pride and Lance Fortune with varying success. He also signed the gravel-voiced Tommy Bruce, and Joe Brown, who steadfastly insisted on keeping his real name. Larry Parnes was now doing very well for himself, although referred to behind his back as 'Mr Parnes, shillings and pence'. His Midas touch deserted him when turning down Cliff Richard, whom he had seen performing at the 2i's. It was Paul Lincoln, the owner, who first spotted Terry Dene, who for a time looked as if he would enjoy enduring stardom. His recordings of 'A White Sport Coat' and 'Stairway of Love' were huge hits. Although Dene had a particularly good recording voice, he was also an early believer in an outrageous and yobbish rock 'n' roll lifestyle, which was still frowned upon by the press and British public opinion. He was arrested for smashing a shop window when drunk and subsequently for vandalising a telephone kiosk. Pretty tame stuff by today's standards, but he was labelled 'the bad boy of British rock'. In trying to evade National Service he attracted more bad publicity. Forced to serve, he was victimised by fellow squaddies. The press continued to insist that Dene represented everything that was wrong with the youth of Britain. Mentally fragile, he was discharged from the Army. Despite his being signed by the opportunistic Larry Parnes, his career never recovered. In the early 1960s, he walked away from the pop scene and turned to evangelism.

Still, legions of hopefuls beat a path to the 2i's. Would-be rockers Vince Taylor, Rick Hardy and Wee Willie Harris all took the stand as did Mickie Most, who worked as a singing waiter. In the sixties, Most went on to become one of Britain's highly successful record producers. Terry Nelhams was managing and performing with The Worried Men skiffle group, who became the resident band at the 2i's. Terry attracted the attention of record producer Jack Good, who arranged a recording contract with him. He also changed Nelhams's name to Adam Faith. His looks and unique singing voice set him apart from the current crop of popular singers. His first record releases failed to make much impression and again it was his regular appearances on television that kept him on the public's radar. Even collaboration with star producer Tony Hatch failed to give him the sought-after hit. Eventually, in 1959, it was his long association with John Barry that provided the breakthrough with his distinctive recording of 'What Do You Want?' His pronunciation of 'baby' as 'bay-bee' did the trick. It proved to be the first number one hit for the Parlophone label, whose list of artists were later to include the Beatles.

Many of the stars who made their debuts at the 2i's were Londoners but the coffee bars' fame had spread, attracting youngsters from the provinces. Two Geordie lads supplemented their earnings working the coffee and orange machines at the 2i's, when not playing their guitars for an increasingly appreciative audience. Bruce Welch and Hank Marvin were paid 18s an hour and it was only later that they found out that the going rate was normally £1, but the 2i's manager, Tom Littlewood, was taking 10 per cent commission. They eventually teamed up with two other young hopefuls, Jet Harris and Tony Meehan. They were then taken round to a tailor's in Dean Street to meet Cliff Richard, which led to the formation of the Shadows and international fame.

The arrival of the Shadows led to an enormous demand for electric guitars. Youngsters across the country pictured themselves as strutting pop stars. Höfner, who advertised themselves as 'the last word in electric guitar gear', were based at 114 Charing Cross Road. Their 'new line' console was incorporated in all their acoustic and electric guitars. They claimed that this revolutionary control panel could effect a quarter beat or, at the flick of a switch, go from rhythm to edgy round tone, all achieved in a flash at prices ranging from twenty-eight to sixty-five guineas. Soho remained a centre for musical instruments of all types. Further down Charing Cross Road, Jennings had their London showrooms offering drum kits, trumpets, saxophones and clarinets, all on easy terms with a down payment and monthly repayments. Most streets in Soho had instruments and sheet music for sale, with the accordion, surprisingly, remaining popular. Sid Phillips advertised a correspondence course on learning to play the clarinet, and the trade press was full of similar offers for a whole range of instruments. Reg Morgan, who claimed to have been the singing coach to the late Steve Conway, offered lessons. Everyone, it appeared, wanted to get in on the act. Music offered youngsters from humble backgrounds an escape route, in a less painful way than boxing had for the previous generations.

Whilst Britain's youth had now established its own culture, the country overall was not at ease with itself. This became obvious with the outbreak of race riots in Notting Hill during the late summer of 1958. Soho, as the most cosmopolitan area in London, had experienced little tension. The music industry had also a long history of generally harmonious integration, so it was no surprise that the *Melody Maker* issued an editorial appeal for a rejection of racial discrimination. It concluded, 'we appeal to our audiences everywhere to join us in opposing any kind and every aspect of colour prejudice, wherever it may occur'. The appeal was endorsed by twenty-seven leading musicians, including Johnny Dankworth, Lonnie Donegan, Tubby Hayes, Humphrey Lyttleton and Tommy Steele. Thus, Soho was in the vanguard of changing public opinion on race and in the explosion of interest in popular music. A small cellar in Old Compton Street could claim to be the birthplace of what was to become a multimillion-pound business, whose export earnings were to be treasured by successive governments. It also laid the foundations for the Swinging Sixties.

20

The Girl with the Red Beret

Springtime is not just for lovers, but for the young too. For renewal and fresh hope after a long and depressing winter. Picture a fine spring day in 1958. A slender, attractive young girl leaves the 2i's Coffee Bar in Old Compton Street. She turns left and walks, as we would all like to walk, with a guileless confidence. Spring has seen her emerge from awkward adolescence and develop into a stunning young woman. She almost skips along Brewer Street, past the admiring glances and catcalls of the barrow boys at the intersection to Berwick Street. She wears a red beret tilted at a jaunty angle. Her first pair of high heels accentuate the length of her legs. The dawning of her new-found attractiveness excites her and she feels quite liberated and at home in the narrow streets of Soho, despite its dubious reputation.

Sipping coffee at the 2i's, she had fallen into conversation with Perin Lewis, a vivacious young woman – one of the famous Windmill girls. Their chat intrigues the girl with the beret. It appears that the Windmill can prove a route to breaking into the exciting world of show business. Stage-struck since she was a child, Jill (the girl with the beret) ponders this as she makes her way towards Piccadilly Circus underground station. Glancing up, she sees the entrance to the stage door of the Windmill as she cuts through Archer Street. On impulse, and with the confidence of youth, she enters to be greeted by Ben Fuller, the doorman. He has seen thousands of hopefuls arrive at his door. He feels he can pick likely candidates almost as well as Vivian Van Damm himself. This youngster looks just the ticket. 'You are in luck,' he tells her. 'The old man is in today.' A quick phone call and she is climbing the Windmill stairs for the first time. The air is a mixture of greasepaint, perfume and sweat. She breathes it in, filling her lungs, a heady smell she can still recall half a century later. A tannoy is relaying the show currently on stage. She squeezes her way upstairs, being passed by lines of scantily dressed dancers. She is aware of whirring sewing machines as she skirts the wardrobe department. Tap dancers are practising a new routine in the rehearsal room, whilst a singer accompanied by a pianist tries to compete with the tannoy. The girl in the beret marvelled at it all. This is for me, she thought, this is the life I would love.

To a young girl, Vivian Van Damm was an old man – older than her father, serious and rather intimidating. Nervously, she stood before him whilst he remained seated at his desk. His office was a male oasis set amidst a building devoted to feminine beauty. The smell of cigars hung in the air. The furniture was solid and somehow comforting. The walls were lined with family portraits, old posters and past souvenir programmes. A fish tank helped to create a sense of calm. He had watched her carefully as she was shown in – how she walked, held herself – noting her shy smile that seemed to light up her face. His speech was slow and deliberate. He asked her only two questions. 'Can you dance?' 'Yes,' she replied. 'Sing?' Yes, she had a good voice. He paused for a moment, still assessing her. Then, looking her straight in the eye, he said simply, 'I like you. I'm going to take a chance on you.' No audition. No having to sing or perform a dance routine. He was taking her quite literally on face value. This was the moment that was to define Jill Millard's life. Drawing out a contract, Van Damm signed it with a flourish and informed her that she would start rehearsals the following week. Once more he was backing an instinct that rarely failed him. A brief moment of elation for the young girl was followed by a sinking heart. 'I can't start next week,' she blurted out. 'I'm still at school.' She assumed he would be angry with her for wasting his time. He wasn't, just a trifle bemused. This was not the first time such a problem had presented itself. The film star Jean Kent had misled him about her age when she had auditioned for the Windmill, but had managed to get away with it. At the tender age of fourteen, the girl with the red beret had no chance, but she was sent home with a contract, promising to return.

Jill, with the backing and support of her mother, left school at the earliest possible moment and set about pursuing a career on the stage. Initially, she appeared at the Edinburgh Fringe and

took small parts in a few television dramas. The attraction of the
Windmill remained and saw her return the following year. It is
where she spent the next happy, rewarding, rollercoaster years.

The enormity of what she was taking on finally sunk home with
her introduction to Keith Lester. He was a leading British dancer
and choreographer, who had trained in the Diaghilev tradition.
He had partnered some of the greatest ballerinas of the previous
two decades. He was a frightening taskmaster. He set out to try
and make the young girl's body do things it had not been designed
for. She was stretched and bent and contorted to the point where
her limbs screamed at her in complaint. He terrified her. He puffed
out his chest and flared his nostrils. He pouted and posed, but
most of all he shouted. She felt intimidated and, for the first time
in her life, clumsy. One of the girls whispered in her ear, 'Don't
let him make you cry. You mustn't let him get the better of you.'
And she didn't. She submitted her body to the daily gruelling
test. She met his goading with a smile and a steady eye. Martinet
he may have been, but his fierce regime was working. What had
seemed impossible just days before now came easily to her. It
was Keith who had created the Windmill's famous Fan Dance in
the 1940s. The routine was the most a nude figure was allowed
to move on stage by law and required considerable skill on the
part of the dancer. The performer had to remain covered whilst
manoeuvring two huge ostrich feather fans. In theory, the Lord
Chamberlain could have the dance removed from the show during
an unannounced visit by one of his sidekicks. It was a dance that
Jill was to perform many times over the coming years.

Soon the anxiety of her first live appearance on the Windmill
stage was behind her and Jill threw herself into the hectic life
that was to be hers for the next four years. Live shows, endless
rehearsals, snatched snacks in the canteen and snatched kisses on
the stairs with one of the handsome Windmill boys. There were
tasty meals at the nearby New Yorker restaurant with friends.
Lifelong friendships were formed, fleeting romances. Life was
an endless whirl of hard work and excitement. She still managed
visits to the 2i's, where she mixed with many of the emerging rock
stars, including Vince Eager, Wee Willie Harris and the Italian
singer Little Tony. Lionel Bart was a regular visitor and she became
friendly with Mickie Most.

One day she was summoned to Van Damm's office. Had she
been reported for one of her innocent kisses on the stairs? Surely

her stage performances were up to scratch? Although in many ways a benign boss, he was also a strict disciplinarian. His stern face suggested trouble. It appeared he had received a letter of complaint from the Mother Superior of her old convent school. There had recently been a headline in the national press: 'Convent girl in Windmill show'. Van Damm was furious that the Mother Superior and sisterhood of St Mary's did not want to be associated with the theatre and were demanding he stopped using her name for publicity purposes. He reacted as if Jill had been accused of walking the streets. 'They are ashamed of you,' he blustered, 'but they should be proud of you. I am.' With that, he sent his young protégée back to work and issued a new press release headed, 'It's a far cry from the Woodford convent schoolgirl days to London's Palais de Glamour.'

Jill's dancing continued to improve under the gentler promptings of John Law. He was the principal male dancer and a skilled choreographer. It was John Law, who had started at the Windmill during Laura Henderson's time, who discovered her singing potential. He immediately thrust her on stage with one of the leading boys, where they performed the rock number 'Hey Good Looking'. Over fifty years later, Jill is still word perfect. It was John who taught her how to project her voice and it was on his instructions that she spent hours in front of her bathroom mirror perfecting her technique. The resident comedians during her time at the Windmill included star names – Arthur English, Bill Pertwee, Jimmy Edmundson and Rex Jameson, best known for his Mrs Shufflewick character. Jill described the Windmill as being like a large family with Vivian Van Damm overseeing it all like a fussy father. With over seventy people employed backstage as well as the performers, it was a huge undertaking, but for the most part it all ran like clockwork. Van Damm was ambitious for his girls to make socially acceptable marriages. The cast were not encouraged to mix romantically. The humble hoofers of the male chorus were certainly not considered suitable catches. In this respect he was like any caring father, trying to guarantee the best for his girls. Protective and not a little snobbish, his concern was generally appreciated. Jill had her fair share of stage-door johnnies trying to make contact, but the nearest she got to an aristocratic admirer was Lord Charles, who arrived in 1960. He was a randy, slightly sloshed, monocled toff. Unfortunately for her, he was also a dummy, the creation of the ventriloquist Ray Alan. He would leer from the stage as Jill waited in the wings, an almost believable character who was to go on to achieve nationwide fame on television. Not that Jill needed to be looking for romance at the time as she was going out with the good-looking Canadian film star Lee Patterson. They went to fashionable restaurants, including the popular Isow's, where the banquettes had metal plates listing famous celebrities who had occupied the table previously. She was also mixing with some of the new stars, including Shirley Bassey.

Mostly, her life was taken up with performing and rehearsing for the next show. Sometimes, during a break, she would slip across the road to watch well-known boxers train in Jack Solomons' gym. Nearby was Mac's Rehearsal Rooms, where West End stars put the final touches to their act. After a tiring day it was a quick walk to the underground and home to bed. Past the lines of prostitutes who were probably jealous of her glamorous life, but who always had a friendly word. She felt as happy and unthreatened in Soho as she would have in an idyllic English village and it was much more fun.

The 317th *Revudeville* saw the arrival of Ray Alan and Lord Charles. Unfortunately, it was a fateful one for the Windmill company. For only the second time since she had joined, Jill was summonsed to the old man's office. Just as she had those years before, she stood in front of him whilst he remained seated. He looked tired and frail. He told her that he continued to be pleased with her, but there appeared to be no particular reason for this sudden meeting. Following a long pause she enquired about his health. 'I've been unwell,' he said. 'I pulled a hair from my nose with tweezers and it set up an infection. Let that be a warning to you. Never pull your nose hairs out – it can cause all sorts of problems.' She sensed that this was his way of saying goodbye. A very British way, oblique and avoiding too much emotion. She felt a great sadness come over her. Although shaking from the effects of Parkinson's disease, he managed to retain both his dignity and authority. Within days, Vivian Van Damm was taken into hospital. He died shortly after, but the show had to go on. Jill remembers her first entrance after receiving the news. She performed an adagio, arranged by John Law, with a very heavy heart, but no one sitting in the audience that day could have guessed. The old man would have been proud of her.

Like so many of the Windmill girls, life did not end with the closing of the theatre. Jill had a daughter by her first husband, and later married the writer and journalist Milton J. Shapiro. She reinvented herself as a talented photo-journalist and joined him on numerous assignments for Warner Brothers in far-flung locations. Together, they were globe-trotting freelancers. They made a formidable team and her work from that time is still being reproduced. On a trip to north-eastern Siberia she was probably the first woman from Western Europe to visit the area, travelling through five time zones to get there.

Now, on a spring day fifty-three years after the young girl with the red beret entered the stage door to the Windmill, I have arranged to meet her for lunch. The location is Archer Street, just a few yards from the theatre. As I turn off Great Windmill Street, I sense her, rather than see her. Turning, I recognise her. Now she walks, not with the guileless confidence of youth, but with the presence of someone who has commanded a stage. As I wait for her to join me I note that people still pause to stare. There is no red beret set at a saucy angle, but stunning grey hair pulled back in a dramatic ponytail. Why, I pondered, as we enjoyed our meal, had so few of the Windmill girls gone on to be stars in their own right. 'Easy,' she replied, 'we were all too happy just being the Windmill girls.' Let that be their epitaph.

61. The mood of Soho's drinking culture captured by Ruth Willetts, a teacher at the St Martin's School of Art.

62. Like many of his talented contemporaries, Dylan Thomas was a regular at the Colony Room and other Soho 'watering holes'.

63. A sketch of 'Ironfoot Jack', a Soho character to be avoided. He was a boozer and a conman, and his lack of personal hygiene was particularly off-putting.

64. Archer Street, where the Windmill girls heading for the stage door had to run the gauntlet of dozens of musicians waiting around in the hope of being hired.

65. Heaven and Hell Coffee Lounge and the 2i's were the places for the young to congregate.

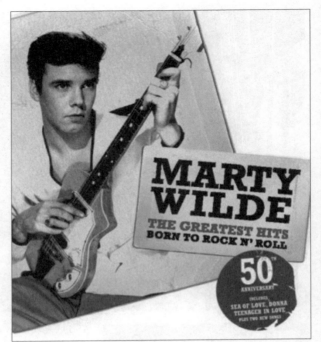

66. Marty Wilde, thought by many to be Britain's answer to Elvis Presley.

67. Convent-educated Windmill girl Jill Millard meets up with Cliff Richard.

Above: 68. Pop scene movers and shakers Mickie and Alex Most.

Left: 69. Jill Millard with Vince Eager, one of the exotically named singers from the Larry Parnes stable.

70. Vivian Van Damm, directing from the stalls.

71. A frail-looking Van Damm with his granddaughters Susan and Jane.

72. A shot that every Windmill girl wanted recorded.

73. Jill Millard poses for the Windmill's production of *Aladdin*, which was produced shortly after Van Damm's death.

74. A publicity shot for the 1962 film *The Window Dresser*. For this performance Pamela Green was bizarrely charged with corrupting a Scottish schoolboy who confessed to his father that he was 'ruined forever'. The judge didn't agree and the case was dismissed, with the judge requesting a copy of the film to take home.

75. Pamela Green prepares a model for a shoot whilst a rather satanic Harrison Marks looks on.

This page: 76 & 77. *Solo* and *Panama* were added to the stable of magazines being produced by Harrison Marks, although his interest was being diverted to film production.

78. By 1960 Marks was veering to outright pornography and staged a daring exhibition of his work at his studio in Gerrard Street.

79. Larry Parnes was not alone in creating crazy names for his performers, as fans beat a path to Denman Street to view the charms of Alma Caddilac.

80. A busy Carnaby Street, the Mecca of 1960s fashion.

81. Songwriter Mitch Murray with Freddie and the Dreamers in Denmark Street.

Above: 82. Market day, with the popular Isow's restaurant in the background.

Left: 83. Ray Alan with Lord Charles. The Windmill continued to be a launch pad for future stars.

Foreword

ANY show that has run continuously for over 32 years has done pretty well; when in addition it has presented, amongst others, John Tilley, Kenneth More, Jimmy Edwards, Harry Secombe, Alfred Marks, Michael Bentine, Eric Barker and Pearl Hackney, Arthur English, Arthur Haynes, Dick Emery, Dickie Murdoch and Peter Sellers, one may well ask, was the Windmill Theatre really the home of beauty unadorned or God's gift to the entertainment world.

So no tears for our final curtain—let it come down to-night to end the long day of striving and glory, as it has always come down, to laughter and applause.

Keith Lester
31st October. 1964

MRS. LAURA HENDERSON

VIVIAN VAN DAMM

SHELIA VAN DAMM

84. The last Windmill programme acknowledging the three guiding lights, Laura Henderson, Vivian and Sheila Van Damm.

THE WINDMILL GIRLS 1944-1964

MOIRA MURPHY · MAUREEN CLAYTON · MARGARET COOPER · JILL MILLARD · JEAN MARA

MANDY MAYER · SADIE COMBEN · MARGARET NICOLSON · IRIS CHAPPLE · WENDY CLARKE · PEGGY MARTIN

85. A montage of some of the lovely girls who appeared at the theatre during its final twenty years.

86. Once a Windmill girl…!

Winkie Winkfield and Jill Millard

87. Jean Mara (Winkie Winkfield) and Jill Millard- Shapiro, still exuding the personality which was the most important characteristic required to become a Windmill girl.

THE WINDMILL GIRLS
17th July 2011

Moira Murphy, Maureen Clayton, Jill Millard, Jean Mara, Mandy Mayer, Sadie Comben, Margaret Cooper, Margaret Nicholson, Iris Chapple, Wendy Clarke, Peggy Martin.

88. Undiminished after all these years, the girls take a bow at their reunion.

PART 4

SWINGING INTO THE SIXTIES

21

Trouble at Mill

A new year evokes hope for many, but also a degree of anxiety about what the future holds. These feelings are magnified when a new decade beckons. In Britain, the euphoria heralding a new Elizabethan era has already cooled. Friday 1 January 1960 dawns dry and mild for the time of year. The previous night's revellers have finally gone home. Maybe a couple of hours' snatched sleep and then it's back to work (New Year's Day has yet to become a national holiday). Soho had witnessed its usual night of excess. The restaurants and clubs full to overflowing, the clip joints and working girls never busier. The streets in the early morning are unusually, and somewhat eerily, almost deserted. A few discarded beer cans rattle along in the morning breeze and come to a rest against an empty champagne bottle. As usual, Soho represents diversity – even in the gutter. The bakers have been at work for hours, but now the publicans and bar owners survey the carnage of the night's celebrations. There are tables to be cleared, glasses and crockery to be washed. Even the stallholders in Berwick Street arrive later than usual – quieter and red-eyed. Many of the Windmill girls have also partied well into the night and need to be back on stage in a couple of hours, looking their best as usual. Only the working girls lie asleep still, dreaming perhaps of a different life of suburban comfort and respectability.

Vivian Van Damm is at his desk on time, as ever. Last night the theatre had played to a full house, but he is worried about a recent fall-off in attendances. The organisations run by Van Damm and Binkie Beaumont continue to run roughly in tandem. Both had enjoyed an extended heyday and now, as if choreographed, they are about to experience severe difficulties.

The Windmill's problems can partially be attributed to Van Damm's failing health. H. M. Tennent and Binkie's demise are more gradual and difficult to pinpoint. It was as if Binkie underwent a personality change with the arrival of a new decade. Some unkindly attributed it to the male menopause. He was tetchy, waspish and out of sorts. For the first time in a long career he found he was unable to book a West End theatre. Perhaps it was the subject matter of a play by Frederick Dürrerhart that was the problem. Cannibalism, bestiality and murder were not subjects that appealed to the theatre owners. More likely, though, it was due to Binkie's previous dominance and condescending manner – it was payback time. The production was forced out to the Royalty Theatre in Kingsway and, despite good reviews, did not enjoy a long run.

Binkie's strange behaviour now went into overdrive. He fell out with his long-time friend Noël Coward, resulting in him missing the chance to present a series of musicals including *High Spirits* and *The Girl Who Came to Supper*. It is also possible that the success of a new wave of writers, led by John Osborne, was finally getting him to doubt his own judgement. He still loathed this 'kitchen sink' school of drama but his response was deeply flawed. During 1960 he presented a number of very poor plays using his old ploy of signing up star names, which had the effect of making the poor plays seem even worse, with the actors really not having their heart in the production. In addition, several of Beaumont's leading playwrights, including Terence Rattigan, were also falling out of favour with the public. There was a new school of young managers making an impact on the West End, including John Gale and Michael White. Each had their own stable of authors and actors, and now agents were not sending their best plays to Binkie; as a result, he was losing what had been a virtual monopoly of West End theatres. For the fifty-three-year-old Binkie, life was becoming increasingly irritating. He had become used to ruling the roost and everyone deferring to him. His arrogance, duplicity and double-dealing were catching up with him, but at least he was in good health.

Vivian Van Damm was not so lucky. For years he had been suffering a debilitating combination of Parkinson's disease and asthma. Happily, his daughter Sheila had joined the company in 1955 and was a popular and resourceful assistant. This was important because Van Damm was becoming increasingly frail and he no longer had the energy that had made him such a force. Rumours spread that the old man was ready to sell the Windmill. A number of prospective buyers came forward at the beginning of 1960 for what they imagined was a thriving business. There was a particularly attractive offer from a leading cinema chain, which fell through when they were given sight of the balance sheet. The myth that the Windmill continued to be 'a little gold mine' was exposed. For several years audiences had been declining against the competition of the growing numbers of explicit strip clubs, particularly Raymond's Revue Bar. The Windmill was considered by many as a relic of the past in a fast-changing world. Certainly, the shows continued to be polished and professional. The girls were as pretty and talented as ever, but public taste had moved on. The Windmill was just not sexy or raunchy enough.

Van Damm went on holiday to Capri in the summer of 1960 in an attempt to restore his health. Whilst there he collapsed, and again in his office in October. Like most men he avoided doctors when possible. Finally he was persuaded to go and see a leading specialist, who gently broke the news to the family that the old showman had cancer in his chest and there was no hope. Cancer still had something of a pariah status. Somehow it was considered to be unspeakable in public – rarely acknowledged. Van Damm was informed that an ulcer was suspected, which required further investigation. Today, patients tend to be told outright about their condition and it is quite possible that the old man read the coded message fed to him. He was admitted to the London Clinic in mid-November. He now badgered his doctor non-stop to give him a knockout pill so that he wouldn't have to endure a lingering death. Eventually, the doctor succumbed. Van Damm duly swallowed the pill when he was left alone. Death did not overcome him, but he had to make a dash for the toilet. Annoyingly, a laxative had been prescribed.

Despite his continuing decline in health, Van Damm insisted on knowing every detail on what was happening at the theatre. A few days after entering hospital, he issued a rallying call to all his employees, congratulating them on how well they had supported Sheila. His condition continued to decline and finally he contracted bronchial pneumonia and died on 14 December. Sheila withheld news of his death until the final curtain call that night. Next morning she pinned up a notice informing the company that there was to be no mourning. She requested them 'to show your love and affection by going on stage and giving it all you have got'. The funeral was to be a private family affair, with a memorial service arranged for Sunday 8 January, so that all who wanted to attend could do so. The service was held at Hampstead synagogue. His death received full coverage in the national press, outlining all the stars he had introduced to the public. Most were known for their time at the Mill but it was news to most that the actor Kenneth More had been employed as a stagehand back in 1935. It had been his job to bolt down the seats each day after the usual scramble to get to the front to get a better view. It was also not known that, with the aid of binoculars, he kept an eye on the audience and ejected anyone seen to be nursing a newspaper or hat on his lap.

Despite these errant punters, Van Damm had, within thirty years, created a theatrical phenomenon, 'London's Modern Temple of Venus'. His daughter now faced the formidable task of reviving the Windmill's fortunes. She set about trying to improve the shows. She took a detached approach, trying to view it as a member of the paying public. She wrote in her diary the day after his death, 'Three good acts, including Ray Alan. Comic very good.' Her father's training was already proving invaluable. She was not going to give up without a fight. The prospects were truly daunting. She was to be responsible for producing up to eight completely different shows, totalling some 1,500 performances a year. The break-even figure of £3,200 a week was going to be extremely difficult to achieve and, based on the latest figures, the company was set to make a loss of over £6,000 for the year.

Her immediate response was to spend and invest, rather than cut back. The vestibule and auditorium were completely redecorated. A new heating system was installed in response to customer complaints, giving a regulated temperature of 65 °F. The front of house staff were issued with smart new uniforms. These investments, whilst welcome, were not in themselves going to turn the business round. The Windmill continued to pay its staff well above the Equity minimum. In 1960 the girls were being paid £12 a week, and Sheila reckoned the unions would fight any cuts and that it would also be bad for morale. So the theory was to throw everything into producing superb shows and the theatre's fortunes would improve. They didn't. By the beginning of 1961 takings continued to fall to around £1,800 a week. The losses could not be sustained. It was decided at an emergency board meeting that the theatre would have to be closed and the freehold sold. Devastated by her failure so soon after her father's death, Sheila promptly went down with flu. Feeling sorry for herself, she was jolted out of her negative frame of mind by her friend Joan Werner. She laid into Sheila, ridiculing her passive response to the intended closure. 'How on earth did you become a rally champion?' she enquired. 'You are absolutely gutless.' Sheila was lectured on the fact that it was her father's bad management that had created the crisis. She was shocked and outraged. In her eyes her father could do no wrong. The criticism did at least shake off her lethargy. She began to look at what cutbacks could be made. Nothing was sacrosanct. She had a meeting with her sister Betty and they agreed to invest a further £10,000 of family money. In addition, some sacred cows were sacrificed. The first house, which normally started at 12.15 p.m., was to be scrapped. Her father had always warned against this course of action, as he had about offering reserved seats. Again, she flew in the face of his advice by allowing reservations for the circle. Still she was not done. She now had a steely determination. Management salaries were cut and twelve artistes were sacked. These were terribly difficult and upsetting decisions, but it was better than closing down. She was humbled by the way everyone accepted the need for cuts. It was estimated that the changes instituted lowered the break-even figure to £2,500 a week.

The remaining artistes were informed that the A and B companies appearing on alternate days would also be scrapped. This system had been in existence since 1932. Now they would have to work every day. They would take it in turns in either performing the first two or the last three houses. The draconian measures ensured an eleventh-hour reprieve for the Windmill. The final fight for survival had begun. Sheila Van Damm emerged from her father's shadow with a series of further brave decisions. She cut the advertising budget and made substantial savings on costume designs, but her instinct was still to invest. The management salary cuts were short-lived and she had plush new seating installed. Joan Werner, who was editor of *She*, redesigned the Windmill souvenir programme into a glossy colour magazine. Sheila was worried that being a woman producing a show designed to appeal to men would be seen as a negative. Unlike her father, she decided not to seek any publicity for herself. She also co-opted the help of two male colleagues when auditioning for new Windmill girls. She reckoned a male perspective in making the choice was essential. They even devised a method that came up with the ideal measurements for a Windmill girl – 38-inch bust, 23-inch waist and 36-inch hips. They went further. The perfect girl would measure 20 inches round the thigh and 8½ inches around the ankle. The length of leg was particularly important and should be 30 inches and measure 15 inches from ankle to knee. There were obviously variations within the company, including a precocious fifteen-year-old who measured 42–24–38. She was quickly promoted to perform the famous Windmill fan dance. She practised and rehearsed for weeks until her performance was perfect. Unfortunately, there was a particularly raucous and appreciative audience for her debut performance. Unnerved by the howls of approval, she completed her act by raising her arms in triumph. Suddenly, realising what she had done, she made a dash for the wings. The roars of applause were reckoned to be the loudest witnessed in the theatre's history.

This event strangely underlined the pressures the Windmill would continue to encounter despite all the changes made. The public demanded real, live, sexy girls, not discreet statues. By August 1961, at least the losses had been staunched. Turnover was averaging the magic £2,500-a-week break-even figure. The shows had never been more professional or better choreographed. The effect was of a charming, nostalgic, rather dated show and yet all around them in Soho there were mountains of bare flesh on show. A more demanding, fickle audience were looking to spend their money elsewhere.

Money was Paul Raymond's prime interest and loads of it was going his way. The membership of his club had mushroomed to almost 50,000 by 1960. In November the wily Raymond negotiated the purchase of the freehold of the Revue Bar in Walkers Court. Jack Isow, his landlord, was furious that he had allowed Raymond a lease that contained a clause which precluded him from increasing the rent. This glaring error, allowed through by his negligent lawyers, had led to real animosity between the two men. Isow salvaged some pride by managing to secure what appeared at the time to be a hefty price of £14,000 for the building. Isow was astonished when Raymond arrived at his restaurant with a briefcase full of cash. Some of it had turned green with mildew. Raymond had obviously not been keeping it under his bed, but the deal was done. This was the first of many which would eventually lead to Raymond becoming Soho's leading property owner. The Revue Bar's annual turnover was now in excess of £250,000 and Raymond reckoned that property was still cheap in Soho and would be a sound investment, and how right he was. Although it was his clubs that were generating the cash to make these purchases possible, he was worried about the future of striptease as he felt that every possible variation had been attempted. Still, he had enough cash to invest in two new clubs. Regular appearances in court did nothing to stem his expansionist activities. He started to acquire all the trappings of a successful entrepreneur. He bought a rather grand house overlooking Wimbledon Common for £25,000. The Bentley was parked in the drive. An early exponent of bling, he wore gold watches and jewellery that gave further evidence of his wealth, and yet all was not well. Strains were beginning to show in his marriage. He rather ungallantly attributed the problems to Jean's lack of ambition. Paul Raymond was obsessed by money and anyone who wasn't was unambitious in his eyes. The real problem was due to his increasing number of affairs and his heavy drinking. For Paul Raymond, the answer to any problem could always be solved by money. When Jean confronted him with his infidelities his answer was to shower her with expensive gifts. It didn't work. Like so many successful couples who have started with nothing, worked hard and relied on each other, when success finally comes it sours their relationship. Jean felt upset and humiliated. Not to be outdone she started having affairs, including several with well-known actors. For Raymond, the financial risks he was taking gave as big a buzz as the sex, booze and drugs he came to rely on.

With neither of his two new clubs doing particularly well, he was forced to seek extra revenue from the Revue Bar. He decided to introduce gambling. London, as epitomised by Crockfords, had become a global centre for heavy rollers from around the world. He was convinced that he could attract a wealthier clientele. He sought to introduce roulette and chemin de fer, which were particularly favourable to the house, providing 5 per cent commission on all winning bets. Roulette, with the wheel having the usual zero slot, would have been illegal if used at the club under existing legislation. Therefore, Raymond opted for a wheel that excluded the zero known as 'Legalite'. Money was made for the house by charging the player a fee for each designated twenty-minute session. With Raymond now advertising his casino at the Revue Bar, the police, again, started taking an interest in his activities. Not for the first time he found himself in the dock at Great Marlborough Street Magistrates' Court. He was found guilty and fined a derisory £10. A more serious threat arrived in the formidable shape of Detective Sergeant Harry Challenor. He had served in the Special Air Service during the war, winning the Military Medal. Known as 'Trunky', Challenor was a loose cannon heading for a fall. He saw himself as a saviour in defeating the underworld, single-handedly, whilst operating his own protection racket. He was not only corrupt but violent and intimidating. Strutting through the streets of Soho he became a feared figure. Paul Raymond soon realised that refusing to pay protection to local crooks was possible, but when Challenor came calling it was pay-up time. He knew the Challenor often resorted to violence, and planting false evidence was a speciality. A complaint to the authorities would merely heap more trouble on himself, so for the time being Raymond kept 'Uncle Harry' happy, leaving him to terrorise others.

By the early 1960s, organised crime had moved in on the strip club scene. Whilst Murray Goldstein's clubs made a passing nod at producing professional shows, 'Big Frank' Mifsud had no such pretensions. A former Maltese traffic policeman, he was another much feared character who, with Bernie Silver, ran about twenty strip clubs, including the Carnival in Old Compton Street and the Blue Moon in Frith Street. He had no interest in even pretending to present a slick show. He employed almost any girl turning up for a job irrespective of looks or talent. If they were prepared to bare all, the job was theirs, but they had to work endlessly, running from club to club. They became a regular sight in Soho. Pale-faced and tottering on high heels, they click-clacked through the streets until the early hours. Although they earned much more than the respectable Windmill girls, these haunted-looking creatures were burnt out within months. They were at the bottom of the pile, constantly harassed and abused by the punters, a life only considered by those who were desperate.

The 1960s had heralded a harsher, outspoken (some thought liberated) era. Long-held perceptions on morality and decency were challenged. Politicians were ridiculed, authority spurned. The young were setting the agenda as never before. Against this background Sheila Van Damm and Binkie Beaumont were swimming against the tide. They had been slow to sense or acknowledge the danger. Like its founder before, the Windmill Theatre was now terminally ill. It would enjoy a few remissions, but the grim reaper beckoned.

22

Where There's Muck, There's Money

By 1960, the streets of Soho had been transformed. What had happened, where were they? For the first time in centuries, it was possible to wander through the naughty square mile without being asked if you were looking for a good time. The 1959 Street Offences Act made soliciting for sexual purposes in public places a criminal offence. If those who had been offended by lines of prostitutes thought the legislation would herald an age of a puritanical Soho, they were to be sorely disappointed. Others actually mourned the absence of the girls, whom they felt had added to the unique atmosphere of the area. However, it was naïve to expect the girls and their controllers to simply walk away. Almost overnight, Soho acquired an uglier face, tacky and sordid. The poorly drafted legislation did not preclude the working girls transferring their trade to clubs, cafés and hostess bars. Within weeks there was an outbreak of outlets devoted to the sale of sex. The gangsters and dodgy entrepreneurs sniffed the chance of making some serious money.

Unforeseen consequences flowed as well from the Obscene Publications Act, also passed in 1959. Ostensibly, this was introduced following lobbying from well-known, established authors who wanted to be allowed to include detailed descriptions of sex without running the risk of being prosecuted. The problem was trying to establish a legal definition of obscenity. In October 1960 Penguin Books were prosecuted under the Act for publishing *Lady Chatterley's Lover*. The publisher's acquittal was to have a profound effect on Britain's cultural outlook. It was an early signal for the floodgates to open and herald a far more liberal attitude to be voiced and generally accepted in Britain. Censorship in Scandinavia had become even more relaxed, resulting in a wave of hardcore pornography arriving in the dirty bookshops of Soho. It was not on open display but secreted away behind a curtain at the back of the shops. No one was quite sure how far the law could be pushed, unless you were on good terms with the local police, that is!

The vagueness of the law left George Harrison Marks with something of a dilemma. He had, increasingly, been producing more explicit material. In January 1960 he held an *Exhibition of the Nude* in Gerrard Street, which was opened by the popular actor Harry H. Corbett. Many of the photographs, whilst still paying lip service to classic artistic photography, were teetering on the edge of pornography. For an entrance fee of 5s you were able to make your own mind up. Whilst his current format of magazine distribution was still extremely profitable, George was becoming greedy. Maybe he was selling thousands of magazines a month, but he was jealous of the hardcore merchants. He suggested to his partner Pam that they should enter the market, but she was violently opposed. She was convinced that porn was demeaning, whilst glamour photography was simply stimulating and, somehow, wholesome. Importantly, it was also above board and not confined to grubby underground distribution. It may have been a fine line, but not one she was prepared to cross.

In April 1960 the premiere of *Peeping Tom* was held at the Plaza cinema, Piccadilly. A monster cut-out of Pam, sporting a sexy red waspie and black stockings, towered above the entrance with a caption, 'Introducing Pamela Green'. The film was panned and damned by the critics. Pam's subsequent film roles were restricted to those made by George. Her flirtation with mainstream fame was brief, although much later *Peeping Tom* became a cult movie.

Increasingly, George appeared to be becoming bored with photography. His ego and sense of self-importance were expanding in unison with his girth. Pam and the staff laughed at him behind his back as he took to wearing a corset, presumably to make him appear more attractive to the increasing number of girls he was bedding. He scarcely bothered to hide his infidelities from Pam, who was concerned and upset by his callousness. She was also alarmed by his seeming lack of interest in the business. Somehow, his visits to the set of *Peeping Tom* the previous year had convinced him that his fortune lay in making films. He felt inspired; unfortunately, that inspiration did not transfer itself to the quality of the films he made. He fancied himself not only as a producer and director, but as an actor too. His films for the most part were amateurish and, viewed today, embarrassingly bad. His first effort *Artist's Model* featured just Pam and her friend Jean Sporle. A hammy plot was contrived just to allow a little saucy nudity. Made in the spring of 1960, it was quickly followed by a further twenty glamour films, made in 8 mm or 16 mm format, by the end of the year. Although each was advertised in *Kamera* and the other magazines in the Harrison Marks stable, sales were disappointing. George had failed to realise that very few people owned the necessary projectors. Poor sales of hardback books and calendars were also causing concern. In addition, employment costs had increased with a burgeoning staff. George now preferred to delegate the jobs that no longer interested him.

He had lost sight of the reason the *Kamera* concept had been so successful. A pocket-sized book could easily be tucked away from the prying eyes of a mother or wife. Pam constantly warned him of the dangers of straying from their original format, but he refused to listen. By now his vanity and self-importance, coupled with his boozing, made it difficult to hold a sensible conversation with him. He had grown lazy and was, seemingly, not prepared to face up to the decline in business. He was by now treating Pam with contempt, by openly boasting of his affair with the busty model Paula Page. He was in turn monosyllabic or cuttingly critical. By the end of 1960 the couple were arguing constantly. There is an uncanny similarity between Harrison Marks and Paul Raymond. Both relied on their wives (although it isn't certain that George did marry Pam) to help them establish successful businesses. Both men, having become wealthy, shared a love of outward extravagance – large cars, brash jewellery, booze and a succession of compliant women. Although they mixed socially on occasions, it is not known how much George was influenced by Raymond. Their similarities ended when it came to investing the wealth they had acquired. Paul Raymond's real passion was for making money – George Harrison Marks was more interested in spending it.

So it was at a time when George and Pam should have been enjoying themselves that everything turned sour. Early in 1961 matters came to a head and Pam moved out. Whilst happy to be away from the emotional turmoil, she was not about to abandon eight years of scheming and hard work she had invested in the organisation. George remained convinced that it was the availability of hardcore porn rather than his indolence that was affecting them so badly. It wasn't long before Pam learned that George was now filming porno sessions after she had left work to go to her new flat in Charing Cross Road.

The desire to make a full-length feature film was now high on his list of priorities. He stayed on the right side of the law by making *Naked as Nature Intended*. Set largely in a nudist camp, it was all beach balls, bums and strategically placed towels. After the censor had made his cuts the film was awarded an X Certificate and ran for sixty-five minutes. The film was premiered at the Cameo Moulin in Windmill Street, which previously had shown only cartoons and newsreels. With no meaningful budget for publicity the launch was a low-key affair, and yet still managed to generate enough interest for the police to be called to control the waiting crowds. Pam and George showed a united front by attending the opening performance together. The film ran for over a year and prompted a series of copycat productions. George now turned his attention to making a series of short comedy films, which he directed, produced, wrote the scripts for, and starred as the lead in. The results owed much to early silent films, but were not as funny. Whilst huge fortunes could be made in films it was more common for a newcomer to encounter losses. Sales of their magazines continued to fall. Publication dates were missed. *Kamera* was now only being printed three times a year and satellite magazines like *Solo* were also falling behind schedule. In 1962 George fell under the spell of seventeen-year-old model Vivien Warren. Although she was twenty years his junior, they married later that year. The wedding was widely covered by the national press. Although Pamela Green and George continued to work together, she must have felt a tinge of regret as he committed himself to an increasingly hedonistic lifestyle. His marriage to Vivien was not to last and George was cast adrift to indulge in his growing list of human weaknesses.

It was reckoned that up to 5,000 girls were driven from the streets of London by the 1959 Act. There had been something of a hiatus in Soho since the demise of Jack Spot and the semi-retirement of Billy Hill. Various factions, mostly Maltese, had attempted to take up the vice-trade baton since the break-up of the Messinas. No one had managed to gain overall control, but the new legislation created the opportunity for a new duo who became known as the Syndicate. Bernie Silver had a blue-chip pedigree to enable him to become king of the sex industry. Together with his partner, 'Big Frank' Mifsud, they were able to extend their control for the next two decades. Silver was Jewish and was born in Stoke Newington. Like Jack Spot, he had volunteered for wartime military service, joining a crack parachute regiment. Just like Spot, he was also discharged on medical grounds in 1943. Moving from the building trade, he served his apprenticeship with the Messinas, before going on to run brothels in the East End. He appeared at the Old Bailey in 1956 charged with living off immoral earnings, but was discharged by an eccentric judge on a technicality.

Silver's partnership with Mifsud was a perfect marriage of brain and brawn. 'Big Frank' had the ability to spread terror, although outwardly he appeared polite and was known for his generosity to those he liked. The pair acquired a toehold in Soho with a strip club in Brewer Street. They expanded rapidly, backed by a small army of thugs who would administer beatings to anyone who did not conform to the Syndicate's rules. Silver insisted that there was to be no rivalry, nor inter-club warfare. It was easy for him to insist on this as the pair controlled 80 per cent of the strip clubs in Soho and for a time no one risked challenging them.

These clubs and nearby beer joints were usually run by Maltese under the supervision of Silver and Mifsud. Punters were lured in by scantily dressed girls and raunchy photographs displayed in the foyer. Overpriced drinks were served to the hapless punters alongside vague promises of sex later after the club closed. Some desperate men were stupid enough to give the girls money up front on a promise of meeting them later. Many a forlorn figure stood for hours at an appointed spot in the hope that his lady would turn up. Eventually the penny would drop, but a visit back to the club to seek recourse was met by a frightening bouncer and a hurried, shameful retreat.

The face of Soho was changing. Small shops were swallowed up by a sea of outlets devoted to the sex industry. Mucky bookshops, strip clubs and clip joints swept all before them. Silver and Mifsud were behind all these activities and the Syndicate prospered. Vast sums were being made. It was reckoned that by the early 1970s the pair were trousering an incredible £100,000 a week. None of this would have been possible without the connivance of the police. Members of the Obscene Publications Squad, known as the Porn Squad, received increasingly huge pay-offs as a hardcore pornography boom developed. It appears that corruption was rife throughout all ranks. Well-orchestrated arrests were made of working girls on a rota basis, minimal fines were imposed by the courts and business then continued as normal. Some girls managed to move upmarket. They needed to be good-looking and have some social skills to enable them to work as an escort hostess. Agencies employing the girls would send them off to meet clients in some of London's swankiest hotels in return for a sizeable introduction fee. For the girls further down the scale, life was far harder. Whether by force or circumstance, or as a career choice, street girls would often entertain up to thirty clients a day. They had to pay inflated rents on their flats and were frequently controlled by a 'boyfriend' who lived off their earnings. The life of Soho prostitutes is brilliantly described by Barbara Tate in her book *West End Girls*.

The police organised prearranged swoops on bookshops to seize pornography. Usually, a frontman who managed the shop paid the fine and the books and films were then sold back by the police. A blind eye was generally turned to the blue film scam. Here, touts would usher punters into an attic or basement with graphic promises of seeing explicit films. Nothing would be shown until the small makeshift cinema was full and the entrance money collected. Then, if they were lucky, the audience would be shown an innocuous nudist film. Any complaints had to be addressed to massive bouncers who, trying to keep a straight face, told the aggrieved punters that they couldn't possibly show films that broke the law. It was not unknown for the tout, having collected the money, to do a bunk, leaving a room full of angry clients staring at an empty screen.

Scams and police corruption were endemic, filtering right through the criminal elite to the humblest conman. Soho's own version of Houdini was not much higher up the criminal scale than the three-card-trick operators. The scam was similar in that a crowd was encouraged to form whilst the escapologist was secured in a straightjacket. As he writhed on the floor a collection was made from the crowd of fascinated onlookers.

With the money safely pocketed, enter, as prearranged, a uniformed policeman who moved the crowd on as he pretended to book our erstwhile Harry Houdini. Instead, he collected a ten bob note from the scammers and everyone (except the paying public) was happy.

Ingenuity has never been lacking in Soho. With working girls being forced from the streets, they set about honing their marketing skills. Shop windows and telephone kiosks advertised their wares in thinly disguised messages. 'French mistress gives lessons in discipline' or 'Swedish chest for sale' created endless interest and amusement to a passing public. As fast as increasingly explicit cards were removed from telephone kiosks, they reappeared again days later.

Although Soho remained the home of the mainstream film industry, and many restaurants and legitimate businesses were profitably run, it is impossible to ignore the fact that huge fortunes were made primarily by selling sex. Whilst the old trades of Soho were closing down and dying out, the oldest of them all was prospering as seldom before. Sex sells and Soho sells sex. Young women, either through choice, circumstance or coercion, chose to pose for increasingly explicit photographic sessions, appear in films or sell their bodies. Almost exclusively it was men who prospered from their activities. The relaxation on nudity that had started innocently with Vivian Van Damm's productions at the Windmill had led to a change in what was considered acceptable. True, prostitution had existed since time began, but displays of nudity by the 1960s scarcely warranted a second glance. The gangsters, porn merchants, pimps, ponces and strip-club owners still continued to profit from an insatiable demand from a constant procession of men visiting the area. Paul Raymond was to become one of Britain's wealthiest men on the back of displays of female flesh. Other even less savoury characters also made fortunes. Some of the girls involved did earn enough to walk away, but for most ageing prostitutes the outlook was dire. Soho, however, shrugged its collective shoulders, for it was at its very heart that the Swinging Sixties were about to be born.

23

A Youthful Revolution

The heady atmosphere of London in the early 1960s was palpable. The young were particularly aware of a fundamental shift in society. For once, it was the exuberance of youth that was setting the agenda. Days passed in a whirl, borne on a tide of new sounds from the pop world and the creation of trendsetting fashion. The introduction of the contraceptive pill encouraged increased sexual activity, no longer overwhelmed by worry or guilt. Against this background a patrician government and the establishment was pilloried as satire took centre stage. Although it was 1966 before 'Swinging London' was defined by an article in *Time* magazine, Soho was already humming with excitement, a focal point for change in attitudes and behaviour.

At the centre of this social revolution was Carnaby Street, formerly a drab thoroughfare populated by suppliers to the catering trade and numerous small workshops. By the early 1960s, it was drawing fashion-conscious youngsters from across the country. Foreign visitors flocked to the new tourist hotspot together with buyers from the top American stores. They all wanted to be part of a young Glaswegian's vision for the future of male fashion. John Stephen had created a retail phenomenon in the space of a few years. Leaving the military department of Moss Bros, Stephen had moved on to work for Bill Green, who was the original instigator of supplying what was originally thought to be outrageous men's clothing. In an era dominated by tweed sports jackets and cavalry twill trousers, his tight black sweaters imported from Paris and garish shirts in primary colours were thought to be shocking. Selling by mail order and targeting the relatively small, underground gay market, Stephen saw a far greater potential for this type of clothing. By the end of the 1950s, he had moved from Beak Street to open his first retail outlet in unfashionable Carnaby Street. Just a stone's throw from Piccadilly Circus, the rents were still cheap and affordable. By 1961, he had four shops trading within a few yards of each other, including His Clothes and Male West One. The designs were far more flamboyant than had been available to young men who wanted to stand out from the conventional crowd. Previously, anyone prepared to wear outlandish clothes was thought to be camp or queer. Stephen was an astute trader, setting rather than following trends. He bought at keen prices and constantly introduced new styles. Shop windows were redesigned almost daily to keep the interest high. He started targeting the youthful 'Mods', the Vesta and Lambretta brigade. They dressed neatly and sported short 'College Boy' hairstyles as opposed to their arch rivals, the leather-clad 'Rockers'.

Famous pop stars started frequenting his shops and he always had a photographer on hand to publicise his celebrity clientele. By 1962, 'Lord Kitchener's valet' was popularising ex-military uniforms sporting Union Jacks. Suddenly, being British was cool. Middle-class parents looked on quite horrified as their sons paraded like peacocks. Their offspring just didn't care, they were out to shock and no outfit was too outrageous. John Stephen was unique in his achievement of becoming one of Soho's self-made millionaires without owing his success to sex or crime. For him it was down to hard work and an ability to read the runes in the fast-changing world of the 1960s.

Meanwhile, the fashion designers for young women were slower to catch the mood. It was as if the girls were more conservative than their attention-seeking boyfriends and brothers. There was a gradual evolution from the 1950s, with pencil skirts, tight sweaters and cardigans remaining popular. Skirt levels did venture just above the knee, but the miniskirt was still a couple of years away – an innovation that transformed many a young girl thought to be plain, but sporting legs that seemed to go on forever, into sex goddesses. For the moment, attention was on the demise of nylon stockings and the much-loved suspender belt as they made way for the more practical tights. Girls tottered delightfully in winkle-pickers with long pointed toes and high stiletto heels, but for the moment it was the young men who were the centre of attention.

Coffee bars still flourished in Soho during the 1960s. Paul Lincoln, at the 2i's, drew in hopefuls from around the country to attend auditions frequented by established and aspiring agents, but the music world had moved on. Record executives had decided that rock 'n' roll was finished. In a sense they were right. The instant star, thumping out a basic self-taught beat, was gone. The producers were anxiously trying to predict the next big sound. A *New Musical Express* survey in 1962 listed Elvis Presley, Cliff Richard, the Shadows, Billy Fury, Frank Ifield and Acker Bilk as the most popular performers. Presley and Cliff Richard were increasingly turning to ballads whilst, apart from Billy Fury, the rest were churning out safe, unchallenging music for the middle ground. All this changed in the same year with the arrival of the Beatles.

Denmark Street, Soho's own Tin Pan Alley, features strongly in British pop history and there is a link to the Beatles. Mitch Murray, like many song writers and musicians, used the Tin Pan Alley studios at No. 22 to cut demo discs. Murray, a handbag salesman, used his selling experience to cheekily gain access to the boss of the giant EMI. Impressed that the young man had managed to bypass receptionists, secretaries and security, he put him in touch with George Martin at Parlophone, a subsidiary label of EMI. Martin was convinced that 'How Do You Do It?' would be a smash hit. He persuaded the Beatles that the song should be their first release. They were unhappy with the result and instead Paul McCartney's 'Love Me Do' hurtled the Fab Four forward to fame and fortune. Martin was proved right though when Gerry and the Pacemakers had a massive hit with 'How Do You Do It?' This was to be the first of a string of hits written by Mitch Murray, including 'I Like It' and 'You Were Made for Me'. The Rolling Stones also rehearsed at the TPA studios before making their first album across the road at the Regent Sound studios. Suddenly, music was exciting again, matching the mood of the young. Artistes, soon to become famous, like Elton John, the Moody Blues and the Pretty Things, beat a path to Denmark Street, along with the majority of the future leading players in the British pop scene. The new sounds formed a backdrop to British life. It was everywhere. Blaring out from cars, cafés and discos until in January 1964 it was anointed by the BBC with the launch of *Top of the Pops*, introduced and hosted by Jimmy Savile.

Earlier in 1961, Ronnie Scott was the first to offer American musicians the opportunity to play at his jazz club which, at the time, was in Gerrard Street. This followed an agreement between the Musicians' Union and the American Federation of Musicians. Now, Ronnie's was able to offer a line-up of top American stars like Stan Getz, Zoot Sims and Al Cohn, and the club was already a Mecca for British jazz fans before moving to its present home in Frith Street. Soho continued to be a draw for a broad church of musicians. By 1960, the home of the famous Skiffle Club in Greek Street had morphed into the Soho Grill, serving classic French cuisine. Four years later, Les Cousins was opened in the cellar as a discotheque, but was to become a meeting place for emerging musical talent. Crowds would sit through weekend all-night sessions, listening to the likes of Bob Dylan and Jimmy Hendrix. Weekends at the Flamingo in Wardour Street featured Georgie Fame and Alexis Korner. The Monday night slot was given over to the emerging talent of the Rolling Stones in 1964. Wardour Street also saw the arrival of the legendary Marquee Club transferred from its previous base on Oxford Street. By then it had forged a reputation for being perhaps the most influential venue for British rock 'n' roll and pop music. The Stones, the Who, Manfred Mann and the Yardbirds all strutted their stuff there.

Music was erupting throughout Soho, but so were drugs. They had always been part of the Soho Scene but became far more widespread during the early 1960s. This was allied to the growing club scene, many of which stayed open all night. The initial attraction was the taking of purple hearts, which were cheap and helped the purchaser to stay awake. Glass vials known as 'poppers', containing amyl nitrate, were cracked open and sniffed, giving an instant high. Marijuana was also widely available. Suddenly, a new generation of youngsters thought taking drugs was cool. The press were less than impressed and sensed a story. Early in 1964, the *London Evening Standard* sent an undercover reporter to investigate. She was able to report that drugs were being sold quite openly at clubs in Wardour Street and that large numbers of youngsters were taking amphetamines. Although in truth the drug culture was in its infancy, middle England was appalled. An older generation didn't like what was going on generally. In an echo from previous generations, they mourned the lack of respect for authority. They resented their conservative beliefs being questioned and ridiculed. They didn't like the music, the clothes or even the hairstyles of their young. A form of youthful anarchy had set in and it was being stoked by educated young men who should have known better.

The boom in satire can be traced back to 1960 with a revue staged at the Edinburgh Festival featuring Jonathan Miller, Alan Bennett, Peter Cook and Dudley Moore, four uniquely talented performers. Although all Oxbridge educated, they were seemingly ill-matched, coming from different social backgrounds. The revue offered a type of humour rarely seen before in Britain. They impersonated and lampooned leading political figures, including Prime Minister Harold Macmillan, and generally attacked the establishment. Following positive reviews a lengthened show containing new and even more controversial material opened in London in 1961. It caused a sensation. It was undoubtedly extremely funny and, to the young, somehow exhilarating as it took to task the typical traditional British values of the stiff upper lip. It was as a direct consequence of the show's success that Peter Cook, in partnership with Nicholas Luard, opened the Establishment Club in Greek Street. Peter Cook envisaged a club similar to those that had thrived in Berlin during the 1930s. By the opening in October 1961 over 4,000 two-guinea subscriptions had been sold. There were chaotic scenes as the doors were shut leaving dozens of frustrated members locked out. For a time the club prospered, with people flocking to see Dudley Moore playing the piano and well-known comics like Frankie Howerd. New cutting-edge material was offered by budding comedians such as John Bird and John Fortune. As a private club the Establishment remained outside any interference from the Lord Chamberlain. A young Australian, Barry Humphreys, was popular, but generally the comics were out to shock, culminating in the appearance of the controversial American Lenny Bruce. *Beyond the Fringe* continued to play to full houses and for a time the Establishment became a favourite haunt of the rich and famous, 'the place to be seen'.

Within a year, television was getting in on the satirical boom with the first screening of *That Was the Week that Was*. It was an irreverent look back at the previous week and it persuaded millions of viewers to stay in on a Saturday night to watch.

In April 1962, *Private Eye*, a satirical paper, hit the news-stands. Its only competition was the long established *Punch*, whose strength lay mainly in the quality of its cartoons. The *Eye* was targeting a younger readership similar in age and outlook to its founders. It was edited and produced by a group of young men who had been educated at Shrewsbury School. Its early editions were, in effect, an extension of a school magazine. Richard Ingrams, Christopher Booker, Willie Rushton and Paul Foot were joined by John Wells, a friend of Ingrams from their Oxford University days. The first edition was published shortly after the opening of the Establishment. It formed a double-pronged attack on the old order. Although the two outfits had much in common, there were tensions when they met socially. The Establishment and *Beyond the Fringe* groups had state-educated members who were generally more left wing than the public-school types at *Private Eye*. 'Satirical' lunches between the groups were not a success. The *Eye* founders were thought to be greedy, ambitious and supercilious, who loved boozing and throwing up in pubs, whilst the Establishment group were supposedly hard, downmarket and confined their drinking to coffee.

Private Eye took some time to establish an identifiable style and, due to a poor distribution, was not widely available. It had yet to establish a reputation for investigative reporting. Despite Christopher Booker's wanting the magazine to adopt a more serious approach, it was generally thought to border on the juvenile. Gradually, circulation improved, encouraging an unwanted approach to buy it from a young Michael Heseltine, which was declined. Perhaps surprisingly, it was Peter Cook and Nicholas Luard who acquired the magazine in the summer of 1962. Cook's involvement proved vital as comic situations came to him easily and the magazine was much improved. Within a year, *Private Eye's* circulation had soared to almost 50,000, prompted largely by word-of-mouth recommendations. It appeared that Peter Cook could do no wrong until it became obvious that the Establishment Club was struggling. He was spreading his talents too thinly. Vitally, he had failed to institute proper financial procedures. It is all too easy in a business dealing largely in cash to lose control. Money was 'borrowed', stolen and filched. The Soho gangsters demanded protection money, making life even more difficult, but it was also partly due to satire being offered to a huge television audience. This was a deadly combination and the Establishment closed its doors in 1964. Much had changed in the intoxicating atmosphere of Soho in the early 1960s, but greed and criminality remained firmly embedded, impervious to the young who thought they could change the world.

24

The Final Curtain

When a friend or loved one is terminally ill, life seems even more traumatic as the world around you carries on oblivious to your feelings. The Windmill was dying a slow, inevitable death. From the day Sheila Van Damm took over control of the theatre the odds were stacked against her. Despite being steeped in the theatre's history, the determination she had shown as a champion rally driver was just not enough. Ten years had elapsed since she had become Ladies European Champion and part of the prizewinning team, including Stirling Moss, competing in the Monte Carlo Rally. A brief boom in business during September 1963 was reversed by the advent of winter. The losses were mounting once more to unsustainable levels. Each morning Sheila drove to work, parking her car at the Lex Garage in Brewer Street. The short walk down Great Windmill Street and the familiar sight of the theatre caused her to postpone the inevitable. The thought of killing everything she and her father had worked to create was almost too painful to bear. The closure would result in the ninety-five staff being sacked. Many of the backroom employees were no longer young and would have little prospect of obtaining another job. Like many small family businesses at that time, no pension provision had been made for the staff. Whilst she had shown she was capable of taking tough decisions, she was too involved on a personal level with her team to be detached. Outwardly strong and calm, she cleverly camouflaged her emotional nature. Again she hesitated, hoping for a miracle. There wasn't one. Sadly, the Windmill had become an anachronism.

Whilst Sheila was fretting about the future of her beloved theatre, her nemesis, Paul Raymond, was swanning around the streets of the West End in his chauffeur-driven Bentley. His business was now so successful that he no longer worried about the dozens of small strip clubs clustered around the Revue Bar. He even went out of his way to befriend Jimmy and Rusty Humphreys, who had opened their operation next door in Walkers Court. Humphreys went on to be one of Soho's most powerful pornographers. It was his systematic bribery of police that eventually led to the downfall of the Obscene Publications Squad in the 1970s. Another policeman, the formidable but deranged Harry Challenor, had already fallen from grace. He had been involved in roughing up protesters objecting to the visit of Queen Frederika of Greece and had planted bricks in their clothes to incriminate them. He was found to be unfit to plead at his trial at the Old Bailey. He was another irritation removed from Raymond's dream of single-mindedly pursuing staggering wealth for himself.

It was another, ostensibly more respectable, club that helped spawn one of the twentieth century's most notorious political scandals. Murray's Cabaret Club in Beak Street was where Christine Keeler met Stephen Ward, the society osteopath and organiser of sex parties. It was also at Murray's that Keeler became friendly with Mandy Rice-Davies, who was also to be central to the downfall of John Profumo, the Tory Secretary of State for War. Although much of the drama would take place elsewhere in the country, it was an event in Soho that helped kick-start the whole affair. In October 1962, the Allnighters Club in Wardour Street was the setting for a vicious attack. Christine Keeler had become involved with Aloysius Gordon, who was known as 'Lucky'. A violent small-time crook, he had become obsessed with Keeler. He was a dominating bully, subjecting her to a series of degrading rapes. She sought the help of Thomas Edgecombe, another former lover. Confronted at the club by Edgecombe, 'Lucky' Gordon turned violently on Keeler. Edgecombe then pulled out a razor and went to work on Gordon's face, causing slashes that required seventeen stitches. After the fight, Keeler decided to go and live with Edgecombe, who had gone into hiding. Tiring of their squalid, drug-fuelled existence, she opted for the more comfortable surroundings of Wimpole Mews, the home of Stephen Ward. Here, she joined her friend Mandy Rice-Davies. Worried that he would be sent to jail for slashing Gordon, Edgecombe rang Christine Keeler, asking her to find him a good lawyer. Edgecombe was now history as far as Christine was concerned and she told him to get lost. Worse, she even threatened to testify against him. Furious, Edgecombe arrived at Stephen Ward's front door on the morning of 14 December, wielding a pistol. He was further enraged when Keeler, in a calculated gesture of utter contempt, threw a pound note down to the street from an upstairs window. Now totally out of control, Edgecombe attempted to gain entry by shooting out the door locks. A shooting in this respectable part of London was unheard of. The popular press went to work on a story that, intriguingly, included girls of doubtful virtue, guns, West Indian hoodlums and a respected osteopath with impeccable social connections. From a shady club in Wardour Street, this story was to lead to not only the downfall of a leading politician, but ultimately the government. Whilst it was Christine Keeler who was at the very eye of the storm, it was her friend Mandy Rice-Davies who had a real gift of one-liners when she said later, 'My life has been one long descent into respectability.'

Meanwhile, in 1964, The Talk of the Town was still attracting the respectable middle classes. It offered a relatively affordable and glamorous night out, where the stars appearing in cabaret were normally of a far higher standard than the food served. There was a buzz about the place, with waiters darting between the banked tables. It was at its height of popularity, still attracting the world's leading performers. In February the legendary Ethel Merman let rip in her only cabaret appearance in Britain. She was followed in July by Lena Horne, another American superstar. One of her performances was given extra frisson by the arrival of Judy Garland. Later that month Judy made an unscheduled appearance in *Night of 100 Stars* at the Palladium, where she knocked them dead with 'Over the Rainbow'. That night, she was introduced to Jessie Mathews, Soho's own troubled star of the 1930s. By November Garland was back at the Palladium for a week's concert appearance alongside her daughter, Liza Minnelli.

Four years earlier, Judy was staying at a rather swish country club close to Elstree Studios. It was a rather grand mock-Tudor manor house, with superb views at night over the shimmering sprawl of London set out in the distance as far as the eye could see. Although I had neither money nor influence, I had managed to become a member of the Exclusive Club based on a misunderstanding by the snobbish owners that my father was a very senior member of the armed forces whom they had met years previously. I never let on, although I was always worried that the General or Air Vice Marshall, whoever he was, would turn up one day and reveal me as a fraud. In the meantime, I was able to invite my friends to stargaze at the likes of Sophia Loren and Roger Moore and a host of other celebrities who visited the club. I was playing snooker there one afternoon with a friend when Judy Garland swept in and joined us. Her behaviour was somewhat erratic and the baize cloth was in constant danger as she sent the balls careering round the table. Later she asked if we would take her daughter to the cinema. So it was that night I sat in the back row of the Ritz cinema in Edgware with Liza Minnelli.

One of the main attractions of Soho is the huge variety of restaurants. Although many are short-lived, old established favourites like Kettner's, Csarda, L'Escargot and Quo Vadis continued to flourish. They sought to offer what is known today as 'fine dining'. Another Soho institution catered for those seeking a more basic cuisine. Jimmy's was London's oldest existing Greek restaurant, founded in Frith Street in 1949 by Jimmy Christodolous. A regular visitor described the stark whitewashed walls and wooden tables, some covered in traditional seersucker cloths. Back in the sixties, the food served was truly basic – moussaka, salad and chips all piled high on huge platters. Fiery red wine was slurped from kitchen tumblers. The place was usually as crowded as a tube train with a wonderful cross-section of Soho life. Old Greek men and large ladies sat smoking and drinking strong, sweet coffee from tiny cups. Peering through a fug of cigarette smoke, the eclectic mix of diners seemed at ease with each other. They were drawn from the theatrical and artistic community. Well-known writers and painters chatted to actresses, stagehands and a few dodgy-looking small-time crooks, all competing to be heard above the deafening Greek music. This was real Soho for Soho-ites rather than the casual visitor.

By 1964, the established rock stars were touring all over the country. As the industry became more professional, Soho was the base for many leading agents. Arthur Howes represented the Kinks from his office at 34 Greek Street. The Rick Gunnell

Agency, who looked after Georgie Fame, Chris Farlowe and the Shevells, worked out of 47 Gerrard Street. The supply of musical instruments remained an important sector of Soho's business life and Music Piccadilly in Denman Street had a perfect location to supply the constant needs of both professional and aspiring musicians. Instruments were being changed frequently, prompted in part by improved technology. *New Musical Express* advertised the Rickenbacker, 'the world's greatest 12-string guitar', the choice of George Harrison and Gerry Marsden.

By April 1964, Sheila Van Damm had realised that the situation at the Windmill was impossible. Each week they were making losses approaching £1,000. She informed the board she could see no prospect for a sustained improvement and that a buyer would have to be found. She was due to meet lesbian friends Joan Werner and journalist Nancy Spain up at Aintree for the Grand National, only to learn on her arrival that they had been killed in a tragic air crash. The loss of her greatest friends concentrated her mind in disposing of the theatre as a way to try and forget her personal grief. It was a particularly dark period of her life. She was contacted by Michael Klinger and Tony Tenser of the Compton Cinema Group, who were interested in buying the freehold. Asked by Klinger why she wanted to sell, she poured her heart out to him. The responsibility for ninety-five people was proving too much. The constant worry and pressure was affecting her health, but if he wasn't prepared to pay the asking price of £200,000 she was going to soldier on. The glorious summer of 1964 passed her by as she struggled to keep news of the impending sale from the staff and press. Losses continued to mount as she played hardball with Klinger. It worked: contracts were due to be exchanged on 10 August. She drafted a letter to the staff which had to be typed at her accountant's to ensure the news didn't leak out. Just as well, because there was a snag with some minor details and the exchange of contracts was delayed. Uncharacteristically, she ran away, staying with friends on the south coast. For the first time she failed to turn up for rehearsals for *Revudeville* No. 342, which she had assumed would never be staged. Eventually, after numerous delays, contracts were exchanged on 30 September. It had been one of show business's best-kept secrets. Now the whole of Fleet Street descended on the theatre. Much to Sheila's relief, the staff took the news with a great generosity of spirit and understanding. This only increased her feeling of guilt. *Revudeville* still had a month to run and some of the artistes left to take up other jobs. Van Damm now insisted that journalists interviewing staff must pay them for the privilege. It was a chance for the staff to prepare for their new, if temporary, freelance status.

The BBC sent a film unit for a two-day filming session during the show's final week. Star presenter Richard Dimbleby provided the commentary and conducted the interviews. Sally Crow was selected to perform the fan dance on the last day and Dimbleby interviewed her stark naked except for the two fans.

There were to be four separate performances on the final Saturday, 31 October, all of which were pre-booked. The final show had to be special, and it was. Former members who had subsequently become famous were invited, including Richard Murdoch, Eric Barker, Charmian Innes, Michael Bentine, Harry Secombe, Arthur English, Dick Emery and Arthur Haynes. There were telegrams from those unable to attend, including Peter Sellers and Bruce Forsyth. The final show started at 10 p.m. and an emotional Sheila Van Damm stood outside in a corridor unable to watch, but listening to the warm applause. As the show concluded, the curtain remained aloft and Sheila gave a short speech before asking all the assembled stars who had worked at the Mill to take the stage. They were introduced individually as they climbed up stairs and stepped over the footlights to huge applause. In the bar there were 500 bottles of champagne waiting to be cracked open for a huge party and reunion. Memories were shared and enlarged upon as the drink flowed. It was the early hours before the party broke up. A party or a funeral? The reaction for most was similar. Real sadness, yet softened by each individual's memories as they stepped out into a cold, autumnal morning.

Appearing in that last performance was Maggie Nichols, who is the youngest surviving Windmill girl. A year earlier she had joined B Company as a fifteen-year-old. She was already an accomplished dancer, having trained at the Italia Conti Academy. Maggie lived in Soho and really didn't fit into the squeaky-clean image maintained by most of the Windmill girls. By her own admission, she was something of a 'wild child'. Whilst most of the girls went straight home after the last performance, Maggie trawled some of Soho's less reputable nightclubs, including the Limbo in Wardour Mews. Being a local girl, she felt quite safe wandering alone, knowing she could rely on the protection of known criminals and working girls who would fend off any unwanted attention. Any punter approaching the young girl was informed most graphically that she wasn't looking for business.

The news that the Windmill was to close was greeted with alarm and tears, and yet there were no recriminations. Sheila Van Damm continued to be viewed with affection. Maggie reckoned she was tough but also kind and fair. The last night became a blur of farewells and tears aided by an endless supply of champagne. For the young Maggie this was just the start of a career that led to the Moulin Rouge in Paris and, subsequently, performing all over the world. Today she is a respected jazz singer, whose style encompasses the avant-garde.

Just around the corner Paul Raymond, nursing a glass of his favourite brandy, was contemplating another new venture. He had been approached by Connor Walsh to start a publication mirroring the hugely successful *Playboy* magazine that generated such vast profits for Hugh Hefner. It would be a classy magazine, featuring articles by leading writers but, more importantly, with pages of enticing nudes. *Kamera* was now in decline. *King*, the new magazine, would command a premium price of 7s 6d and provide yet another source of revenue. Harrison Marks had failed to develop or invest in his titles. It was time for a real professional to take up the reins. Even in the world of glamour photography it was fatal to stand still.

On the Monday following the Windmill's closure, Sheila Van Damm returned to the empty building. For the first time in thirty-two years the theatre was quiet. No high heels clattering on the staircase, no tannoy, no life. She sat in the stalls, a lone figure except for the ghosts of her imagination. So much had changed and it was the change in public attitudes that had really caused the theatre's demise. Outside, Soho itself was going through an ugly, largely unattractive phase. Too many sex shops and clip joints. It was a hiccup in its long history and soon its own citizens, represented by the Soho Society, started a regeneration. Today, licensed sex shops are limited in number and small businesses are thriving again. Old Compton Street has become a Mecca for the gay community, whilst further south Gerrard Street is home to Chinatown. Working girls are still controlled and trafficked by unscrupulous men and a murky underworld continues to exist, but still Soho intrigues. It remains edgy, enticing fresh devotees. It is generous in the pleasure it gives, but seductive in the dangers on offer to the weak-willed. Soho, like a good wine, should be savoured, not abused.

There remains one living legacy from the Windmill years. Each summer a reunion is held by the remaining Windmill artistes, many now into their eighties. Mostly, it is the girls who survive and they offer a direct route back to a different age. One where a very special type of innocence managed to flower in the midst of London's most colourful or, some would say, naughty square mile.

Select Bibliography

Cryer, Barry, *The Chronicles of Hernia*, Virgin Books 2009

Golstein, Murray, *Naked Jungle*, Silverback Press 2006

Granger, Pip, *Up West*, Corgi Books 2009

Henderson, Peter, *A Picture of Loveliness*, private publication 2009

Hugget, Richard, *Binkie Beaumont*, Hodder & Stoughton 1989

Hurst, Anthony, *Soho and St Anne's Church*, Soho Society 2010

Kynaston, David, *Austerity Britain: 1945–1951*, Bloomsbury 2007

Laver, James, *Costume and Fashion*, Thames & Hudson 1969

Linane, Fergus, *London Crime and Vice*, Sutton Publishing 2003

Moynahan, Brian, *The British Century*, Random House 1997

Morton, James, *Bent Coppers*, Little Brown 1993

Morton, James, *Gangland Soho*, Piatkus 2008

Melly, George, *Owning Up*, Penguin Books 1965

Richardson, Nigel, *Dog Days in Soho*, Victor Gollancz 2000

Sandbrook, Dominic, *Never Had It So Good*, Little, Brown 2005

Soames, Mary (ed.), *Speaking for Themselves*, Doubleday 1998

Summers, Judith, *Soho*, Bloomsbury 1989

Tames, Richard and Sheila, *Covent Garden and Soho*, Historical Publications 2009

Tames, Richard, *Soho Past*, Historical Publications 1994

Tate, Barbara, *West End Girls*, Orion 2010

Thomas, Donald, *An Underworld at War*, John Murray 2003

Van Damm, Sheila, *We Never Closed*, Robert Hale 1967

Van Damm, Vivian, *Tonight and Every Night: The Windmill Story*, Stanley Paul 1952

Waugh, Evelyn, *The Diaries of E.W.*, Penguin Books 1982

Willetts, Paul, *Members Only: The Life and Times of Paul Raymond*, Serpent's Tail 2010

Acknowledgements

The author and the publisher are grateful to the following for permission to reproduce the illustrations used in this book: Susan Angel and Jane Kerner, the grandchildren of Vivian Van Damm; Jill Millard-Shapiro; Maurice Poole; Yak El-Droubie; the Arthur Lloyd website; Mary Evans Picture Library; Mirror-Pix; Gerry Atkins; Soho Books; the Museum of Soho; Jean Picton; Jean Sporle; Marty Wilde; Mitch Murray; Paul Willetts; James Morton; James Petter; Gary L. Moncur, and Lianna Law; Windmill Theatre Company Ltd.

My thanks to the following, whose help made this book possible: Maurice Poole for his generosity in sharing his considerable knowledge; Jill Millard-Shapiro; Jean Picton; Yak El-Droubie; Marty Wilde; Mitch Murray; Maggie Nichols; Tony Shrimplin; the staff of Westminster City Archives; and finally to Joan Beretta for transcribing my illegible writing and for her advice on the photographic content.

Index

Regent's Park

From Tudor Hunting Ground
to the Present

PAUL RABBITTS

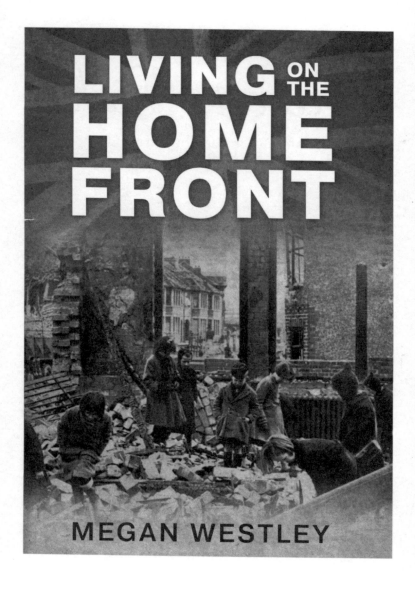